Engaging Student Voices in Higher Education

"The idea of higher education as a transformational process for students is a key ambition for many higher education institutions to fulfil. However, as mass higher education is currently evolving, it is a challenge to engage and cater for the needs of an increasingly diverse student population. Giving students a voice, and understanding better the many different voices of students is of crucial importance for those involved in higher education, and the current book is a must-read for those interested in bringing (all) students in as partners in learning, as change agents or as co-creators in their own transformational process. Through a range of critical and reflective contributions, this book offers theoretical and practical insights into the current and future ways and forms of student involvement in higher education."

—Professor Bjørn Stensaker, *University of Oslo, Norway*

"Much has been written about the contemporary student in higher education, but 'the student' has quite often been conceptualized and portrayed in stereotypical ways. This volume rightly breaks the tradition and offers a much more nuanced perspective on issues related to student identity, engagement, voice … and silence, without falling in the trap of arguing that every student is unique. A must-read for anybody interested in listening to what students really say."

—Professor Jeroen Huisman, *Ghent University, Belgium*

Simon Lygo-Baker · Ian M. Kinchin · Naomi E. Winstone
Editors

Engaging Student Voices in Higher Education

Diverse Perspectives and Expectations in Partnership

palgrave
macmillan

Editors
Simon Lygo-Baker
Department of Higher Education
University of Surrey
Guildford, UK

Ian M. Kinchin
Department of Higher Education
University of Surrey
Guildford, UK

Naomi E. Winstone
Department of Higher Education
University of Surrey
Guildford, UK

ISBN 978-3-030-20823-3   ISBN 978-3-030-20824-0   (eBook)
https://doi.org/10.1007/978-3-030-20824-0

This Palgrave Macmillan imprint is published by the registered company Springer Nature Switzerland AG
The registered company address is: Gewerbestrasse 11, 6330 Cham, Switzerland

Foreword

This is an important and timely book. It finds itself situated at a moment where, despite increasing marketisation of higher education and the dominant neoliberalist political discourse, there are signs of resistance within the landscape of higher education. With increasing competition for students, tertiary sector institutions have almost unilaterally responded by placing significant energy and resources into understanding and enhancing the student experience. The result has been a detectable shift across policy and process by which the student has been put at the centre of academic endeavour in both the space of learning and teaching and academic life. This book focusses on undergraduate and postgraduate voices, and carefully considers the weight and impact of these voices and resulting actions across different detailed settings. Through a carefully curated collection of chapters, it takes a considered view on access into and through education, distinguishing where and which voices are heard. It considers how minority and non-traditional learners find their way into tertiary education and how universities are responding to the expectations of their funders and communities. This book offers new perspectives on the often complicated and dynamic nature of students' lives that is interwoven with the fabric of a modern university setting that intersects both private and professional boundaries. A distinctive international flavour is captured through studies that examine the student voice in different non-European settings where commonalities and differences are made visible in the ways that new forms of partnership are being forged between academic, student and institution.

The chapters presented in this volume also signal a growing maturity within academia whereby faculty now recognise the empowered student voice as a vital, rather than threatening, lever for change and enhancement in areas such as curriculum development and course design. Certainly, in the UK, the National Student Survey (NSS) has served to catalyse a sharpening of sensitivity to the various intersects where student, academic and institution come together. This and other surveys that institutions promote have provided touch points to gauge student sentiment and, on the surface at least, provide actionable insights. It is difficult to argue with the notion of listening and acting on the views of academia's primary 'customer', yet the question remains, is this at the correct granularity and cadence? Do these instruments provide the pulse check of student sentiment in a timely enough fashion for meaningful action? This highlights the value in recognising both the breadth and depth of the student voice in its multiple forms. For example, student teaching feedback systems which are meant to be *'feedback'* are only one point that help faculty triangulate the shifting centre of what constitutes excellent learning and teaching. When thoughtfully contextualised, this particular student voice has legitimacy and weight and must not be misinterpreted nor devalued.

Reading across the chapters in this book, it becomes clear that the nature and value of the student voice have changed. Early passive representation models of the student voice have shifted towards more active participatory formulations of student action. Taking a nod from design and software industries, approaches such as design thinking and co-design have become popular within many of our higher education establishments. We are experiencing more open and dynamic patterns of interaction with a positive shift from a wariness of listening and acting on the views of our students to the incorporation of multiple viewpoints within groups and committees that cut vertically and horizontally across the organisation. Prime examples include the recent focus of tertiary institutions on student success through whole of journey mapping, articulating transition pathways and scaffolding the first year experience to achieve articulated goals in access and progress. Whatever form these efforts take, the agency of the student within these activities has become more prominent.

Looking forwards, the future will provide more moments of disruption as digital technologies continue to transform the higher education sector. With the changing nature of work, the growing power of artificial intelligence and data analytics, we can expect the student voices and actions of today to be empowered and reengineered in new and exciting configurations. Acknowledging these changes, the chapters within this book take the reader on a journey that criss-crosses individual and personal with institutional and formal structures.

In conclusion, this book offers insights that cross theoretical and practical boundaries to provide new positions on the complicated nature of evolving student voices and the actions that surround them. The work challenges the reader on a number of levels and it offers a touch point for senior leaders looking to forward an institutional agenda around engaging student voices in deep and meaningful ways. I wholeheartedly recommend this book to all those involved in managing and promoting student success and engagement.

Wellington, New Zealand

Professor Steven Warburton
Assistant Vice-Chancellor
(Digital Futures)
University of Wellington

Preface

This book aims to challenge, or at least promote critical reflection on, the dominant discourses within higher education that focus on the student voice as a singular entity. The implications of considering a multiplicity of student voices are explored from a variety of perspectives: the chapter authors have been selected to represent a variety of institutional roles typically found across a university and thus to maximise the diversity of views that might be heard across any campus. Whilst the idea for this book originated with colleagues at the University of Surrey, it includes chapters written by colleagues from other institutions in and beyond the UK, providing insights from across the sector which are supported by the international literature on the subject.

This book will be of interest to policy-makers as well as to strategic leaders in universities and to academics who work with students as teachers, mentors, advisors and personal tutors. It challenges the tired trope of the 'feckless, snowflake millennial', and presents well-informed and thoughtful analyses of students as engaged members of the higher education community, rather than as homogenous objects of study within it.

The editors start the book in Chapter 1 by laying out their view of the 'single voice fallacy'. This is explored in depth in Part I, which commences with an account of a single student voice and then considers the diversity of student voices and the ways these intersect with contemporary themes such as partnership and consumerism.

Part II considers the various ways that diverse student voices have been masked by consideration of the 'average voice' in ways which have contributed to presenting a simplified student landscape which has in turn shaped and supported the development of policy. Part III goes on to consider events in the student journey and the different ways that institutions have engaged with student voices within the messy landscape of competing perspectives on a huge number of issues encompassing, for example, student transitions, well-being and employability.

Part IV explores the ways in which consideration of diversity in student voices may alter our perspectives on well-established themes including the evaluation of teaching and the research-teaching nexus. The editors conclude with a synthesis and suggestions concerning how future progress can draw on the enhanced perspectives afforded through being attuned to heterogeneous student voices. They anticipate that the reader may be unsettled by some of the ideas presented within the book, and indeed that is its aim—to prompt critical reflection on institutional practices in this new and uncertain era for higher education.

Guildford, UK

Professor Jane Powell
Vice-Provost Education
University of Surrey

Contents

1   The Single Voice Fallacy   1
    Simon Lygo-Baker, Ian M. Kinchin and Naomi E. Winstone

Part I   Engaging with Diverse Student Voices

2   Finding an Identity in the Crowd: A Single-Case
    Framed Narrative of Being in the Invisible Majority   19
    Ian M. Kinchin and Alexander M. Kinchin

3   The Value of Working with Students as Partners   37
    *Kathryn A. Sutherland, Isabella Lenihan-Ikin
    and Charlotte Rushforth*

4   The Voice of the Student as a 'Consumer'   55
    Louise Bunce

5   International Student Voice(s)—Where and What
    Are They?   71
    Anesa Hosein and Namrata Rao

6   Developing Oracy Skills for Student Voice Work   89
    Marion Heron and David M. Palfreyman

Part II   From Voice to Voices: Engaging Student Voices
          Beyond Metrics

7   Developing Assessment Feedback: From Occasional
    Survey to Everyday Practice   109
    Naomi E. Winstone and David Boud

8   What Happens After What Happens Next? The Single
    Voice of DLHE and Its Distortions on the Student
    Learning Journey   125
    Keith Herrmann

9   Mechanisms to Represent the Doctoral Researcher Voice   143
    Shane Dowle, Sam Hopkins and Carol Spencely

Part III Engaging Student Voices Across the Higher
          Education Experience

10 'Duck to Water' or 'Fish Out of Water'? Diversity
    in the Experience of Negotiating the Transition
    to University   159
    Naomi E. Winstone and Julie A. Hulme

11 Making Learning Happen: Students' Development
    of Academic and Information Literacies   175
    Karen Gravett

12   Collaborating with Students to Support Student
     Mental Health and Well-being   191
     Dawn Querstret

13   Reconciling Diverse Student and Employer Voices
     on Employability Skills and Work-Based Learning   209
     Katarina Zajacova, Erica Hepper and Alexandra Grandison

14   Students' Perceptions of Graduate Attributes:
     A Signalling Theory Analysis   225
     Anna Jones and Judy Pate

Part IV   The Influence of Student Voices on Academic
          Work

15   Valuing Uncertainty   245
     Simon Lygo-Baker

16   Pluralising 'Student Voices': Evaluating Teaching
     Practice   261
     Adun Okupe and Emma Medland

17   Student Voice(s) on the Enactment
     of the Research-Teaching Nexus   279
     Ian M. Kinchin and Camille B. Kandiko Howson

18   Engaging Students as Co-designers in Educational
     Innovation   297
     Karen Gravett, Emma Medland and Naomi E. Winstone

19   When All Is Said and Done: Consensus or Pluralism?   315
     Simon Lygo-Baker, Ian M. Kinchin and Naomi E. Winstone

Index   327

Notes on Contributors

David Boud is Alfred Deakin Professor and Foundation Director of the Centre for Research in Assessment and Digital Learning, Deakin University, Australia; Professor in the Work and Learning Research Centre, Middlesex University, UK; and Emeritus Professor at the University of Technology Sydney. His research on teaching, learning and assessment in higher and professional education is highly cited internationally. His current areas of interest are assessment in higher education and learning in the workplace. His most recent books are *Developing Evaluative Judgement in Higher Education*, (Routledge, 2018) and *Re-imagining University Assessment in a Digital World* (Springer, forthcoming) each with various others.

Louise Bunce is a Senior Lecturer in Human Development and Teaching Excellence Fellow at Oxford Brookes University, UK. She is also a Fellow of the Higher Education Academy and a Chartered Psychologist. Her research applies psychological theory to understand the factors that support or hinder children's and adults' learning and development and ability to thrive. In collaboration with her students, she has conducted internationally recognised research to explore the impact of the marketisation of higher education on student engagement and academic performance.

Shane Dowle is the manager of the Doctoral College at the University of Surrey, UK, and he is also a part-time Ph.D. researcher at Royal Holloway, University of London. Shane's research interests focus on the doctoral student experience with a particular focus on what enables Ph.D. students to complete their projects successfully and on time. Shane is an advocate of postgraduate issues at the sector level and has served on advisory boards for the QAA and HEA.

Alexandra Grandison is a Senior Lecturer in Psychology at the University of Surrey, UK, and a Senior Fellow of the Higher Education Academy. She has been a lecturer in Higher Education since 2010 and has taught and supervised students at all Undergraduate and Postgraduate levels. Alexandra has a keen interest in employability and work-based learning and how students engage with these concepts throughout their time in education. Through her role as Senior Professional Training Tutor, she has supported students in preparation for, during and after their professional training year and co-developed an innovative skills-based module to facilitate employability in psychology.

Karen Gravett is a Lecturer in Higher Education at the University of Surrey, UK. Her previous posts have included information skills librarian, academic liaison and electronic information roles at the University of Surrey and Royal Holloway. She completed her B.A. (Hons) at Cardiff University in 2003, and a Masters in Library and Information Studies at University College London in 2006. Her interests include: digital and information literacy, pedagogy in Higher Education, and electronic information and technologies.

Erica Hepper is a Lecturer in Psychology at the University of Surrey, UK. She obtained her Ph.D. from the University of Southampton in 2007 and has taught at all HE levels since then, including holding the roles of Director of Undergraduate Studies and Senior Professional Training Tutor. Erica is a social/personality psychologist and her research focuses on understanding individual differences in self-relevant emotions and motivation in social contexts such as education, the workplace and close relationships.

Marion Heron (Engin) is a Senior Lecturer in Higher Education at the University of Surrey, UK. She has worked in higher education institutions in Turkey and Dubai. She is an applied linguist with a particular interest in the application of sociocultural theory to examining the relationship between talk and learning.

Keith Herrmann was at the time of writing the Director of Employability at the University of Surrey, UK, where he was strategic lead on employability, careers and the university's renowned student placement programme. Keith was previously Deputy Chief Executive at the Council for Industry and Higher Education (CIHE) focusing on research about entrepreneurship education, innovation, university-business collaboration, career guidance and STEM education. Keith worked previously at Durham University Business School as Director of Programmes where he led a team specialising in entrepreneurship and economic policy. Keith also pro bono convenes the Careers Alliance, a network of 25 national organisations with an interest in career guidance.

Sam Hopkins works for the Researcher Development Programme (RDP) at the University of Surrey, UK, developing a range of training and support activities for researchers. Sam now manages the mentoring programmes and the part-time and distance provision. Sam studied B.Sc. Zoology in the UK and then completed her M.Sc. and Ph.D. in South Africa, subsequently taking a position as a lecturer. She continued her postdoctoral research career in biological sciences at the University of Surrey and spent a short time at the Zoological Society of London. Sam is now applying these experiences to her role in the RDP team.

Anesa Hosein is a Lecturer in Higher Education at the University of Surrey, UK. After teaching and studying in the areas of physics and manufacturing engineering, she moved to the UK as an international student to pursue a Ph.D. in Educational Technology. Her research focuses on how affective and social factors influence academics' and students' experiences in Higher Education for various groups, such as migrant academics and persons in STEM.

Julie A. Hulme is a Reader in Psychology at Keele University, UK, and Chair of the British Psychological Society (BPS) Division of Academics, Researchers and Teachers in Psychology. A UK National Teaching

Fellow, and Principal Fellow of the Higher Education Academy (PFHEA), she applies psychology to learning, teaching and assessment. Julie's own experiences as a mature student helped her to recognise the importance of transition to university, and of skills and confidence for successful university study. She strives to create engaging learning opportunities which help all students to achieve their aspirations, through the application of psychology to everyday life (psychological literacy).

Anna Jones is a Senior Lecturer in Clinical Education at King's College London. Her research interests include institutional change, graduate attributes, disciplinary cultures, medical education, academic practice and the role of higher education. In her previous roles, she was responsible for the design, coordination and delivery of a range of transition, student learning and academic development programmes.

Dr. Camille B. Kandiko Howson is Associate Professor of Education in the Centre for Higher Education Research & Scholarship at Imperial College London. She researches higher education with a focus on pedagogy and student engagement; quality, performance and accountability; international and comparative education; curriculum change; and gender and prestige in academic work. She has worked on using concept mapping in educational research and practice. Previously she was Academic Head of Student Engagement and Senior Lecturer in Higher Education at King's College London.

Alexander M. Kinchin was an undergraduate student at a south coast university at the time of writing, where he was studying electrical and electronic engineering, after gaining A-levels in biology, chemistry, mathematics and physics. His academic interests were triggered by his passion for electric guitars and heavy metal music. He is also heavily engaged in airsoft and table-top gaming, having been involved in running university societies for both of these activities. Alexander is also interested in internet culture and science fiction literature. He is currently considering employment options in a variety of fields—away from engineering.

Ian M. Kinchin is Professor of Higher Education at the University of Surrey, UK. He is engaged in the professional development of academic staff, whilst undertaking research into university pedagogy and the application of Novakian concept mapping. Ian is the editor of the *Journal of Biological Education*, a Fellow of the Royal Society of Biology, a Senior Fellow of the Higher Education Academy, and has been a member of the Governing Council of the Society for Research into Higher Education. He is currently developing a model for academic development that is framed by the concepts of pedagogic frailty and resilience.

Isabella Lenihan-Ikin is completing a conjoint degree in Law and Biomedical Science at Victoria University of Wellington. Isabella served as the Academic Vice President of the Victoria University of Wellington Students Association (VUWSA) in 2017 and was elected to the University Council as one of two student representatives in 2018.

Simon Lygo-Baker is a Senior Lecturer in the Department of Higher Education at the University of Surrey, UK. He also holds a visiting position at the School of Veterinary Medicine, University of Wisconsin-Madison. He completed a Masters in Political Science at Warwick University before undertaking a Ph.D. in Education looking at identity and values in university teaching. He initially worked on projects with marginalised communities such as refugees and asylum seekers and those in recovery from addiction. More recently, he has worked at King's College London and the University of Surrey in academic development and researching aspects of learning and teaching within the disciplines.

Emma Medland is a Lecturer in Higher Education at the University of Surrey's Department of Higher Education and has been an academic developer for twelve years in the UK. Her research interests focus on assessment and feedback in higher education, particularly in relation to assessment and feedback literacy, the subjectivity underpinning assessment and feedback practices, the role of assessment in curriculum development, and the concepts of 'grade inflation' and contract cheating. Emma is a Senior Fellow of the Higher Education Academy and is Programme Director for the M.A. in Higher Education.

Adun Okupe is the director of the Sahara Centre which focuses on advancing sociocultural development in Nigeria. She is also a Senior Advisor at Compass, a customer engagement and insights firm focused on working with organisations to engage better with their customers. Her research interests along the lines of leadership, societal change and tourism are influenced by her practical applications which all include aspects of teaching, be it in the classroom, disseminating research findings or providing advisory services to organisations. She is particularly interested in how the feedback process can be improved. She is a member of the Institute of Chartered Accountants of Scotland and a Fellow of the Higher Education Academy.

David M. Palfreyman works in the College of Education at Zayed University in the United Arab Emirates. His experience includes twenty-five years of teaching on undergraduate and postgraduate programs in English language and teacher education, in higher education institutions and international organisations. His research interests include the role of sociocultural context and discourse in learning by students and practitioners, as well as multilingualism and biliteracy in educational settings. He is the founding editor of the journal *Learning and Teaching in Higher Education: Gulf Perspectives* (LTHE).

Judy Pate is a Senior Lecturer (Management) in the Adam Smith Business School at the University of Glasgow. She has expertise in human resource management, sociological theory, trust and the sociology of professions.

Dawn Querstret is a Lecturer in Workforce Organisation and Wellbeing at the University of Surrey, UK. She is chartered with the British Psychological Society and is a Registered Practitioner Psychologist (Health) with the Health Care and Professions Council. Dawn is currently leading research investigating the efficacy of online mindfulness interventions for mental health and well-being in a variety of samples. For example, for depression, anxiety and stress in occupational and student samples; and for emotional resilience, quality of life and resilience in samples of people with long-term health conditions (multiple sclerosis, stroke, irritable bowel syndrome and fibromyalgia).

Namrata Rao is a Senior Lecturer in Education at Liverpool Hope University in the Centre of Education and Policy Analysis. She has a background in biological sciences and a Ph.D. in Education. She is a

Senior Fellow of the Higher Education Academy, executive member of the British Association of International and Comparative Education (BAICE), member of the Research and Development Working Group of the Association for Learning Development in Higher Education (ALDinHE). Her research focuses on international and comparative education, various aspects of learning and teaching in higher education, and factors that influence academic identity and practice.

Charlotte Rushforth was the Student Representation Coordinator for the Victoria University of Wellington Students Association (the only such full-time paid position in the country), from 2017 to 2018. Charlotte completed her M.A. in Communication in 2017 at the University of California Santa Barbara.

Carol Spencely is a Teaching Fellow for Learning Development at the University of Surrey. She completed her Ph.D. in Immunology at the University of Liverpool before moving to Imperial College London for a postdoc position at the National Heart and Lung Institute. Following further postdoc contracts and a teaching fellowship, she decided to move away from lab-based research. Carol worked as a medical writer for a communications company, but she was then drawn back to Imperial where she helped to set up the Postdoc Development Centre before joining the Researcher Development Programme at the University of Surrey in 2012.

Kathryn A. Sutherland is an Associate Professor in the Centre for Academic Development at Victoria University of Wellington, New Zealand. She recently returned to this role after a six-year term as Associate Dean (Students, Learning and Teaching) in the Faculty of Humanities and Social Sciences. Kathryn's research and teaching both focus on the socialisation, retention and fulfilment of early career academics (ECAs). Through programmes like Ako in Action, she encourages ECAs to work more deliberately and effectively with students as partners in teaching design and curriculum development.

Naomi E. Winstone is a Reader in Higher Education and Head of the Department of Higher Education at the University of Surrey, UK. Naomi holds B.Sc., M.Sc. and Ph.D. degrees in Psychology and has extensive experience of academic leadership, having occupied the roles of Director of Learning and Teaching and Associate Dean (Learning and Teaching) at the University of Surrey. Naomi is a cognitive psychologist, specialising in learning behaviour and engagement with education. Naomi's research focuses on the processing and implementation of feedback, educational transitions and educational identities. Naomi is a Senior Fellow of the Higher Education Academy and a National Teaching Fellow.

Katarina Zajacova is a Senior Professional Training Tutor and a Teaching Fellow in Psychology, Sociology and Social Sciences at the University of Surrey, UK. She has worked in Higher Education since 2006 and has supervised, taught and supported students in preparation for and during their professional training year. Katarina has convened a number of employability-related UG modules and has worked on the development of innovative skills-based learning and teaching methods and assessments. Through her role as Faculty Senior Professional Training Tutor, she has liaised and collaborated with numerous placement providers and employers in the UK and abroad.

Abbreviations

AQA	Academic Quality Agency
AUSSE	Australasian Survey of Student Engagement
CEQ	Course Experience Questionnaire
CUAP	Committee on University Academic Programmes
DLHE	Destinations of Leavers from Higher Education
EMI	English as a Medium of Instruction
ESL	English as a Second Language
GTA	Graduate Teaching Assistant
HE	Higher Education
HEA	Higher Education Academy
HEI	Higher Education Institution
HEPI	Higher Education Policy Institute
HESA	Higher Education Statistics Agency
LEO	Longitudinal Earnings Outcome
MEQs	Module Evaluation Questionnaires
NSS	National Student Survey
NSSE	National Survey of Student Engagement
NTFS	National Teaching Fellowship Scheme
NUS	National Union of Students
NZ	New Zealand
NZUSA	New Zealand Union of Students' Associations

OFFA	Office for Fair Access
OfS	Office for Students
PRES	Postgraduate Research Experience Survey
QAA	Quality Assurance Agency
REF	Research Excellence Framework
TEC	Tertiary Education Commission
TEF	Teaching Excellence Framework
UK	United Kingdom
UKPSF	UK Professional Standards Framework
US	United States
VLE	Virtual Learning Environment
WBL	Work-Based Learning

List of Figures

Fig. 2.1   A concept map of the discourse of teaching and learning
           (MEQ = Module Evaluation Questionnaire, a mechanism
           that allows students to rate the quality of their teachers)   24
Fig. 2.2   A concept map relating the pedagogy of the discipline
           with the practice of the discipline   25
Fig. 2.3   A concept map of the research-teaching nexus   27
Fig. 2.4   A concept map of the regulation and evaluation of teaching   29
Fig. 5.1   Non-UK students' distribution across the constituent
           countries (HESA 2015/2016 dataset)   77
Fig. 5.2   Number of UK international students from the top 5
           countries (HESA 2015/2016 dataset)   78
Fig. 10.1 Mean confidence ratings across academic skills at Time 1
           (start of year 1) and Time 2 (end of year 1). Paired
           t-tests: * p <0.05 ** p < 0.01 *** p < 0.001   165
Fig. 17.1 A wholistic model for research-based learning
           decision-making (modified and redrawn from Brew, 2013)   286
Fig. 18.1 Top-down and bottom-up approaches to design   299
Fig. 18.2 Concept map interview with project lead   306

List of Tables

Table 5.1 Review of literature on Chinese international students
with reference to the UK   80
Table 6.1 Oracy skills framework (Mercer et al. 2017)   97
Table 7.1 Assessment and feedback items in the 2017
UK National Student Survey (NSS)   114
Table 17.1 Disciplines and authors represented in the special issue 283

1

The Single Voice Fallacy

Simon Lygo-Baker, Ian M. Kinchin
and Naomi E. Winstone

When considering issues of power and control in any social system, the concept of 'voice' often comes to the fore. Within the higher education sector, this concept brings with it a wealth of underpinning ideas, such that consideration of a 'voice' represents more than 'noises made' or 'utterances spoken'. The notion of voice is bound up with ideas such as identity (who am I to have a voice?), agency (how can I use my voice?), and responsibility (how should I use my voice?). Cook-Sather (2006) argues that the concept of voice 'signals having a legitimate perspective and opinion, being present and taking part' (p. 362). In addition, the ideas that have increasingly become aligned with the idea of voice have tended towards an implication of 'pro-active voices' rather than passive or re-active voices.

S. Lygo-Baker (✉) · I. M. Kinchin · N. E. Winstone
Department of Higher Education, University of Surrey, Guildford, UK
e-mail: s.lygo-baker@surrey.ac.uk

I. M. Kinchin
e-mail: i.kinchin@surrey.ac.uk

N. E. Winstone
e-mail: n.winstone@surrey.ac.uk

© The Author(s) 2019
S. Lygo-Baker et al. (eds.), *Engaging Student Voices in Higher Education*,
https://doi.org/10.1007/978-3-030-20824-0_1

In a hierarchical system that is not used to engaging with a diversity of proactive voices, there is likely to be competition to be heard. As a consequence, there might be a number of 'lost voices', where the loss may be felt by individuals who feel marginalised, but also where loss represents missed opportunities for organisational learning. To avoid drowning in a sea of voices, universities may have developed selective hearing—where certain voices are allowed to become dominant over others, and the voice of the 'ruling stratum' becomes the accepted voice (Hobden & Wyn Jones, 2017, p. 138). This seems to run contrary to the widely espoused goals of diversity and inclusion. This book aims to throw light onto these issues so that diverse (and possibly contradictory) voices can engage in the discourses that will shape higher education in the coming years.

In this chapter, we frame our broad conceptual framework and introduce some key themes that will be developed throughout the chapters in this book. The aims of the book are threefold:

1. to explore how notions of the student 'voice' as a single, monolithic entity obscure the divergence in experiences of students;
2. to consider how placing emphasis on what is brought to the fore under the banner of the 'student voice' might lead educators and policymakers to miss important messages from students themselves communicated through their actions and what they *don't* say;
3. to consider different ways of working in partnership with students to develop their own experiences as well as to influence the nature of academic work more broadly.

Student Experience, Student Engagement, and Student Voice

As the learning environment evolves within the twenty-first century, the notion of the student experience has become increasingly prevalent. Articulation of the student experience has noted the importance of establishing a dialogue with a range of stakeholders. Whatever the stimulus, it is evident that the strategy to provide greater access to higher education and to encourage universities to become more adaptable has heeded the argument that key stakeholders, such as employers, need to have greater input into the system. This is based on the (perhaps flawed) premise that members of each stakeholder group hold identical, or at least highly similar, views. In a fluid sector (Bauman, 2000), this is surely unlikely as needs are constantly in flux and employers, for example, may have little idea what their future requirements are. Despite this, a rise in the authority of stakeholder groups within the academic community has been recognised (Jongbloed, Enders, & Salerno, 2008). Within these stakeholder groups sit the students themselves, whose many differing voices often become homogenised. The student voice, as a seemingly singular sound, is then more easily aligned with those of other stakeholder groups, such as employers, to suggest greater demands on the sector, such as higher quality teaching. With a rise in discourse of students as 'customers' in higher education, the student voice has been framed in a similar way to the consumer voice in wider society; as paying customers, students can and should give feedback and express (dis)satisfaction with their experience of the service.

Alongside discourse around the student experience and the notion of the student voice sits the concept of student engagement, which is often seen as overlapping with student voice (Seale, Gibson, Haynes, & Potter, 2015). Engaged students are, in many cases, seen as the ones who are willing to contribute their voices to debates and developments. This view of engagement, as participation in the wider work of the university, is arguably different to discussion of student engagement with the academic pursuit of their programme of study, such as engaging in independent study, asking questions, and participating in discussion. Perhaps, therefore, it is not surprising that the concept of student engagement has been described as 'an uncritically accepted academic orthodoxy' (Brookfield, 1986, p. 96), and that in higher education, with reference to student voice, 'definitions and conceptualisations are underdeveloped' (Seale, 2010, p. 995). Canning (2017) argues that the distinction between the concepts of student engagement and student voice is fuzzy, with student voice perhaps best seen as a form of student engagement. Whilst it is possible to argue that a student who makes their voice heard is engaged in some way, in this book we consider other ways in which students 'speak' to us; through their actions, through their participation, and even through their silence. Indeed, viewing student engagement as solely characterised by active and observable participation is described as the 'tyranny of participation' by Gourlay (2015, p. 403).

The Increasing Volume of the Student 'Voice'

Articulation of students' authority has been represented by the concept of the 'voice' that the students have found or perhaps been given. The concept of student 'voice' has a long history in the compulsory education sector (e.g. Kane & Chimwayange, 2014; Quaglia & Corso, 2014), where voice is conceptualised as:

> listening to and valuing the views that students express regarding their learning experiences; communicating student views to people who are in a position to influence change; and treating students as equal partners in the evaluation of teaching and learning, thus empowering them to take a more active role in shaping or changing their education. (Seale, 2010, p. 995)

In the wider sphere of educational research, attention to surfacing the voice of children represents the new sociology of childhood (l'Anson, 2013), and a response to critiques that children's perspectives were often overlooked in research. For example, Fullan posed the question 'what would happen if we treated the student as someone whose opinion mattered?' (Fullan, 1991, p. 170). Paying attention to opinions as representing more than just points of data is central to this approach.

Returning to the higher education context, whilst the definition of the student voice varies, the concept itself has surfaced across a range of locations. Policymakers with an interest in influencing the behaviour of those working with learners, as well as universities themselves, have become increasingly interested in a dialogue with the student voice. Students themselves have been drawn to use the term, developing conferences that run under the banner of the student voice (which began in 2014), and the concept is also integrated within researchers' conceptual frameworks and resulting publications (Bishop, 2018; Brooman, Darwent, & Pimor, 2015; Seale, 2016).

The most common manifestations of the student voice can be seen through the canvassing of students' opinions through metrics such as the National Student Survey (NSS) in the UK and the Course Experience Questionnaire (CEQ) in Australia, institutional teaching evaluations, students' contributions to programme design and revalidation, Student Union fora, staff-student liaison committees, and student-led teaching awards. Arguably, the main focus in higher education is on forms of voice carrying 'external currency' (Canning, 2017, p. 522), such as the NSS. Seale et al. (2015) raise the possibility of 'voice fatigue' (p. 548) as a result of students being inundated with requests to give voice to their experience. This raises the question of the rationale underpinning attempts to surface the student voice. Do we assume that students are not satisfied and feel ignored (Seale et al., 2015)? Or is there a sense of 'ticking a box' to show that students have been consulted in quality assurance and enhancement processes (McLeod, 2011)? Many quality assurance bodies such as the Quality Assurance Agency in the UK (QAA) and Professional Statutory and Regulatory Bodies make it a requirement for programmes to include students in quality enhancement and assurance activities (Bishop, 2018). Crucially, involving students more heavily in governance does not necessarily lead to greater democracy; in fact, it may serve to reinforce the consumer identity of students (Bishop, 2018). Seeking student input into validation and accreditation processes can, if taken in isolation, embody a 'consumer panel' model of student voice which reinforces the business/consumer roles of university and student, respectively (Canning, 2017). Cynically, this approach could be seen as more about serving the reputation of the institution than engaging student voices, merely representing 'a zeitgeist commitment to voice alongside a concern for client and stakeholder interests' (Ruddock, 2006, p. 133).

When these different approaches are examined, a potential dichotomy emerges. Whilst the emphasis has been upon the student 'voice', suggesting a singular and unified perspective, within these narratives there is often a recognition of the complexity that listening to particular perspectives may provide as issues around diversity and inclusion abound, suggesting the presence of multiple voices. As so often where complexity exists there is a tendency to attempt to simplify, with a view to being able to explain past responses and predict future actions. As Mayring (2007) argues, observations and data are often undermined by overhasty generalisations that may miss the very learning they seek to promote. In this case, the loudest or dominant 'voice' within a particular context can become the one that is repeated, to the point it appears unanimous and is used to inform responses. Whilst we know that the student voice is by nature diverse, and with the impact of globalisation arguably becoming even more so, there is potential that we take the 'loudest' perspective to be representative of all. However, researchers have argued that such an approach is flawed (Lincoln & Guba, 1985) and that attempts to reduce complexity to create simplicity are problematic (l'Anson, 2013). Instead, we should recognise and take seriously the messiness that characterises the world around us (Law, 2004; Thrift, 2008).

The Single Voice Fallacy

Students do not speak with a single unified voice; a cursory examination of student evaluations demonstrates often wide fluctuations of opinion. As argued by McLeod (2011), 'Any voice-based equity interventions need to be able to allow and respond to dissonance, to the likelihood of discordant voices and to all students not speaking as one' (p. 187). Even if we were to accept that student voices are uniform, there is limited evidence that student feedback has a transformative impact on the evolution of higher education teaching practice. Despite our increased knowledge of how people learn, the sector remains somewhat wedded to lengthy lectures and examinations that privilege those who can recall through short-term regurgitation, retaining a focus on knowing and understanding rather than applying and creating. Why is this?

The assumption remains that learners will become more engaged if they are able to participate in decisions about their learning. The movement to increase student involvement has led to different conceptualisations emerging. For some, it has been about students as partners in learning (Cook-Sather, Bovill, & Felten, 2014), for others as change agents (Dunne & Zandstra, 2011) and others as co-creators (Bovill, Cook-Sather, & Felten, 2011). For teachers, this remains potentially problematic unless the learners are distilled to a singular voice, because pluralism creates potentially different learning directions and requests. Seale (2016) argues this has led to a shift away from a focus on a recognition of voices to more centralised initiatives that are more likely to work with a distilled version; in other words a singular funnelled voice. Cook-Sather (2006) identifies a potential negative aspect of student voice, the idea that this is 'monolithic' (p. 367), and Seale (2010) cautions that by adopting a unitary concept of the student 'voice', we rely on assumptions about what the dominant voice desires.

So whilst there are increased suggestions that the student voice is listened to through metrics such as the NSS and CEQ, student module evaluations, or staff-student committees, this remains somewhat limited and hides individual voices. It may be that a reduced perspective is advantageous to those developing policies, where the temptation to demonstrate compliance through engagement with the student voice may be overwhelming. The result, a sleight of hand that suggests different voices have an impact. However, evidence may suggest that these voices become condensed and all that actually occurs is the distillation of a particular, often recognisable voice that is promoted and used for political ends by various stakeholders.

As Parmenter (2017) recently suggested in the Washington Post, this leads to individual students merely being viewed as data points, losing their individual voice. As argued by McLeod (2011):

> In social research, the attitude to voice tends to take two main directions. First, there is a privileging and celebration of voice: voice is given to, and heard from, the excluded, the neglected, the ordinary…This celebratory mode, however, is countered by recognition of the ethical and epistemological dangers of speaking for, or on behalf of, others: this includes questions not only about the violence of speaking for others…but also about whose voice speaks loudest. (p. 183)

This reminds us of the importance of not paying lip service to student voice work by assuming that if dominant voices have been heard then we have successfully and equitably engaged students' voices in shaping academic work. Not only is the concept of student voice necessarily plural, many voices go unheard (Canning, 2017).

Engaging with Student Voices

In this book, we examine the potential for engaging with student voices as a pluralistic but complex concept and consider how we may conceive of these differences as sources of insight into the student experience. The continuous process of change in higher education means that finding a singular voice of consensus, whilst appealing, is unlikely to be achievable. Even employing simple delineations that are often used to categorise learners: school leavers, mature students, first generation, distance, or international suggests plurality is likely to exist. Within and across each simplified category, there are likely to be different perspectives and as a consequence attempts to communicate with a single voice may create a dialogue with only a particular group or section of a university within a particular category. A potential outcome of such approaches may be the further isolation of significant numbers of learners who lose their voice or are left unheard. Therefore, attempts to create apparent consensus reduce the pluralism that many have viewed as a core element of the university campus and experience, and in particular the development of a more diverse group of learners.

A consequence may be that as institutions seek to maintain the status quo, they favour a particular voice whenever it is available and can be isolated. The result, a focus on the product of these engagements that provide a more grounded set of actions. These are increasingly established as Key Performance Indicators that can be measured and the impacts more easily defined as a response to the dominant voice: a 'You said, we did' approach.

In a review of student voice initiatives in UK higher education, Seale (2010) criticises a tendency to focus not on the process of dialogue with students, but on the product of our engagements. We therefore need to understand how we engage with individual student voices before we are able to engage with the plurality of voices to appreciate how students experience and explain various aspects of higher education, not necessarily through consensus, but through variation.

This book considers how to engage with the student voices that exist and continue to emerge, providing a reconceptualisation of the current debates. The book also seeks to build on this reconceptualisation, by exploring how to subsequently engage with the results of these conversations to bring a greater understanding of the student experience using the additional data and insight for those teaching and developing learning within institutions. It is important to consider ways that we may celebrate different perspectives, as opposed to a reductionist approach that leads, ironically, to greater fragmentation. On the one hand, institutions seek to engage with the student voice whilst at the same time acknowledging the need to recognise and engage with under-represented or vulnerable groups. This book seeks to initially isolate and recognise these as two different aspects that although linked are best separated for examination. By conflating the two, it may inadvertently have caused a focus on identified groups within the learning environment. As argued by McLeod (2011):

> To align voice with marginalized or under-represented groups is to further stigmatize such students – they are known and heard by their otherness: 'traditional' student groups are 'normal' and are not accorded a problematic voice; and it is also likely to diminish struggles for greater equity. (p. 187)

Ultimately this may represent a lack of balance within the literature where the voices of the 'privileged majority' go unrecorded and unrecognised, except as an aggregated mass (e.g. through the NSS). The student voice, whilst being portrayed as a positive notion through which a dialogue is opened between different groups within an institution, may actually prevent or negate the voices of others being heard. The notion of an institution engaging with a unified single voice that includes representation from different perspectives is appealing. However, the balance may not represent the body to which it purports to give voice. As such, there is an opportunity to examine the dilemma this represents within the notions of *pluralism* (student voices) and yet being aware of the consequent challenge to the notion of *consensus* (student voice).

We consider 'student voices' as they emerge across a wide variety of contexts within the heterogeneous university environment. Within the current literature, there is a growing emphasis on the promotion of collaborative partnerships, with the student being the co-producer or producers (e.g. Cook-Sather et al., 2014). This is significant as one critique of student 'voice' is that students' contributions to learning and teaching processes are often limited to consultation, which arguably limits the agency students have to realise meaningful change (Bovill, Cook-Sather, Felten, Millard, & Moore-Cherry, 2016). Engaging students as true partners, change agents, and co-creators moves the role and agency of students beyond mere consultation (Bishop, 2018).

This highlights an important outcome of student voice work: true engagement with student voices comes not from what students have to say, but enabling action in response to their views. Seale (2010) argues that voice work should involve 'hearing what students say and using what they say to make improvements', where there is 'an implicit emphasis on taking on board and valuing student views' (p. 998). Taking this even further, we might place greater emphasis on students themselves leading these actions; the common 'you said, we did' mantra places students in a passive role where it is the institution that takes responsibility for action. Student agency requires the possibility that not only can students identify areas of change in the first place, they can also lead on endeavours to enact change. As argued by Dunne and Zandstra (2011):

> There is a subtle, but extremely important, difference between an institution that 'listens' to students and responds accordingly, and an institution that gives students the opportunity to explore areas that they believe to be significant, to recommend solutions and to bring about the required changes. (p. 4)

For student voices to have an impact upon the actions of universities and to be heard, they have to refer to issues that already feature within the higher education discourse. Only by achieving this are they perceived to be of relevance and become recognisable. We have therefore sought to investigate student voices within the contexts provided by issues that are recognised and given value by universities (e.g. assessment & feedback, technology-enhanced learning, research, etc.) and these are reflected in the foci of the separate chapters presented here.

Woven through the varied chapters in this volume is a thread of discourse seeking to look beyond 'voices' to consider what we can learn from student actions and inactions. Seale et al. (2015) raise the importance of considering how we interpret students' silence. What can we learn from what students don't say, or where they don't feel able to express their views? Cook-Sather (2006), in a consideration of means through which we engage with student voices, argues that the most common approach is listening; the processes of watching students and reflecting upon their (in)actions are much rarer. She goes on to argue that:

> Using the term "voice" to represent a repositioning of students in educational research and reform also runs the risk of denying the potential power of silence and resistance. Silence can be powerful – a withholding of assent, a political act. Silence can mean the voice is not speaking because it is not worthwhile or safe to speak. (Cook-Sather, 2006, p. 369)

Students' actions also speak as loudly as their voices, and universities should be open to learning from what students do, not only what they say. For example, what might on the surface appear to be minimal engagement with learning opportunities might be students trying to tell us that such opportunities are not appropriately timed or scheduled. Engaging with student voices requires paying equal attention to what students do and do not say, and what actions they do and do not take. As argued by Canning (2017), 'voice needs to be understood more broadly than the expression of the spoken or written word. The unspoken voice, silence and the unconscious student voice need greater consideration' (p. 529).

Outline of the Book

Part I: Engaging with Diverse Student Voices

We begin the book by listening to the voice of a student. Engaging in depth with the experiences and perspectives of a single student powerfully illustrates the importance of recognising nuanced experience. We also use this student narrative as a lens through which to explore many of the other topics covered in this book. McLeod (2011, p. 186) reminds us that 'One further virtue of taking student voice seriously is that it provides a reminder of the presence of embodied students, against the prevalence of abstract, disembodied equity categories that beset discussion of inequality and representation in education'. In this vein, we also bring to the fore in this part some key considerations in embracing diversity and nuance of perspective, including the experiences of international students, and a critical treatment of the 'student-as-consumer' voice. As a counterpoint, we also explore meaningful engagement with the voices of students as partners, and the role of oracy skills in students' participation in voice work.

Part II: From Voice to Voices: Engaging Student Voices Beyond Metrics

One of the most prominent accounts of the singular student 'voice' in higher education comes from the surveys and metrics used to give account to the student experience. In fact, many of these processes that are commonly framed under the auspices of the student voice in reality serve to reduce students to mere 'data points', where many of the nuances in their experiences are lost. The chapters in this part seek to position students as more than data points, exploring what can be learnt through alternative, more meaningful ways of engaging with their experiences. The chapter focuses on different surveys and metrics: the NSS, the Postgraduate Taught Experience Survey (PTES) and Postgraduate Research Experience Survey (PRES), and the Destination of Leavers of higher education survey (DLHE).

Part III: Engaging Student Voices Across the Higher Education Experience

In this part, we move to consideration of the value of engaging student voices as a way of understanding key events and challenges in the student journey. We focus on key milestones in the academic life cycle including the transition to university, the development of academic and information literacy skills, mental health and well-being, employability and work-based learning, and graduate attributes. Within these chapters, we observe different approaches to engaging student voices in higher education. In Chapter 10, we see how students' voices can be used to support subsequent cohorts during transition periods, and in Chapter 14, we witness the value of signalling-theory analysis in surfacing diverse perspectives.

Part IV: The Influence of Student Voices on Academic Work

As argued by Cook-Sather (2006), the expression of views is just one dimension of voice; agency and representation comes from having some control over how the results of these exchanges are enacted and developed. In this part, we consider how the voices of students can more meaningfully contribute to research and development agendas. Many attempts to listen to the student 'voice' are actually less democratic and participatory than they might appear, because such expression of voice operates within constraints of rules and expectations, such as when students are 'allowed' to share their views, and in response to a set agenda (Canning, 2017). This represents what Foucault terms the 'micro power' systems constituting the 'dark side' of what may appear to be egalitarian processes (1977, p. 222). For example, student evaluations of teaching are often limited to set survey questions, the responses to which are processed centrally and can be 'sanitised' by the time they reach the teaching staff who have the power to effect change (Canning, 2017). In this part, we explore alternative approaches to the evaluation of teaching and also consider how the uncertainty that can arise through student voice work influences academic identity and values. We also consider how students' perspectives can shape the relationship between academics' research and teaching work.

Conclusion

In this book, it is not our intention to try and cover all relevant dimensions of student heterogeneity, nor to attempt to address all issues pertinent to homogenising student voices. Rather, we illustrate our premise through the lens of a series of challenges and topics that are at the forefront of policy and practice in higher education. The rhetoric of consumerism and marketisation in contemporary higher education need not prevent meaningful engagement with students, nor attempts to build genuine partnerships. Students do not all speak with the same voice, and higher education has much to gain from listening to and learning from students' voices and actions.

References

Bauman, Z. (2000). *Liquid modernity.* Cambridge, UK: Polity.

Bishop, D. C. (2018). More than just listening: The role of student voice in higher education, an academic perspective. *IMPact: The University of Lincoln Journal of Higher Education Research, 1*(1).

Bovill, C., Cook-Sather, A., & Felten, P. (2011). Changing participants in pedagogical planning; Students as co-creators of teaching approaches, course design and curricula. *International Journal for Academic Development, 16*(2), 133–145.

Bovill, C., Cook-Sather, A., Felten, P., Millard, L., & Moore-Cherry, N. (2016). Addressing potential challenges in co-creating learning and teaching: Overcoming resistance, navigating institutional norms and ensuring inclusivity in student-staff partnerships. *Higher Education, 71*(2), 195–208.

Brookfield, S. (1986). *Understanding and facilitating adult learning.* Milton Keynes, UK: Open University Press.

Brooman, S., Darwent, S., & Pimor, A. (2015). The student voice in higher education curriculum design: Is there value in listening? *Innovations in Education and Teaching International, 52*(6), 663–674.

Canning, J. (2017). Conceptualising student voice in UK higher education: Four theoretical lenses. *Teaching in Higher Education, 22*(5), 519–531.

Cook-Sather, A. (2006). Sound, presence, and power: "Student voice" in educational research and reform. *Curriculum Inquiry, 36*(4), 359–390.

Cook-Sather, A., Bovill, C., & Felten, P. (2014). *Engaging students as partners in learning and teaching: A guide for faculty.* Hoboken, NJ: John Wiley & Sons.

Dunne, E., & Zandstra, R. (2011). *Students as change agents: New ways of engaging with learning and teaching in higher education.* Bristol: ESCalate Higher Education Academy Subject Centre for Education/University of Exeter.

Foucault, M. (1977). *Discipline and punish: The birth of the prison.* London: Penguin.

Fullan, M. (1991). *The new meaning of educational change.* New York: Teachers College Press.

Gourlay, L. (2015). 'Student engagement' and the tyranny of participation. *Teaching in Higher Education, 20*(4), 402–411.

Hobden, S., & Wyn Jones, R. (2017). Marxist theories of international relations. In J. Baylis, S. Smith, & P. Owens (Eds.), *The globalization of world politics* (pp. 129–143). Oxford: Oxford University Press.

Jongbloed, B., Enders, J., & Salerno, C. (2008). Higher education and its communities: Interconnections, interdependencies and a research agenda. *Higher Education, 56*(3), 303–324.

Kane, R. G., & Chimwayange, C. (2014). Teacher action research and student voice: Making sense of learning in secondary school. *Action Research, 12*(1), 52–77.

l'Anson, J. (2013). Beyond the child's voice: Towards an ethics for children's participation rights. *Global Studies of Childhood, 3*(2), 104–114.

Law, J. (2004). *After method: Mess in social science research.* Abingdon, UK: Routledge.

Lincoln, Y. S., & Guba, E. G. (1985). *Naturalistic inquiry.* Newbury Park, CA: Sage.

Mayring, P. (2007). On generalization in qualitatively oriented research. *Forum Qualitative Sozialforschung, 8*(3), 1–8.

McLeod, J. (2011). Student voice and the politics of listening in higher education. *Critical Studies in Education, 52*(2), 179–189.

Parmenter, J. (2017). *What happened when i stopped viewing my students as data points.* Retrieved from https://www.washingtonpost.com/news/answer-sheet/wp/2017/10/11/teacher-what-happened-when-i-stopped-viewing-my-students-as-data-points/?noredirect=on&utm_term=.5b3630addbf0.

Quaglia, R. J., & Corso, M. J. (2014). *Student voice: The instrument of change.* Thousand Oaks, CA: Corwin Press.

Ruddock, J. (2006). The past, the papers and the project. *Educational Review, 58*(2), 131–143.

Seale, J. (2010). Doing student voice work in higher education: An exploration of the value of participatory methods. *British Educational Research Journal, 36*(6), 995–1015.

Seale, J. (2016). How can we confidently judge the extent to which student voice in higher education has been genuinely amplified? A proposal for a new evaluation framework. *Research Papers in Education, 31*(2), 212–233.

Seale, J., Gibson, S., Haynes, J., & Potter, A. (2015). Power and resistance: Reflections on the rhetoric and reality of using participatory methods to promote student voice and engagement in higher education. *Journal of Further and Higher Education, 39*(4), 534–552.

Thrift, N. (2008). *Non-representational theory: Space, politics, affect.* Abingdon, UK: Routledge.

Part I

Engaging with Diverse Student Voices

2

Finding an Identity in the Crowd: A Single-Case Framed Narrative of Being in the Invisible Majority

Ian M. Kinchin and Alexander M. Kinchin

The search for a student voice has been dominated by methodologies that have typically sought to describe the 'big picture first' rather than investigating what goes on at the level of the individual. Typically, the activation of student voice has been achieved through un-targeted and large-scale questionnaires (such as the National Student Survey in the UK) which give a generalised overview, but may not represent the view of any particular or 'average' individual. At the same time, research into the nature of the student voice has often focussed on conferring representation and empowerment to under-represented, marginalised, or persecuted groups (e.g. McLeod, 2011). This has been undertaken with the aim of increasing equality and fairness across an increasingly diverse student body. In this context, it is understandable that much research has had the intention of levelling the higher education playing field and so has tended to focus on

I. M. Kinchin (✉)
Department of Higher Education, University of Surrey, Guildford, UK
e-mail: i.kinchin@surrey.ac.uk

A. M. Kinchin
Brighton, Sussex, UK

© The Author(s) 2019
S. Lygo-Baker et al. (eds.), *Engaging Student Voices in Higher Education*,
https://doi.org/10.1007/978-3-030-20824-0_2

groups such as ethnic minorities, the LGBTQ+ community, and widening participation students. However, the combined result of these approaches is that the diversity of views of those assumed to be within the 'privileged majority' has been relatively under-represented or under-explored. This case study seeks the view of a student from within this majority group who does not fit into any of the marginalised groups that currently receive particular attention, but whose personal identity does not fit with the idea of a dominant group or a privileged majority.

The Value of the Individual

There is a current trend within higher education to focus on large-scale surveys (such as the NSS) and analysis of 'big data' in order to identify trends that may inform policy. However, this is in danger of missing the detail that can only be found in personal stories (Hamshire et al., 2017). The value of analysing a single case is to offer the intensive study of the complexity presented by one individual. The richness of the data produced can be a valuable tool for the bottom-up generation of research questions and for identifying previously unnoticed phenomena of potential importance in order to develop theory inductively (Eisenhardt & Graebner, 2007). The detailed analysis here of an individual provides the opportunity to look at a singular student voice in a way that demonstrates the dynamic interactions between constituent elements that form the messy world of the individual, rather than simply providing lists of attributes where connections can only be inferred. Even when students are 'informed', 'empowered', and 'academically literate', they rarely inhabit a world of controlled experiments, abstracted variables, objective measurement of pre-defined outcomes, average results, or generalised truths. Rather, they live in an idiosyncratic and unpredictable world of a particular person in a particular learning context without necessarily knowing where they fit into the overall landscape of their discipline at any given time. Location of the individual within the wider HE environment may be a positive outcome for the exploration of individual student voices.

The Method

This chapter offers an analysis of the voice of a single student (Alexander) through guided reflections on the products of a concept map-mediated interview. The interview concentrated on four strategic areas that occupy prominent positions in the educational research literature:

- The nature of the discourse on teaching and learning and whether this concentrates on the mechanisms and procedures of teaching (timetabling, assessments, feedback, etc.) or on the underpinning pedagogy (teacher expectations, professional values, student learning approaches, etc.).
- The relationship between the pedagogy and the discipline and whether the programme offers an authentic insight into the discipline by relating theory and practice in a manner that reflects professional practice and not just 'academic study practices'.
- How the research within the department relates to the teaching in the department and how these links are exploited in teaching strategies and made explicit in the programme.
- How the teaching is regulated and evaluated and what appreciation there is of the role of student voices in the decision-making processes of the institution.

Accessing the links students make between key ideas offers a dual outcome. It provides a means to triangulate interpretations of the more superficial data gained by mass surveys. It also offers the possibility of stimulating reflection among students to promote more sophisticated conceptions of learning that help them move beyond the typical non-learning cycles that are promoted by strategic and surface approaches to learning (Kinchin, Lygo-Baker, & Hay, 2008). The methodology mirrors that undertaken with university staff (e.g. Kinchin & Francis, 2017; Kinchin & Winstone, 2018) so that comparisons may be made between teacher and student perceptions. In addition, the process that has been developed to promote reflection among teachers in order to promote more sophisticated and more resilient approaches to teaching at university (Kinchin, 2017) may have a complementary role in developing metacognitive skills and learner resilience. Whilst we have co-authored this chapter, Alexander is referred to as 'he' or 'the student' in the text for simplicity.

The application of concept maps to frame the reflective narrative is a key element in the process that emphasises the dynamic relations between ideas whilst helping the mapper to identify links between elements that may not initially be apparent. As explained by Wilson, Mandich, and Magalhães (2015, p. 4):

> Concept mapping is a medium through which people come to understand more about an event and about themselves. This change of self, re-shapes the meaning of the phenomenon that is being studied, and offers the participants an opportunity to "re-see" the significance the experience and the mapping process offer them. Through this process of "re-seeing," participants develop an artistic expression of self-discovery (the concept map) and their voice resonates on both an individual and a social level.

Heron, Medland, and Kinchin (2018) acknowledge that the talk that occurs during a map-mediated interview means that the maps are (to some extent) a co-construction that emerges from the dialogue about these ideas—though the interviewee (Alexander) has the final say about what is included and what is not. Within qualitative analyses of these maps, the emphasis is on their construction and interpretation by the participant, and the critical filter for inclusion in a map is the extent to which the participant judges it relevant to their own interpretation (Oancea, Florez-Petour, & Atkinson, 2017).

The concept maps are then used as a focus and a frame for the construction of an exploratory narrative by the student. Excerpts from the narrative are used as prompts and illustrations of incidents that are then critiqued and analysed with reference to the appropriate research literature so that in the narrative the 'focus shifts from participants and events in the observed world to an abstracted issue in an academic world' where the 'writer assigns relevance to events beyond the field in which it took place to make them relevant in a given field of academic knowledge production' as described by Hood (2015, p. 121). The in-depth study of an individual student in this way will demonstrate a richness and complexity to the voice that is not captured by more superficial, quantitative tools.

Personal Context

Alexander studied Electrical and Electronic Engineering at a university on the South coast of England. Having dropped a grade in his A Levels, he undertook a foundation year before embarking upon the three-year B.Eng. programme. Those students who had to undertake a foundation year had to do so because they did not get the required grades at A Level to move straight into the 1st year. The reason for this was not that they had not encountered the appropriate content (in Alexander's case, he had studied Physics and Mathematics at A Level), but they had not mastered the content or understood it sufficiently to get a higher grade. It would then seem reasonable to assume that the foundation year would provide innovative and engaging strategies and suggest active learning approaches to help the students gain a better understanding—as recommended in the research literature (e.g. Freeman et al., 2014). However, Alexander's perception was that the content was simply repeated with the implicit assumption that a second exposure to the same content would yield a better result. Ironically, this is anecdotally referred to within STEM subjects as the definition of idiocy—'doing the same thing again and expecting a different result'. Alexander recalls one lecturer stating '*I don't care if you pass or not, you've already paid your tuition fees*'. For him, this summed up the university's attitude to the foundation year. The widening access agenda that is implicit within the use of a foundation year does not seem to extend to epistemological access to the discipline. Academics whose identity is not that of 'teacher' (judging by the comments referred to above by Alexander) may resent having to teach the foundation year group. Alexander spent his first year of study in a hall of residence on the campus and then shared a house with other students. The concept maps and developing narrative were formally collected during the final year of his programme.

Teaching and Learning

The concept map of teaching discourse (Fig. 2.1) suggests that the student is much more aware of the mechanistic instructional discourse (focussing on grading, timetabling, and examining) than on the values-laden

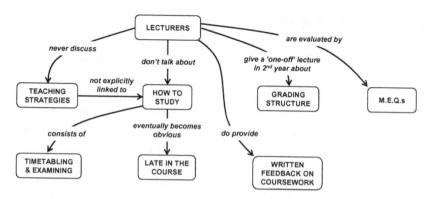

Fig. 2.1 A concept map of the discourse of teaching and learning (MEQ = Module Evaluation Questionnaire, a mechanism that allows students to rate the quality of their teachers)

regulative discourse that might include teaching and learning strategies that would fit with the pedagogic culture of the department. The comment in the map that '*how to study eventually becomes obvious late in the course*' suggests a trial and error approach to achieving alignment between teacher expectations and student actions—a teaching perspective that is somewhat at odds with the scientific, evidence-based approach that is embedded within the culture of the discipline (e.g. Borrego & Henderson, 2014), but none-the-less an approach articulated by teachers of engineering (e.g. Behnejad, 2018). Whilst Alexander is aware that the lecturers are sometimes formally observed in their teaching and that they may periodically be absent to attend a teaching course, the discourse of that professional development never permeates into classroom discussions. The pedagogy of the discipline is never openly discussed.

Whilst there is recognition of the written feedback that is provided on coursework (Fig. 2.1), this is not placed within any broader conception of teaching. The feedback, therefore, appears to be disarticulated from the teaching. If the assumptions and theories that are guiding the disciplinary teaching approach have not been articulated, then it requires a considerable conceptual leap for the student to know how to act on feedback to support further learning. The issue of recipience of feedback has been highlighted by Winstone, Nash, Rowntree, and Parker (2017) as an issue that needs

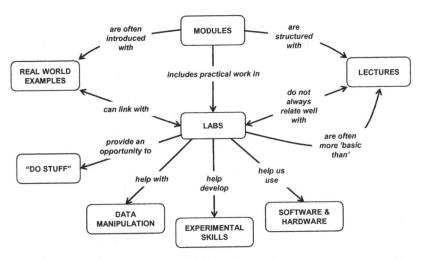

Fig. 2.2 A concept map relating the pedagogy of the discipline with the practice of the discipline

to be addressed across the sector, and so it is no surprise that it should surface within this single case.

Pedagogy and the Discipline

The pedagogy of the discipline is made explicit through the actions of the lecturers and the structure of the programme. The centrality of 'labs' in the concept map in Fig. 2.2 highlights their perceived importance and the amount of time spent on them. It is also here that links are made with 'real world examples' and with the skills that will be needed in the world of work.

However, Alexander comments that the relationship between elements of the curriculum is not obvious: *'Sometimes the labs don't rely on information from the lectures. At other times they are totally dependent upon you having attended a particular lecture to know what's going on. There's no regular pattern'*. From this, it is not clear if the conceptual and contextual forms of knowledge that are a feature of engineering curricula are made explicit to the student to support any kind of knowledge synthesis (Wolff & Luckett, 2013). If not, then the relationship between lectures and labs may not be apparent (Fig. 2.2).

There is no mention of 'talk' within the map, and Alexander reflected that, '*seminars are mostly repetition of key points from the lecture or working through problem sheets with a postgrad*'. The opportunity for students to use the language of the discipline does not appear to be a priority, even though engineering has been described as an intensely oral culture (Darling & Dannels, 2003). This raises questions about the authenticity of the curriculum and the mixed messages about relating to real-world problems, but not necessarily adopting real-world approaches.

The pervasive discourse on employability in higher education (e.g. Yorke, 2004) places a focus on the student as potential worker (see Chapter 8) and is expressed through the terminology of graduate attributes (e.g. Oliver & de St. Jorre, 2018): particular sets of employability skills developed by institutions and embedded in curricula (see Chapter 14). These focus firmly on students' future identity as workers, rather than their current identity as students (Daniels & Brooker, 2014). However, the assumed connection between undergraduate studies and eventual employment are not universally applicable. Alexander reflects: '*Whilst I did enjoy some of the modules, I decided fairly early on in the course that I didn't want to pursue a career in engineering. So all the talk of work placements and the like was all a bit of a turn-off for me*'. This seems to place Alexander in the 10% of students who prefer a 'here-and-now' disciplinary focus to their time at university rather than a 'distant' employment focus (O'Leary, 2017). Ironically, Alexander's engagement with the extra-curricular life on campus (arranging activities and acting as treasurer for a student society and working with the local 'table-top gaming community') probably enhanced his employability skills to a greater extent than anything that was 'provided' within the bounds of the degree programme—perhaps because these were seen by him as authentic activities rather than contrived simulations related to abstract problems.

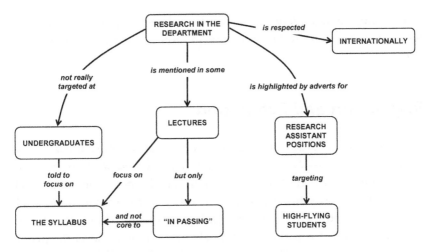

Fig. 2.3 A concept map of the research-teaching nexus

Research and Teaching

The outward-facing view of research at the university and the internal-facing view seem to be very different. Whilst the student is aware of the international reputation of the institution, he feels that this is not really targeted at him, other than through occasional passing reference in a lecture (Fig. 2.3).

The research-teaching nexus is a contested concept in which there are numerous perspectives operating within any given institution that vary according to discipline, job role, motivation, and so on (Hosein, 2017). Some of these perspectives view the teaching environment as research-rich, in which research activities and teaching activities are mutually beneficial, whilst others may perceive their professional environment as research-drained—where resources are diverted towards research to the detriment of the teaching environment. The student perspective of the research-teaching nexus has rarely been investigated. Where it has (e.g. Kandiko & Kinchin, 2013), it can be seen that some students will have a negative opinion of the value of research to their own taught programmes. Where research seen by academics as a product (such as research outputs for the REF) rather than as a process that helps to develop disciplinary ways of thinking, then student access will be reduced to passing reference to research within lectures (Fig. 2.3), or as job adverts aimed at the high-flying elite.

Regulation and Evaluation

The management of learning seems to be a fairly opaque subject for the student (Fig. 2.4)—'*I am not sure who is in charge now as the management keeps changing*'. In addition, the student has the perception that teaching is not a priority for either the university or the student union. The union's perceived focus on politics and on marginalised minorities seems to reflect comments in the literature about working to 'level the playing field' (McLeod, 2011). But as the union does not explicitly focus on the student's own cultural identifiers, he essentially feels part of a community that is marginalised by the establishment. The lines between 'the majority' and 'minorities' start to become quite blurred as the student's individual identity starts to intersect the boundaries of several communities across the campus—the engineering community, the metal community, the gaming community, etc.

The unbalanced structure of the map morphology in Fig. 2.4 is particularly marked in comparison with the previous three maps and suggests an uneven view of the topic (Buhmann & Kingsbury, 2015). In this case, the external management and internal self-regulation of learning are only considered as marginal components of the learning environment, and this omission might be construed as an indicator of potential problems ahead (or 'pre-frailty' in the connection between the student's identity as a learner and the university's homogenised view of students) resulting from a mismatch between personal and institutional expectations (Kinchin & Winstone, 2017).

A Metal Identity

For students who do not yet feel part of the engineering community, the academic environment can feel like a 'chilly climate' (Marra, Rodgers,

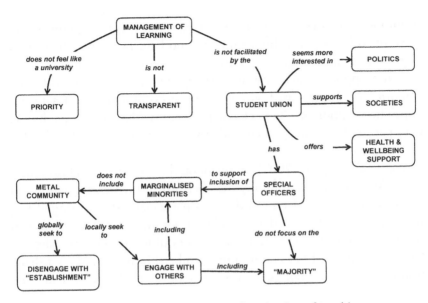

Fig. 2.4 A concept map of the regulation and evaluation of teaching

Shen, & Bogue, 2012). Disciplinary in-jokes may fall flat if the recipients do not feel part of the joke. For example, Godfrey and Parker (2010, p. 10) cite the following 'well known joke': 'You know you are an engineer if you haven't got a life and can prove it mathematically'. The funny side of such comments will not be appreciated by students who already feel disconnected from the community or disengaged from their teachers. Such jokes may also amplify the student perception of STEM as 'stable, rigid and fixed, and, hence, too narrow a platform for developing and constructing desirable identities' (Holmegaard, Madsen, & Ulriksen, 2014, p. 186). Not 'having a life' is not an aspirational driver to engage with the community.

So if you are not identifiable by your academic tribe (sensu Trowler, 2001), other identifiers will be used such as gender, race, and socioeconomic background. Being a member of the 'privileged majority' may be seen as being part of 'the problem' of social inequality. Therefore, we might expect to find some white, male, straight, middle-class students choosing an alternative identity, rather than accepting the hegemony of an imposed identity that might be forced upon them by groups with a powerful voice (e.g. for those students who have no wish to be labelled by their gender or sexuality). This may be helpful in removing oneself from the 'oppressive majority' and placing yourself on a plane with other 'minority' or 'marginalised' groups as a process of deliberate fragmentation. The adoption of a 'heavy metal persona' by Alexander might be seen to be part of that strategy when students feel that the dominant voice does not represent them.

Snell and Hodgetts (2007) comment on the ways in which heavy metal stylisation reaffirms community membership and represents rejection of mainstream dictates of taste and style—particularly the wearing of long beards and metal T-shirts that provide entry routes for conversations with other community members. These authors (ibid., p. 438) also describe less overt expressions of community membership that build on a shared history of the genre alongside knowledge of the intricacies of bands and their music:

> Discussions between Metallers regarding band preferences and concerts attended were used to interweave participants' own personal histories with a co-constructed community history.

Brown (2011, pp. 223–224) explains how the dominance of research into metal culture from disciplines such as criminology and psychology has negatively shaped the discourse, removing it from the mainstream consideration of 'what students want', and pushed it in a particular direction:

> Academic psychology views the music and culture of heavy metal as a problem, one that needs to be scientifically studied in order to identify an objective measure of the 'effect' or influence of the music culture on antisocial, delinquent and deviant behaviour.

This viewpoint appears to say more about the assumptions of the researchers rather than an objective observation of reality and is reminiscent of dominant discourses used to describe other minority groups in earlier periods of history before they found their voices in society. Adopting a counterculture identity offers the individual a feeling of freedom, what Malott (2006) has termed spaces of temporary autonomy. The suggestion here is that the adoption of a metal identity, rather that offering an aggressive posture, may in fact represent the opposite social position, of non-aggression towards other socially defined groups on campus (see Fig. 2.4). Therefore, the metal identity is perceived as a mechanism of engagement rather than one of alienation as is often represented (Hines & McFerran, 2014; Rowe, 2017), even though this may not be recognised by the wider university community.

Conclusions

After spending four years studying engineering, Alexander decided to abandon the academic tribe that should have nurtured him as an undergraduate. The major factors that have been found in the literature to be responsible for students' decisions to leave engineering include poor teaching and a lack of belonging to the academic community (Marra et al., 2012), whilst the construction of a disciplinary identity is thought to be impeded by a modular structure where programmes can be felt by students to consist of a series of disconnected subjects (Ulriksen, Holmegaard, & Madsen, 2017). The 'talk' and 'sense of belonging' that Alexander felt did not come from the academic community at his university was effectively filled on campus by extra-curricular activities and the metal community. Loosely targeted and conflicting discourses within higher education (such as widening participation and employability) are also seen to contribute to difficulties in constructing a non-conformist student identity.

The big data survey approach to student engagement has been selective in its acknowledgement of the 'cultural groups' that are significant on campus and only acknowledges those that have worked to develop a voice through the strong advocacy of support groups (such as widening participation) or who have a strong financial pull (such as students paying overseas fees). The personal story within this chapter also highlights the inherent dangers of universities disproportionately focussing their supportive energy on 'vulnerable' or 'minority' groups in a manner that reflects national policy rather than local need. It has been commented in the literature that the language of widening participation straddles a number of competing and potentially contradictory discourses (e.g. Wilkins & Burke, 2015), and that rather than smoothing out inequalities, as intended, in the context of a marketised higher educational system it has in fact produced different inequalities by limiting its reach to those who are felt to be deserving of support (e.g. Mavelli, 2014; Rainford, 2017).

Whilst the idea of employability is embedded within the higher education discourse, the one group whose voices have been examined the least in this context is the undergraduate population (Tymon, 2013). Critics of the employability discourse have commented on implicit assumptions about level playing fields and the neglect of social inequalities (e.g. Moreau & Leathwood, 2006). Frankham (2017, p. 629) goes further and comments that claims about employability are based on 'a series of lies, fictions or half-truths that are made into the rule of the world'. Student agency is diminished through 'the habit of homogenising and simplifying who students are, where they come from, and what their experiences are' and 'ignores the ways in which students' experiences are intimately connected to the quality and strength of their relationships with academics' (Sabri, 2011, pp. 664–665). The result of this confusion is that many undergraduates disengage from this world during their first years of study (Tymon, 2013) so that their voice no longer registers, and, as in the case here of Alexander, may reduce their motivation to re-engage with it later on.

In combination, the mismatches, 'follies', and tensions inherent in the discourses of widening participation and employability that are described in the literature (e.g. Frankham, 2017; Rainford, 2017) do not augur well for the development of a nurturing environment from which informed student voice(s) might emerge. Indeed, competing agendas within universities seem to encourage certain discourses over others, adding to the pressures of work, whilst political changes in the system appear to be at odds with the values that drew many academics into academia in the first place:

> Academics are experiencing a growing sense of disconnection between their desires to develop students into engaged, disciplined and critical citizens and the activities that appear to count in the enterprise university. (Manathunga et al., 2017, p. 526)

This may result in an 'avoidance of minds' (rather than a meeting of minds) if academics are distracted by other priorities within the university from engaging with their students about such issues. If we have an environment full of disconnections and mismatches, then we might characterise the 'sacred aura' surrounding the notion of student experience (Sabri, 2011) as an isolated bubble that exists within an environment of pedagogic frailty (Kinchin & Winstone, 2017). Indeed, considering any of the four strategic areas that were used as the focus for the map-mediated interview with Alexander, there are issues of disconnection between the student and the university. Whilst at the outset of his undergraduate career Alexander may have been seen as a member of the privileged majority, he did not see himself this way. In terms of his need to undertake a foundation year, he was in a minority group. In terms of his lack of interest in the employability agenda, he was in a minority group. In terms of aligning with the metal culture, he was in a minority group. Indeed, his position at the intersection of these minority groups probably makes his perspective unique—an individual. This emphasises the need to recognise the distinctiveness of personal stories (Hamshire et al., 2017) and highlights the dangers of constructing policy (such as widening participation and employability) by observing students exclusively through the unfocussed, homogenised gaze provided by big data. This loss of personal perspectives may have had unanticipated outcomes and rather than levelling the playing field, from the undergraduate perspective, many initiatives within higher education have simply adjusted the slope.

References

Behnejad, S. A. (2018). Engineering. In I. M. Kinchin & N. E. Winstone (Eds.), *Exploring pedagogic frailty and resilience: Case studies of academic narrative* (pp. 33–45). Leiden: Brill/Sense.

Borrego, M., & Henderson, C. (2014). Increasing the use of evidence-based teaching in STEM higher education: A comparison of eight change strategies. *Journal of Engineering Education, 103*(2), 220–252.

Brown, A. R. (2011). Heavy genealogy: Mapping the currents, contraflows and conflicts of the emergent field of metal studies, 1978–2010. *Journal for Cultural Research, 15*(3), 213–242.

Buhmann, S. Y., & Kingsbury, M. (2015). A standardized holistic framework for concept map analysis combining topological attributes and global morphologies. *Knowledge Management & E-Learning, 7*(1), 20–35.

Daniels, J., & Brooker, J. (2014). Student identity development in higher education: Implications for graduate attributes and work-readiness. *Educational Research, 56*(1), 65–76.

Darling, A. L., & Dannels, D. P. (2003). Practicing engineers talk about the importance of talk: A report on the role of oral communication in the workplace. *Communication Education, 52*(1), 1–16.

Eisenhardt, K. M., & Graebner, M. E. (2007). Theory building from cases: Opportunities and challenges. *Academy of Management Journal, 50*(1), 25–32.

Frankham, J. (2017). Employability and higher education: The follies of the 'productivity challenge' in the teaching excellence framework. *Journal of Education Policy, 32*(5), 628–641.

Freeman, S., Eddy, S. L., McDonough, M., Smith, M. K., Okoroafor, N., Jordt, H., & Wenderoth, M. P. (2014). Active learning increases student performance in science, engineering, and mathematics. *Proceedings of the National Academy of Sciences, 111*(23), 8410–8415.

Godfrey, E., & Parker, L. (2010). Mapping the cultural landscape in engineering education. *Journal of Engineering Education, 99*(1), 5–22.

Hamshire, C., Forsyth, R., Bell, A., Benton, M., Kelly-Laubscher, R., Paxton, M., & Wolfgramm-Foliaki, E. (2017). The potential of student narratives to enhance quality in higher education. *Quality in Higher Education, 23*(1), 50–64.

Heron, M., Medland, E., & Kinchin, I. M. (2018). Interview talk and the co-construction of concept maps. *Educational Research, 60*(4), 373–389.

Hines, M., & McFerran, K. S. (2014). Metal made me who I am: Seven adult men reflect on their engagement with metal music during adolescence. *International Journal of Community Music, 7*(2), 205–222.

Holmegaard, H. T., Madsen, L. M., & Ulriksen, L. (2014). To choose or not to choose science: Constructions of desirable identities among young people considering a STEM higher education programme. *International Journal of Science Education, 36*(2), 186–215.

Hood, S. (2015). Ethnographies on the move, stories on the rise: Methods in the humanities. In K. Maton, S. Hood, & S. Shay (Eds.), *Knowledge-building: Educational studies in legitimation code theory* (pp. 117–137). London: Routledge.

Hosein, A. (2017). The research-teaching nexus. In I. M. Kinchin & N. E. Winstone (Eds.), *Pedagogic frailty and resilience in the university* (pp. 135–149). Rotterdam: Sense.

Kandiko, C. B., & Kinchin, I. M. (2013). Student perspectives on research-rich teaching. *Higher Education Research Network Journal, 6,* 1–98.

Kinchin, I. M. (2017). Visualising the pedagogic frailty model as a frame for the scholarship of teaching and learning. *PSU Research Review, 1*(3), 184–193.

Kinchin, I. M., & Francis, R. A. (2017). Mapping pedagogic frailty in geography education: A framed autoethnographic case study. *Journal of Geography in Higher Education, 41*(1), 56–74.

Kinchin, I. M., Lygo-Baker, S., & Hay, D. B. (2008). Universities as centres of non-learning. *Studies in Higher Education, 33*(1), 89–103.

Kinchin, I. M., & Winstone, N. E. (2017). Pedagogic frailty: Opportunities and challenges. In I. M. Kinchin & N. E. Winstone (Eds.), *Pedagogic frailty and resilience in the university* (pp. 211–225). Rotterdam: Sense.

Kinchin, I. M., & Winstone, N. E. (2018). *Exploring pedagogic frailty and resilience: Case studies of academic narrative.* Leiden: Brill/Sense.

Malott, C. (2006). From pirates to punk rockers: Pedagogies of insurrection and revolution: The unity of Utopia. *Critical Journal of Education Policy Studies, 4*(1), 159–170.

Manathunga, C., Selkrig, M., Sadler, K., & Keamy, K. (2017). Rendering the paradoxes and pleasures of academic life: Using images, poetry and drama to speak back to the measured university. *Higher Education Research & Development, 36*(3), 526–540.

Marra, R. M., Rodgers, K. A., Shen, D., & Bogue, B. (2012). Leaving engineering: A multi-year single institution study. *Journal of Engineering Education, 101*(1), 6–27.

Mavelli, L. (2014). Widening participation, the instrumentalization of knowledge and the reproduction of inequality. *Teaching in Higher Education, 19*(8), 860–869.

McLeod, J. (2011). Student voice and the politics of listening in higher education. *Critical Studies in Education, 52*(2), 179–189.

Moreau, M. P., & Leathwood, C. (2006). Graduates' employment and the discourse of employability: A critical analysis. *Journal of Education and Work, 19*(4), 305–324.

Oancea, A., Florez Petour, T., & Atkinson, J. (2017). Qualitative network analysis tools for the configurative articulation of cultural value and impact from research. *Research Evaluation, 26*(4), 302–315.

O'Leary, S. (2017). Graduates' experiences of, and attitudes towards, the inclusion of employability-related support in undergraduate degree programmes; trends and variations by subject discipline and gender. *Journal of Education and Work, 30*(1), 84–105.

Oliver, B., & de St Jorre, T. J. (2018). Graduate attributes for 2020 and beyond: Recommendations for Australian higher education. *Higher Education Research & Development, 37*(4), 821–836.

Rainford, J. (2017). Targeting of widening participation measures by elite institutions: Widening access or simply aiding recruitment? *Perspectives, Policy and Practice in Higher Education, 21*(2–3), 45–50.

Rowe, P. (2017). Becoming metal: Narrative reflections on the early formation and embodiment of heavy metal identities. *Journal of Youth Studies, 20*(6), 713–731.

Sabri, D. (2011). What's wrong with 'the student experience'? *Discourse: Studies in the Cultural Politics of Education, 32*(5), 657–667.

Snell, D., & Hodgetts, D. (2007). Heavy metal, identity and the social negotiation of a community of practice. *Journal of Community & Applied Social Psychology, 17,* 430–445.

Trowler, P. R. (2001). *Academic tribes and territories.* New York: McGraw-Hill.

Tymon, A. (2013). The student perspective on employability. *Studies in Higher Education, 38*(6), 841–856.

Ulriksen, L., Holmegaard, H. T., & Madsen, L. M. (2017). Making sense of curriculum—The transition into science and engineering university programmes. *Higher Education, 73,* 423–440.

Wilkins, A., & Burke, P. J. (2015). Widening participation in higher education: The role of professional and social class identities and commitments. *British Journal of Sociology of Education, 36*(3), 434–452.

Wilson, J., Mandich, A., & Magalhães, L. (2015). Concept mapping: A dynamic, individualized and qualitative method for eliciting meaning. *Qualitative Health Research, 26*(8), 1151–1161.

Winstone, N. E., Nash, R. A., Rowntree, J., & Parker, M. (2017). 'It'd be useful, but I wouldn't use it': Barriers to university students' feedback seeking and recipience. *Studies in Higher Education, 42*(11), 2026–2041.

Wolff, K., & Luckett, K. (2013). Integrating multidisciplinary engineering knowledge. *Teaching in Higher Education, 18*(1), 78–92.

Yorke, M. (2004). Employability in the undergraduate curriculum: Some student perspectives. *European Journal of Education, 39*(4), 409–427.

3

The Value of Working with Students as Partners

Kathryn A. Sutherland, Isabella Lenihan-Ikin
and Charlotte Rushforth

Introduction

Many universities have worked hard to ensure student voices are included at every decision-making level institutionally. In New Zealand, students have long been valued members of various boards and committees at all levels within our universities. Yet, student voices are sometimes unheard or tokenistic, collaboration amongst student representatives themselves (let alone with staff) is often minimal, and student involvement in wider

K. A. Sutherland (✉)
Centre for Academic Development, Victoria University of Wellington, Wellington, New Zealand
e-mail: kathryn.sutherland@vuw.ac.nz

I. Lenihan-Ikin
Law and Biomedical Science, Victoria University of Wellington, Wellington, New Zealand

C. Rushforth
Victoria University of Wellington Students Association, Wellington, New Zealand

© The Author(s) 2019
S. Lygo-Baker et al. (eds.), *Engaging Student Voices in Higher Education*,
https://doi.org/10.1007/978-3-030-20824-0_3

curriculum projects and change initiatives is limited. Furthermore, student voices are barely present at all (as authors) in the international research literature on student experience. The challenge is to move beyond representation and voice, towards partnership.

In this chapter, we reflect first on the student voice and student engagement literature and then provide a brief overview of the growing students as partners approach, arguing that partnership offers a meaningful move towards reciprocal learning that benefits all involved. Welcoming students as partners in curriculum design, research and university-wide change initiatives allows the sharing of different kinds of expertise, professional development for both staff and students, and the development of critical thinking and analysis skills for all partners. Our chapter itself reflects this model of partnership in that the authors are themselves from different communities: academic, undergraduate student and professional staff.

In this chapter, we offer a take on student voice from New Zealand. We highlight New Zealand research that has informed international debates on voice and engagement, and we describe the historic context and our hopes for its future. We pay particular attention to what is happening at our own university, with the hope that others may be similarly inspired to work towards partnership models at their own institutions.

Values

To begin, we draw readers' attention to the title of this chapter. It stresses the *value* of working with *students as partners*. But what do we mean by these terms? Universities worldwide are well ensconced in neoliberal political environments and funding models (Larner & Le Heron, 2005; Roberts, 2009). In this milieu, universities can often appear to put "neoliberal values of entrepreneurialism, competition and market forces, fiscal responsibility and accountability, managerialism, performance measurement, and productivity ahead of the traditional academic values of collegiality, investigation of truth and critical inquiry, academic freedom, openness, and contribution to knowledge" (Sutherland, 2018, p. 28). We do not want to construe "value" in this chapter in solely economic terms; we are not arguing that working with students as partners will save institutions money or generate profit (although that may happen). Rather, we see partnership as valuable for all the joys, challenges, inspiration, and transformation it can bring all those involved. Perhaps, we really mean "value" as in "ideal", as described by Batchelor (2012):

> Ideals are a person's answer to the question of what his or her highest values are, what he or she finds most excellent. They are navigation aids, giving direction and inspiration and holding out an incentive to make something special of one's life.... Listeners' own values underlie qualities in listening that seek to hear the voice of values and ideals in students. The complex reciprocal relationship of listening to students' experiences also reveals and probes listeners' values. (p. 604)

In "students as partners" models, some of those values include respect, responsibility and reciprocity (Cook-Sather, Bovill, & Felten, 2014), the last of which we address later in this chapter. For now, we want to emphasise that we see partnership as moving beyond merely "representing" or "hearing" students' voices. Instead, partnership should be an institution-wide ethos (National Union of Students [NUS], 2015; Varnham, Olliffe, Waite, & Cahill, 2018), where everyone listens to each other. Partnership encourages an environment where, contrary to Alexander's experiences in Chapter 2, everyone cares about teaching and learning. In a university with a partnership ethos, students are fully involved from inception and design, construction and creation, through to implementation and evaluation (and even reimagining and discarding, where necessary) of all aspects that affect student learning, well-being and lives. Below, we provide a brief overview of the literature on student voice and student engagement that leads to a consideration of the emancipatory potential of student–staff partnership in twenty-first-century universities.

Student Voice

A substantial literature on student voice in higher education now exists, particularly from the UK (and is well-cited elsewhere in this book), and also from Australasia (Alkema, McDonald, & Ryan, 2013; Varnham et al., 2018). However, the concept is misunderstood in the literature, and in practice, its focus and purposes are not easily agreed upon, its ideologies and antecedents are not often enough acknowledged, and it is not well problematised (Freeman, 2016).

Too often, conceptions of the student voice are confined to providing fodder for institutional research: student voice is treated as "students' opinions" and collected through surveys, evaluations and research projects for "evidencing impact, (in TEF provider submissions), validating institutional work (in OFFA access statements), supporting professional development (for HEA fellowships) and in the reward and recognition of individuals (for the NTFS)" (Austen, 2018). This conception of the student voice does not necessarily lead to or equate with any sense of empowerment for students over their own learning (their voices are mere data points). Indeed, some student researchers actually found when investigating students' own perceptions of student voice that students had felt more empowered and engaged in high school (Dickinson & Fox, 2016). Nor is "student voice" often enough pluralised or inclusive, as Alexander's story in Chapter 2 implies, to the point that some students perceive it as exclusive, a luxury for a minority of the student population, even as a "myth" (Dickinson & Fox, 2016).

Picking up on the desire for a more inclusive and capacious conception of student voice, John Canning's (2017) interpretation is helpfully broad:

> I not only understand student voice to be plural (students' voices) but also that certain student voices are not always heard or articulated. Student voice encompasses everything [from] the feedback students give universities through formal and informal structures, staff-student partnerships, through to campaigning and protest. (p. 520)

Similarly, Batchelor (2012) identifies more than one dimension to the student voice. She argues that students have and should be nurtured to discover, explore and use, their "epistemological voice, or a voice for knowing; a practical voice, or a voice for acting and doing; and an ontological voice, or a voice for being and becoming" (p. 597). We ascribe to a similarly broad view of student voice that recognises the whole student and embraces not only the desire for inclusion in the quality assurance aspects of the neoliberal university, but also the right to critique the very structures within which one is learning. In the next section, we turn to some key issues from the student engagement literature, which is often conflated with student voice literature, sometimes obscuring our understandings of both terms (Canning, 2017).

Student Engagement

Student engagement is a multifaceted, vague and contested concept. As Ashwin and McVitty (2015, p. 343) note, "the fact that it would be very difficult to be against student engagement is testament to its vagueness". Debates abound in the research literature, to which NZ authors like Nick Zepke and Ella Kahu have contributed significantly. These debates include issues with definitions (Buckley, 2018; Zepke, 2017), influences (Trowler, 2015; Zepke, 2014), purposes (Baron & Corbin, 2012), antecedents (Kahu, 2013) and objects (Ashwin & McVitty, 2015). An entire recent issue of *Higher Education Policy* (Volume 30, 2017) was devoted to "critical or alternative perspectives on student engagement" (Macfarlane & Tomlinson, 2017, p. 2). There is also a lack of clarity about its counterpoint, with the opposite of student engagement being presented variously as apathy (Macfarlane & Tomlinson, 2017), non-engagement (Vuori, 2014), alienation (Kahu, 2013) and disengagement (Baron & Corbin, 2012): all subtly different.

Writing from an Australian context, Baron and Corbin (2012, p. 765) argue that because changes in higher education have led students to be often viewed more "as (passive) consumers, rather than as (active) partners in a learning community" student engagement has become a "quality control indicator, subject to formal quality assurance mechanisms, rather than a subject of meaningful dialogue". In such environments, students may have a voice but no agency, and no meaningful engagement either cognitively or psychosocially (Kahu, 2013), let alone politically (Ashwin & McVitty, 2015).

Several researchers (Buckley, 2018; Varnham et al., 2018; Wimpenny & Savin-Baden, 2013) have made the connection between the student voice literature and the student engagement literature, but the two corpuses do not often speak directly to or with one another. Buckley

(2018, p. 719) in a recent essay on the ideology of student engagement questions "whether they are two sides of the same coin, or fundamentally different ideas that share a name". On the one side is student engagement with learning activities and curricula, for example, and on the other side, student participation (and voice) in decision-making. Arguably, though, student engagement can be, and should be, "concerned with issues like feedback, representation, and involvement in curriculum design, *and* [be] closely related to the concepts of student voice and students-as-partners" (Buckley, 2018, p. 729, our italics).

In this chapter, we conceive of student engagement broadly as "holistic, lifewide and…not confined to classrooms or formal curricula" (Zepke, 2017, p. 226). Following Ashwin and McVitty (2015), we also see its purpose as the formation of knowledge, through students' "behavioural, emotional and cognitive involvement in their studies" (Buckley, 2018, p. 719), the formation of curricula, *and* the formation of community. We also agree that student engagement requires "whole of institution" approaches (Baron & Corbin, 2012; Kahu, 2013; National Union of Students [NUS], 2015). One potential "whole of institution" approach is the growing "students as partners" movement, described below.

Students as Partners

In 2016 and 2017, two new journals appeared with the aim of publishing the growing research on students as partners (Healey, Flint, & Harrington, 2014a), co-creators (Bovill, Cook-Sather, & Felten, 2011), co-producers (Carey, 2013), co-researchers and co-constructors (Bellinger, Bullen, & Ford, 2014), co-inquirers (Bell, 2016) and change agents (Kay, Dunne, & Hutchinson, 2010). The RAISE Network (Researching, Advancing and Inspiring Student Engagement) launched the *Student Engagement in Higher Education Journal* in 2016, described on their website as publishing "research, theory, practice and policy about student engagement…[including] all forms of work around student voice, student participation and students as partners" (SEHEJ website). Then, in 2017, the *International Journal for Students as Partners* was launched, with the vision of publishing "new perspectives, practices, and policies regarding how students and staff…are working in partnership to enhance learning and teaching in higher education" (IJSAP website). The appearance of these two journals is testament to the rapid growth of the "students as partners" movement in higher education, a concept that its proponents claim is less outcomes-focused than it is "process and values-orientated" (Matthews, 2016, p. 3):

> partnership is understood as fundamentally about a relationship in which all involved – students, academics, professional services staff, senior managers, students' unions, and so on – are actively engaged in and stand to gain from the process of learning and working together. Partnership is essentially a process of engagement, not a product. It is a way of doing things, rather than an outcome in itself. (Healey, Flint, & Harrington, 2014b, p. 12)

Influenced by Arnstein's "ladder of citizen participation" which places citizen control and power at the top of a ladder, and manipulation and non-participation at the bottom, the students as partners concept is well summed up in Bovill and Bulley's (2011) "ladder of student participation". Their ladder moves from teachers controlling decision-making at the bottom, to students in control at the top. It acknowledges the role that students *can* play in making decisions about and co-creating their own learning experiences. They can be not just learners, but also partners in the co-design and co-construction of their learning. But partnership requires reciprocity and trust: staff are on the ladder, too. And those staff are not just academics, but professional and support staff as well. Furthermore, the partnerships are not just about teaching and learning, but about the wider student experience (SPARQS, 2011). As the National Union of Students (2015) has argued, "at its roots partnership is about investing students with the power to co-create, not just knowledge or learning, but the higher education institution itself" (p. 8).

Embedded in the students as partners concept are several values that all partners not only need to be aware of, but adhere to, embody and promote. They include respect, reciprocity and shared responsibility (Cook-Sather et al., 2014). We pick up on the second of these three values; in particular, by describing the attempts our university is making to honour a partnership ethos, especially in a country with biculturalism at its core.

New Zealand: Some Context

The Treaty of Waitangi, signed between the British Crown and indigenous Māori rangatira (chiefs) in 1840, is a broad statement of principles that founded our country in partnership (NZ History, 2018) and that underpins a bicultural approach to most aspects of life. For example, the Māori Education Strategy, *Ka Hikitia—Accelerating Success,* embeds this partnership model through the principle of "ako"—a "two way teaching and learning process…where the educator and the student learn from each other in an interactive way. Ako is grounded in the principle of reciprocity" (Ministry of Education [MEdu], 2013, p. 16). This reciprocal approach extends to an expectation that our tertiary education institutions will work "in partnership with Māori" (Ministry of Education [MEdu] & Ministry of Business, Innovation andEmployment [MBIE], 2014, p. 7) to support not only the educational success of Māori students, but also the growth of Māori language, customs and knowledge for *all* New Zealanders. Later in the chapter, we describe one example of an "ako" partnership model. Below, we outline the current situation in terms of national "student voice" and partnerships with students in national quality assurance, decision-making and curriculum development.

While other regions have long-standing student engagement and/or experience surveys, such as the National Survey of Student Engagement, NSSE (North America) and the National Student Survey, NSS (UK), NZ has experimented with, but not settled on, a national survey of students. The Australasian Survey of Student Engagement, AUSSE, an adaptation of the NSSE, ran in NZ from 2007 until 2012, with all eight universities participating at least once, but never all in the same year. Since 2012, various universities have trialled other student surveys including Student Experience, Student Opinion and Student Barometer surveys. Nationally, we are not systematically (i.e. all using the same tool) collecting or benchmarking student experience data. Universities are required, however, to report their student completion, retention and progression rates to the funding body, the Tertiary Education Commission, the TEC, in order to receive funding for teaching and learning.

In NZ, the TEC funds eight universities, sixteen institutes of technology and three wānanga (Māori teaching and research institutions), and the sector also comprises many industry training organisations and private training establishments. Many of the state-funded institutions have student unions or associations who are, in turn, members of the NZ Union of Students' Associations, NZUSA. Section 229A of the Education (Freedom of Association) Amendment Act 2011 came into force from the beginning of 2012 and states that "no student or prospective student is *required* to be a member of a students' association". This effectively created a situation of voluntary student unionism, a problem recognised in Australia (Baron & Corbin, 2012) and NZ (Alkema et al., 2013) as a threat to the power of the student voice at a national level. Encouragingly, however, the NZUSA has maintained a functional membership and is recognised by the government as the peak student representative body. This recognition extends to student representation on the two key national quality assurance bodies through which NZ universities cooperate nationally. The Committee on University Academic Programmes, CUAP (Universities NZ, 2018, p. 7), aims to "maintain and advance standards" in relation to the development, accreditation and moderation of new courses and programmes. The Academic Quality Agency, AQA, is "a body operationally independent of Universities New Zealand, set up by the universities to ensure the quality of their academic activities" (Universities NZ, 2018, p. 3).

While students are represented on both, AQA has very recently moved beyond mere student representation towards including students in a partnership approach to quality enhancement. They conduct quality assurance academic audits of all universities on a 7–8 yearly cycle. For the first time, students or recent graduates will be included in the 2017–2023 cycle as *auditors*. In July 2017, the President of NZUSA and the Executive Director of AQA signed a memorandum of understanding to this effect, acknowledging the shared objective of "having an authentic, enduring, diverse and effective student voice that contributes to academic quality and quality assurance in NZ universities" (AQA, 2017).

This national partnership is reflected institutionally. Our university, for example, has a robust and long-standing commitment to student representation at each level of the quality assurance process, from individual class representatives for every course to student representatives on faculty and university committees and on the university's governing body, the University Council.

International research has lauded this level of representation in NZ (Varnham et al., 2018), and locally funded research emphasises "positive trends in relation to student engagement with representative systems, with numbers of representatives increasing and greater interest being demonstrated in participation in training" (Alkema et al., 2013, p. 34). But there is some concern that while engagement is increasing, partnership is still not realised. In a stocktake of codes of practice in NZ universities, "70% of surveyed organisations noted that they considered students to be learning partners" but only 4% indicated that "students are integrated into the [teaching and learning] policy-making process at all levels" (Gordon, MacGibbon, Mudgway, Mason, & Milroy, 2011, p. 41). People involved in the work of students' associations across the country are working hard to rectify this (as evidenced by the memorandum of understanding described above). However, considerable work still needs doing for partnership to become an ethos, not merely a commitment on paper. We provide a student perspective on these desired shifts from representation to partnership, below, and then outline our university's efforts in this regard.

Student Representation

Below are three different student views, written from the authors' own experiences and taking the reader chronologically through some shifts in student representation.

Historical (Kathryn): When I was a student in the 1990s, students' associations were politically active and noisy. They organised us to protest in the streets over government plans to introduce a user-pays system of higher education. To no avail, as from my second year of university, I paid fees that rose, on average, 13% a year for the next decade. While my abiding memory is of student reps focusing on political activism, I also recall students being represented on most of the important decision-making bodies at all the universities I attended. Indeed, I served on several university committees as a student, myself, though I don't really remember having the courage or opportunity to say much at all. I have no recollection of the deeper level of engagement possible through the class representatives systems we have today, nor of any type of 'students as partners' approach to curriculum development.

Outsider (Charlotte): I completed both my undergraduate and postgraduate degrees in the US, but was not a member of a students' association. I vaguely remember elections, but do not think I ever voted. The extent of my involvement in the Graduate Students' Association was to show up on Tuesday because it was free bagel day. The irony is not lost on me that I moved on to become the Student Representation Coordinator at Victoria University of Wellington Students' Association (VUWSA). However, my position is very much separate from the political side of VUWSA – I am not on the executive; I am staff. My job is not to inform the student executive what to campaign about; rather, I help them think of practical ways to make their voices heard.

Current student (Isabella): I have been a student at three different NZ universities, and am currently one of two student representatives on the University Council. I am also the national student representative on CUAP (the NZ-wide committee mentioned earlier). Despite this wide experience, often it is hard to fully embody the idea that my voice has validity. As a young, non-qualified, 21 year old in a room full of very highly qualified academics, it can be hard to feel confident in speaking and telling our stories. There are also instances of feeling completely tokenised and patronised.

The rhetoric is that "we are the experts in being a student". Whilst this is true, the university often seems to think that because we have a lived experience of being a student it means that we can speak for ALL students. This is never the case. I have been in meetings where the attention is turned to me and I am asked, "what do the students think?" When this happens, I preface my answer with the justification that one academic would never be asked to speak for the entire academic body (as evidenced by the wide representation of staff on the committee), so I should not be expected to speak for all students – I can only speak for my experience as a student.

Beyond the challenge of hearing multiple student voices, funding pressures resulting from voluntary student unionism mean that students' associations rely more on universities for money. While this creates more collaboration, it also puts funding at risk if student associations are too oppositional.

Student Activism as Voice

Student associations are known for their political activism, and the "student voice" was historically often confined to this role. Student unions have occupied a radical space, which has seen very important and significant changes to NZ society. For example, students were instrumental in lobbying on health reforms, and wider social issues, including the Vietnam War and homosexual law reform (NZUSA, 2014). Without diminishing the scale, energy and dedication required to carry them, these are the "glamorous" issues. They excite students and build unity, with media often willing to get behind as well. The successes are celebrated and tightly woven into the history of students' associations. However, the unglamorous day-to-day work of students' associations also focuses on issues of academic quality within the institution: student representatives pushing for small amendments to student workload, for example, or questioning the value (to students—not the monetary or status value to the university) of new programmes, or lobbying for the halt of programme cuts. This work can go unnoticed, undocumented, and is not necessarily deemed worthy of celebration, despite being one of the primary concerns for NZUSA and local students' associations. The trail of student participation in such academic developments is often lost in history. In the next section, we outline the steps our university is taking towards an embedded partnership approach that honours all participants' contributions.

Partnership Case Study: Victoria University of Wellington

Partnership Commitments

Our university has a very clearly *espoused* commitment to partnership. We have a Student Charter[1] that acknowledges partnership as the bedrock of our approach to supporting the student experience. Our new Learning and Teaching Strategy, Te Rautaki Maruako,[2] also embraces a "working in partnership" approach, to the extent even that students co-designed and co-authored the strategy itself.

Students are represented at every level of the decision-making ladder, from individual course level through to faculty committees, up to university-wide boards, and on the University Council. We have had a class representatives system[3] in place since 1997, and, as far as we are aware, we are the only university in New Zealand with a *full-time* student representative coordinator whose focus is completely on supporting student representatives (roles at other universities are part-time and/or focus also on clubs, engagement or advocacy).

Partnership Realities

Recent surveys show that students are satisfied with their overall student experience at Victoria, but less than two-thirds (around 60%) strongly agree or agree that "Victoria works in partnerships with students listening to the student voice".[4] While the class reps model is widespread, long-standing and incredibly beneficial when both parties to the partnership are proactive, it is otherwise a fairly reactive model, snapping into action only in response to problems.

We try to mitigate some of this risk by providing training and support for the hundreds of class reps who volunteer each year, all coordinated through the student representation coordinator. While training and support for class reps is clearly important, arguably academic staff also need such support. In 2018, for the first time, the student association produced a short "refresher" video for academics on the important role that class reps play, as well as an invitation video to attract class reps to step up. We could be doing much more, however, to support academics to develop successful partnerships.

Similarly, we could be doing more to create real partnership in co-construction and co-design of our curricula, inviting students not just on to review panels (after programmes are set), as we currently do, but also on to curriculum design teams (*before* a programme is developed). Real partnership sees students welcomed as *proposers* of new ideas, programmes and policies, and fully involved from the moment of conception, not just consulted as part of a review process.

Our Learning and Teaching Strategy, co-designed and co-authored with students, embraces six key values that give voice to the teaching and learning goals and actions for the wider university. All of these values, but three in particular will, we hope, bring us much closer to the partnership ethos: akoranga (the reciprocity of teaching and learning), manaakitanga (supporting and respecting each other, particularly in relation to the generous fostering of knowledge) and whanaungatanga (acknowledging and nurturing close connections and providing a sense of belonging). One manifestation of these values in practice is our nascent staff–student lecture observation and curriculum development programme, called Ako-in-Action. This programme has been co-designed and is being co-constructed and co-delivered with students as full partners from inception. We look forward to reporting on its development and hopeful success in coming years.

While there is no easily adaptable "partnership" model that will fit all institutions, several resources provide excellent guidelines and suggestions. We conclude by encouraging readers to embark upon a "Partnership Maturity Audit" to work out just what kind of ethos their university currently embraces.

Conclusion

In the Ako Aotearoa and NZUSA-sponsored report on student voice in NZ, the authors note that "Staff at most organisations viewed students primarily as fee-paying customers but also saw the 'students as partners' model as an ideal, preferred or future state" (Alkema et al., 2013, p. 4). To work towards this, we first need to take stock of where we are, and the following questions (adapted in part from Alkema et al., 2013) should help readers and their institutions to assess their own levels of partnership "maturity".

Does my institution…?

– Have a range of representative systems that enable students to have a voice at all levels of decision-making?
– Fund and resource students adequately to undertake representative work in supported, meaningful and knowledgeable ways?
– Have good uptake by students of the various student representation systems available to them?
– Include students in the co-design, construction and creation of new programmes and curricula *as well as* in quality assurance and evaluation?

- View students as co-producers and partners in curriculum, policy and change initiatives?
- Codify and embed student representation in policy, in constitutions of committees and boards and in their terms of reference, etc.?
- Recognise and reward student AND staff (academic and professional) contributions in partnership initiatives?
- Support and train students AND *all* staff in developing and sustaining successful partnerships?

Raising questions such as these, and listening to the answers of staff *and* students, will demonstrate a move towards partnership. Then, working respectfully with each other and taking shared responsibility for next steps in any planned approach will see voices turned into reciprocal action that enhances the learning experience for *all* involved.

Notes

1. https://www.victoria.ac.nz/learning-teaching/partnership/student-charter.
2. https://www.victoria.ac.nz/documents/policy/strategies/learning-teaching-strategy.pdf.
3. Class Reps serve as a liaison between the students in the class and the lecturer/s teaching the course. Their role is to 'assist communication between staff and students in relation to course matters and to provide a point of contact for students', https://www.victoria.ac.nz/documents/policy/academic/class-representative-policy.pdf.
4. https://www.victoria.ac.nz/__data/assets/pdf_file/0003/1197138/student-voice-have-your-say.pdf.

References

Alkema, A., McDonald, H., & Ryan, R. (2013). *Student voice in tertiary education settings: Quality systems in practice*. A report prepared for Ako Aotearoa &

NZUSA. Retrieved from https://akoaotearoa.ac.nz/download/ng/file/group-4/student-voice-full-report.pdf.

AQA. (2017). Retrieved from http://www.aqa.ac.nz/memorandum.

Ashwin, P., & McVitty, D. (2015). The meanings of student engagement: Implications for policies and practices. In A. Curaj, L. Matei, R. Pricopie, J. Salmi, & P. Scott (Eds.), *The European higher education area: Between critical reflections and future policies* (pp. 343–359). Cham: Springer.

Austen, L. (2018, February). *'It ain't what we do, it's the way that we do it'—Researching student voices.* Retrieved from https://wonkhe.com/blogs/it-aint-what-we-do-its-the-way-that-we-do-it-researching-student-voices/.

Baron, P., & Corbin, L. (2012). Student engagement: Rhetoric and reality. *Higher Education Research & Development, 31*(6), 759–772.

Batchelor, D. (2012). Borderline space for voice. *International Journal of Inclusive Education, 16*(5–6), 597–608.

Bell, A. (2016). Students as co-inquirers in Australian higher education: Opportunities and challenges. *Teaching & Learning Inquiry, 4*(2), 1–10.

Bellinger, A., Bullen, D., & Ford, D. (2014). Practice research in practice learning: Students as co-researchers and co-constructors of knowledge. *Nordic Social Work, 4*(1), S58–S69.

Bovill, C., & Bulley, C. J. (2011). A model of active student participation in curriculum design: Exploring desirability and possibility. In C. Rust (Ed.), *Improving student learning (18) global theories and local practices: Institutional, disciplinary and cultural variations* (pp. 176–188). Oxford: The Oxford Centre for Staff and Educational Development.

Bovill, C., Cook-Sather, A., & Felten, P. (2011). Students as co-creators of teaching approaches, course design, and curricula: Implications for academic developers. *International Journal for Academic Development, 16*(2), 133–145.

Buckley, A. (2018). The ideology of student engagement research. *Teaching in Higher Education, 23*(6), 718–732.

Canning, J. (2017). Conceptualising student voice in UK higher education: Four theoretical lenses. *Teaching in Higher Education, 22*(5), 519–531.

Carey, P. (2013). Student as co-producer in a marketised higher education system: A case study of students' experience of participation in curriculum design. *Innovations in Education and Teaching International, 50*(3), 250–260.

Cook-Sather, A., Bovill, C., & Felten, P. (2014). *Engaging students as partners in learning and teaching: A guide for faculty.* Somerset, NJ: Jossey Bass.

Dickinson, L., & Fox, A. (2016). Who owns the student voice? *The Journal of Educational Innovation, Partnership and Change, 2*(1). Retrieved from https://journals.gre.ac.uk/index.php/studentchangeagents/article/view/233.

Freeman, R. (2016). Is student voice necessarily empowering? Problematising student voice as a form of higher education governance. *Higher Education Research & Development, 35*(4), 859–862.

Gordon, L., MacGibbon, L,. Mudgway, S., Mason, T., & Milroy, T. (2011). *Final report: Stocktake of codes of practice in tertiary organisations.* A report prepared for Ako Aotearoa. Retrieved from https://akoaotearoa.ac.nz/download/ng/file/group-4/stocktake-of-codes-of-practice-in-tertiary-organisations.pdf.

Healey, M., Flint, A., & Harrington, K. (2014a). Students as partners: Reflections on a conceptual model. *Teaching & Learning Inquiry, 4*(2), 1–13.

Healey, M., Flint, A., & Harrington, K. (2014b). *Engagement through partnership: Students as partners in learning and teaching in higher education.* Retrieved from https://www.heacademy.ac.uk/knowledge-hub/engagement-through-partnership-students-partners-learning-and-teaching-higher.

Kahu, E. (2013). Framing student engagement in higher education. *Studies in Higher Education, 38*(5), 758–773.

Kay, J., Dunne, E., & Hutchinson, J. (2010). *Rethinking the values of higher education—Students as change agents?* London: Quality Assurance Agency for Higher Education. Retrieved from http://dera.ioe.ac.uk/1193/1/StudentsChangeAgents.pdf.

Larner, W., & Le Heron, R. (2005). Neo-liberalizing spaces and subjectivities: Reinventing New Zealand universities. *Organization, 12*(6), 843–862.

Macfarlane, B., & Tomlinson, M. (2017). Critical and alternative perspectives on student engagement. *Higher Education Policy, 30*(1), 1–4.

Matthews, K. (2016). Students as partners as the future of student engagement. *Student Engagement in Higher Education Journal, 1*(1). Retrieved from https://journals.gre.ac.uk/index.php/raise/article/view/380.

Ministry of Education (MEdu). (2013). *Ka Hikitia—Accelerating success. The Māori education strategy 2013–2017.* Retrieved from https://education.govt.nz/assets/Documents/Ministry/Strategies-and-policies/Ka-Hikitia/KaHikitiaAcceleratingSuccessEnglish.pdf.

Ministry of Education (MEdu) & Ministry of Business, Innovation and Employment (MBIE). (2014, March). *Tertiary education strategy 2014–2019.* Retrieved from http://www.education.govt.nz/assets/Documents/Further-education/Tertiary-Education-Strategy.pdf.

National Union of Students (NUS). (2015). *A manifesto for partnership.* Retrieved from https://www.nusconnect.org.uk/resources/a-manifesto-for-partnership.

NZ History. (2018). *The treaty in brief.* Retrieved from https://nzhistory.govt.nz/politics/treaty/the-treaty-in-brief.

NZUSA. (2014). *History.* Retrieved from http://www.students.org.nz/history.

Roberts, P. (2009). A new patriotism? Neoliberalism, citizenship and tertiary education in New Zealand. *Educational Philosophy & Theory, 41*(4), 410–423.

SPARQS (2011). *A student engagement framework for Scotland.* Retrieved from https://www.sparqs.ac.uk/upfiles/SEFScotland.pdf.

Sutherland, K. A. (2018). *Early career academics in New Zealand: Challenges and prospects in comparative perspective.* Cham: Springer.

Trowler, P. (2015). Student engagement, ideological contest and elective affinity: The Zepke thesis reviewed. *Teaching in Higher Education, 20*(3), 328–339.

Universities NZ. (2018). *CUAP handbook.* Retrieved from https://www.universitiesnz.ac.nz/sites/default/files/uni-nz/CUAP_Handbook_2018_Web.pdf.

Varnham, S., Olliffe, B., Waite, K., & Cahill, A. (2018). *Student engagement in university decision-making and governance: Towards a more systemically inclusive student voice, 2015–2016.* Final report for the Australian Government Department of Education and Training. Retrieved from http://studentvoiceaustralia.com/wp-content/uploads/2018/05/SP14-4595_Varnham_FinalReport_2018.pdf.

Vuori, J. (2014). Student engagement: Buzzword or fuzzword. *Journal of Higher Education Policy and Management, 36*(5), 509–519.

Wimpenny, K., & Savin-Baden, M. (2013). Alienation, agency and authenticity: A synthesis of the literature on student engagement. *Teaching in Higher Education, 18*(3), 311–326.

Zepke, N. (2014). Student engagement research in higher education: Questioning an academic orthodoxy. *Teaching in Higher Education, 19*(6), 697–708.

Zepke, N. (2017). *Student engagement in neoliberal times.* Singapore: Springer.

4

The Voice of the Student as a 'Consumer'

Louise Bunce

Emergence of the Student 'Consumer'

In several countries around the world, higher education funding models are undergoing an ideological shift away from state responsibility towards student responsibility for tuition fees. This is changing the relationship between students and higher education institutions (HEIs) as well as the nature of student engagement and pedagogic relations (Cardoso, Carvalho, & Santiago, 2011; Delucchi & Korgen, 2002; Ek, Ideland, Jönsson, & Malmberg, 2013; Koris, Örtenblad, Kerem, & Ojala, 2015; Pitman, 2000; White, 2007). The impacts of this ideological shift have been increasingly felt in HEIs in England and Wales over the last two decades. Students now bear the major costs of up to £9250 per year of their tuition through income-contingent loans. To put this figure in context, average graduate full-time earnings in the UK for the year 2015–2016 were approximately £23,000 (Higher Education Statistics Agency [HESA], 2017). Before 1998, the

L. Bunce (✉)
Oxford Brookes University, Oxford, UK

© The Author(s) 2019
S. Lygo-Baker et al. (eds.), *Engaging Student Voices in Higher Education,*
https://doi.org/10.1007/978-3-030-20824-0_4

state provided universities with funding for student tuition. Following much political debate and student demonstrations, students entering higher education (HE) in 1998 were charged a means-tested £1000 towards their tuition, which subsequently increased to a maximum of £3000 for students starting their HE in 2006. Based on an analysis by the OECD, the media reported that the current cost of university tuition made England and Wales among the most expensive countries in the world in which to graduate (e.g. Espinoza, 2015).

The personal financial transaction that most students make with their university[1] in exchange for the opportunity to 'get a degree' (Molesworth, Nixon, & Scullion, 2009) does, in many ways, make students 'customers'[2] and universities 'service providers'. We saw evidence of this rhetoric from the experience of Alexander in Chapter 2, and a student in Tomlinson's (2017) study explained that 'If we're paying for it, that's like you are a consumer more or less. So you know, I am paying for education therefore I am a consumer of education' (Tomlinson, 2017, p. 458). This shift towards students being defined and, in some cases, self-identifying as consumers is one reason why the student voice has been amplified over the last couple of decades. It has also resulted in HEIs believing that it is necessary to seek out, listen to, and respond to the student voice. Thus, the HE system in England and Wales represents a relevant context within which to focus a discussion on the impact of the student 'consumer' and their voices on learning and teaching in HE (Woodall, Hiller, & Resnick, 2014).

Impacts of the Marketisation of Higher Education for the Student Voice

The notion that students should contribute to the costs of their education was first announced in the Dearing Report, published in England and Wales, UK, under a Labour government (National Committee of Inquiry into Higher Education [NCIHE], 1997). That report stipulated that students should only contribute to the cost of their education if the 'tariffs offer value for money to customers' (p. 210) and that 'new approaches to quality assurance should focus on the consumer rather than the provider' (p. 60). Over the last few years, this approach to quality assurance has been enacted in several ways. Measures of student satisfaction have assumed substantial importance in the way in which the performance of HEIs is assessed, with the National Student Survey (NSS) in the UK (introduced in 2011) providing statistics on the quality of the student experience (Higher Education Funding Council for England [HEFCE], 2011). In addition, students are provided with Key Information Sets that give them information to help them to choose a course, including the number of contact hours, type of assessment, and levels of employability and income among graduates. These are now all key drivers in assessing the quality of provision in HEIs, fostering a spirit of greater competition among universities (Tomlinson, 2017).

Even more recently, the Teaching Excellence Framework (TEF) has been introduced to assess the quality of teaching that universities are providing for students. The student voice features in this metric (taken from the annual NSS) in terms of their ratings of teaching quality on their course, ratings of the quality of assessment and feedback, and level of academic support they have received. Universities were first ranked in 2017 as providing a bronze, silver or gold level of teaching excellence, which somewhat upset the traditional university rankings provided by the Research Excellence Framework (REF). Although some would argue that excellent teaching is underpinned by excellent research (see Chapter 17), the introduction of the TEF was undoubtedly focused on offering quality assurance to students in a way that the REF was not.

Another change that has emerged in the light of the shake-up of HE funding is the introduction of the Office for Students, which came into being on 1st April 2018. This is a regulatory body for HE in England that puts students at the 'heart of the market' (Boyd, 2018). It has been designed to encourage the growth of a competitive market that informs student choice and protect the interests of its customers. One of its four key objectives is to make sure that HEIs provide students with value for money. To help make this assessment, the annual student experience survey conducted by the Higher Education Policy Institute (HEPI) has, since 2012, asked students whether or not they perceive their universities as providing 'value for money'. Just over 50% of students in England rated their university as providing good or very good value for money in 2012, but this has since declined to just 35% in 2018. This is in stark contrast to home students studying in Scotland, who more consistently rate their (free) education as providing good or very good value for money. This concept of value for money is, however, a nebulous construct, and students state that they do not receive enough information about how their tuition fees are spent, so it is difficult to interpret their judgments. Nonetheless, the introduction of these ways of assessing the teaching quality in HE provides a voice to the student 'consumer'. These changes are in line with the government's belief that students are 'intelligent customers' and should be a major driving force behind improving quality (Department for Education and Skills [DfES], 2003).

The principle of consumer sovereignty suggests students are enjoying a much louder voice in relation to the content and nature of their education. Some academics agree that treating students as 'consumers' has led to a greater awareness among themselves of students' needs, and that this has encouraged staff to reflect on and improve their teaching practices (Lomas, 2007). Universities routinely listen to and act upon the student voice (or 'customer feedback') both at the level of individual modules or courses (see Chapter 16) as well as more broadly across the range of campus services, including careers, sports and even the canteen. Consequently, the teaching and learning environment has become more responsive to students' desires, which seems to be associated with having satisfied students. In 2018, the NSS reported that overall levels of student satisfaction remained high at 83%. This does not, however, necessarily mean that learning and teaching quality has improved (see Chapter 7), but, nonetheless, this would suggest that the student voice, as one of the predominant stakeholders in HE, is being heard and acted upon in a way that results in their satisfaction.

While student 'consumer' satisfaction metrics may be driving up the quality of the student experience, the shift in responsibility for tuition fee payment from the state to the individual student corresponds to a change in who is seen as the primary beneficiary of education. Traditionally, educating people at university level was a public good, paid for from the public purse, because of the contributions that those graduates make to the future economic, social and health status of the nation (McMahon, 2009). Williams (2013) argues that HE has become disconnected from its historical purpose of seeking 'advancement of the mind', enlightenment and understanding, which was the nature of education described by Newman (1852) in 'The Idea of a University'. Instead, HE is now seen as a private good, paid for by the individual beneficiary, supporting 'non-collectivised ambitions of economic prosperity and personalised self-fulfilment' (Jones-Devitt & Samiei, 2010, p. 92). Universities are now under pressure to provide students with an education that translates directly into high-earning professional employment, which is another metric by which students can judge the quality of the services being provided by their university (see Chapter 8).

Undoubtedly, making a link between learning and earning is increasing the connection that students make between a wider societal culture of the unending consumption of goods and services and their education. There are several reasons, however, why this parallel draws short because HE differs from normal kinds of business. Some of these were outlined by Paul Greatrix, Registrar for The University of Nottingham, writing in the *Guardian* (2011). First, he notes that HE is usually a one-off transaction, with minimal opportunities for repeat sales. Second, other people, such as parents or employers, may be heavily involved in the decision about which university a student should attend or which course to complete. Third, the 'customer' cannot try the product before deciding whether to buy. Finally, who the customer is shapes the quality of the final product, that is, the degree classification with which they graduate, and the student must meet particular criteria before they are eligible to consider buying the product in the first place. In addition, it is impossible for students to return the 'product', and almost impossible for them to get their money back. Therefore, the treatment of students as consumers may not be entirely helpful when applied to HE.

Perhaps most importantly, viewing students as consumers and degrees as commodities[3] is considered most unhelpful when it comes to the nature of engagement that universities require from their students. It has been argued that the marketisation of HE has created an environment in which students expect to be served rather than challenged, and this conflicts with many of the goals of effective pedagogy (Delucchi & Korgen, 2002). Many academics believe that academic standards are being sacrificed on the altar of student satisfaction, leading to a 'dumbing down' of academic content because lecturers are resisting innovation and avoiding making intellectual demands of their students (Lomas, 2007; Pitman, 2000; Williams, 2013). This so-called 'safe teaching' (Naidoo & Jamieson, 2005, p. 275) involves a straightforward transmission of pre-specified content followed by conventional assessment of that content. Furthermore, others argue that simply judging universities on the basis of the extent to which their graduates are 'satisfied' or how much they are earning, will create overly passive and instrumental approaches to learning, and place students outside of the intellectual community rather than as active partners within it (Finney & Finney, 2010; Naidoo & Jamieson, 2005; Williams, 2011, 2013; Woodall et al., 2014). This process may then become associated with students feeling a lack of responsibility for their learning, being resistant to engaging in education as a process rather than a product, and having a sense of entitlement, which are not attitudes that are conducive to 'independent lifelong learning and innovation' (Naidoo & Jamieson, 2005, p. 276). Thus, a paradox results from listening to and acting upon the student as consumer voice emerging from metrics because students may end up with what they want rather than what that they need to bring about change in society for the greater good (e.g. graduates with creative and critical thinking skills alongside knowledge and understanding).

The Student as Consumer Voice: What the Research Says

Despite the pervasive treatment of students as consumers within the HE system, little is known about the extent to which individual students themselves identify as consumers and perceive their degree as a commodity. This second half of the chapter considers some emerging empirical evidence to explore these issues and try to answer questions including: How does a consumer identity impact on students' approaches to learning? Does a consumer identity impact on their academic performance? Is the student as consumer voice a monolithic representation of the views of all students, or do individual voices align with a consumer identity to a greater or lesser extent? This section will also consider the experience of teaching staff in terms of the extent to which they hear the voice of the student consumer in the classroom and how they perceive its impact on pedagogic relations.

The first study to investigate systematically the extent to which students identify as consumers, or 'customers', was conducted by Saunders (2014) in the United States of America. After reviewing the limited amount of (largely North American) research, he developed a unidimensional customer orientation questionnaire comprising 18 items to assess students' level of agreement with educational priorities and planned academic behaviours associated with a customer orientation. These included items such as 'I think of my college education as a product I am purchasing' and 'It is part of my professors' job to make sure I pass my courses'. The questionnaire was completed by 2674 first-year students during the induction period at a large public research university. Students rated each statement on a scale from 1 to 5 where 1 = strongly agree and 5 = strongly disagree. While the mean customer orientation score of 3.32 was close to the midway point of the scale (neither agree nor disagree), there was some interesting variation, revealing that individual students accepted some elements of a consumer orientation and rejected others. For example, the majority of students (54%) agreed that their education was a product they were purchasing, but 42% disagreed that their primary identity was that of a customer of their university. However, when it came to planned academic behaviours, many students (43%) agreed that 'As long as I complete all of my assignments, I deserve a good grade in a course' whereas only a small minority (6%) agreed that they would only try and take the easiest courses possible at university. Saunders concludes that while the dominant ideology in HE positions students as consumers, in general students themselves do not express a customer orientation, at least when they initially enter the HE system. These figures also serve to demonstrate that there is heterogeneity in students' perceptions of themselves as consumers, meaning that it is important to listen to individual student voices and not assume that all students think in the same way.

Similar findings have been emerging from recent studies conducted with students in England and Wales. Using an adapted version of Saunders' (2014) scale, Bunce, Baird, and Jones (2017) conducted a survey of over 600 undergraduates studying in England and Wales during early 2015 (when the maximum tuition fee was £9000). The aim was to explore the extent to which students identify as consumers of their education and its impact on academic performance. Students from 35 different HEIs took part, and approximately, equal numbers of students were in their first, second or final year of study. This sample was, therefore, more diverse and representative than the sample in the study by Saunders (2014). Bunce et al. (2017) also considered the extent to which students identified as learners, that is, whether they held a broad set of attitudes and behaviours relating to intellectual engagement. Students rated their levels of agreement on a 7-point scale, where 0 = strongly disagree, 3 = neutral and 6 = strongly agree, for 15 consumer items, e.g., 'If I cannot get a good job after I graduate, I should have some of my tuition fees refunded', and 15 learner items, e.g., 'I want to learn as much as possible while at university'. Similarly to Saunders, the mean consumer score was close to the midway (2.53) indicating that, on average, students tended neither to agree nor disagree with a consumer orientation. However, students who were personally responsible for their tuition costs had a significantly higher consumer orientation than students who, for example, were in receipt of a bursary or support from family or friends. This also suggests that there was variation in the extent to which individual students expressed agreement or disagreement with a consumer orientation. The mean learner score was 'agree' (4.77), indicating that, on average, students tended to identify themselves as learners. Again, however, there was also individual variation, with some students expressing disagreement with some of the items. When looking at the impact of a consumer orientation on learner identity and academic performance, Bunce et al. (2017) found some interesting and concerning results. Most notably, they found that the more that students held a consumer orientation towards their studies, the poorer their academic performance.[4] Furthermore, consumer orientation mediated the traditional relation between learner identity and academic performance whereby a lower learner identity was associated with a higher consumer identity and subsequently poorer academic performance. It seems likely that a consumer orientation 'competes' with learner identity, which is consistent with Saunders' (2014) finding that students agreed with some consumer statements and rejected others in favour of a more traditional learner attitude towards studying.

This broad pattern of findings is fairly consistent with results from a qualitative study conducted in England and Wales by Tomlinson (2014, 2017), in which only some students perceived themselves as consumers. Tomlinson interviewed 68 undergraduates from seven HEIs about their attitudes towards the marketisation of HE and the impact of fees on the way they thought about teaching and learning. The analysis revealed three sets of attitudes held by students that varied in the extent to which they held a consumer orientation. On the one hand, some students held an 'active service-user' attitude, recognising that a consumerist approach was inevitable given the level of fee they were paying. On the other hand, there was a group of students who explicitly rejected the consumer approach, recognising that it was a passive approach signalling 'lower intellectual merit' (Tomlinson, 2014, p. 11) and resulting in tension with the overall goals of academic growth: '...You've earned that opportunity to be there, so you should work hard...' (Tomlinson, 2017, p. 12). Finally, there was a third group of students expressing a mixed or ambivalent attitude to a consumer orientation, having 'internalised discourses of student rights and entitlements' (Tomlinson, 2017, p. 6), however, these attitudes sat alongside a sense of personal responsibility for their education (see White, 2007, for a similar perspective among Australian undergraduates and Todd et al., 2017, for Canadian students).

An interesting study conducted with students studying at one university in Estonia sheds further light on the finding that the student 'consumer' is not a universal identity. Koris and Nokelainen (2015) explored whether there were elements of their university education in which students may expect to be treated more as customers than learners. Four hundred and five second- and third-year business students, both fee paying and non-fee paying, completed a questionnaire to assess the extent to which they felt that they should be treated as customers in relation to 11 categories of educational experience. These included, among others, grading, classroom teaching, curriculum design, communication with staff, and feedback. Some students expected to be treated as consumers in some, but not all, categories. For example, students expected the HEI to collect and act on their feedback, that classroom teaching material should be presented concisely for ease of studying, and that teachers should employ methods that are interactive and stimulating. In contrast, they did not feel entitled to receive good grades because they were customers, and did not feel that they should be able to graduate without putting in the necessary amount of work.

A consumer orientation, therefore, is not one to which all students universally subscribe, again, demonstrating the importance of engaging with the heterogeneity of multiple student voices. However, it seems that the direction of travel in HE is one of embedding and reinforcing the voice of the student consumer. The extent to which individual students will embrace or resist the consumer identity remains to be seen; however, research is beginning to emerge that suggests this voice may be having a negative impact on students' attitudes towards studying, and ultimately, their degree outcomes. Recall that Bunce et al. (2017) found that the more that students held a consumer orientation towards their studies, the lower their level of academic performance. In a follow-up study, Bunce and Bennett (in press) examined how levels of academic performance may be being impacted by a consumer orientation in relation to its impact on student approaches to learning. They assessed students' approaches to learning (Biggs, Kember, & Leung, 2001; Marton & Säljö, 1976), their consumer orientation and their academic performance. The findings replicated those obtained by Bunce et al. (2017) by showing that the more that students identified as a consumer, the lower their level of academic performance. But how did this relate to students' approaches to learning?

According to Marton and Säljö (1976), there are two major ways in which students may approach their learning: deep approach and surface approach. A deep approach involves using higher-order thinking skills with the intention of understanding, synthesising and evaluating material to make meaning. In contrast, a surface approach involves reproducing material or simply learning information by rote with the intention of passing by expending the minimal level of effort. Adopting a deep approach to learning is largely consistent with enhanced academic performance (Diseth & Martinsen, 2003; Duff, Boyle, Dunleavy, & Ferguson, 2004; Marton & Säljö, 1984) while adopting a surface approach tends to be consistent with lower performance (Duff et al., 2004; Eley, 1992). Bunce and Bennett (in press) found that students who took a deep approach to learning had higher levels of academic performance, and did not identify as strongly as consumers as students who took a surface approach. Furthermore, deep approach to learning mediated the negative relation between identifying as a consumer and academic performance: students who identified as consumers reported lower academic performance because they were less likely to take a deep approach to learning.

These data thus provide a warning about the potential impact of students relying on their voice as a consumer to achieve a change in their educational experience, because a consumer voice may interfere with attitudes and behaviours that support a deep approach to learning. For example, a consumer orientation may create an 'us' (students as customers) versus 'them' (the university as a service provider) attitude, which is at odds with the pedagogic assumption that knowledge is co-created by students in partnership with teaching staff (see Chapter 18). This experience of some students holding consumerist notions of 'us' versus 'them' was also described in a study exploring the impact of the voice of the student consumer on staff perceptions of students' motivations for learning (King & Bunce, under review). All ten academics that were interviewed by King and Bunce perceived some students as being intrinsically motivated: 'There are still the *absolute* gems, the highly motivated, you know, students reading for pleasure'. Seven academics, however, perceived these students as being in the minority: 'I seem to get more comments about, "I pay your wages", "I'm paying for my degree". [...] I think they've lost the... the feeling of... sort of collegiality'. Importantly, academics did not see this approach as being entirely the fault of the students, but as being associated with the political changes that have marketised HE: 'I'm not having a go at students here, because I see them simply reacting to a culture that has been created years and years before they reach university'. Academics seemed to sympathise with students' position, while also feeling challenged to maintain academic standards when students are being told to seek value for money above other forms of educational value. One academic summarised: 'It's a strange irony really, by them paying more [...] we give them more, but actually [...] the outcome for them is less'. This interviewee seems to be suggesting that students may well get better support services or a better student experience, but in the long term, their academic potential may not be fulfilled.

In summary, the available research into the extent to which students identify as consumers seems to demonstrate that, in general, students are not wholly resisting the student as consumer voice, and neither are they embracing it. Again, it is important to emphasise that individual student voices are not represented by average levels of agreement with a consumer orientation in large-scale surveys. Instead, HEIs should also listen to individual student voices that are not captured in these metrics. It seems likely that students experience some tension between the traditional role of students as learners, that is, students who engage critically with new concepts and create new insights, and the modern role of students as consumers, that is, students who expect to be told what they need to know in order to pass. What is clear, however, is the impact of identifying as a consumer on how students approach their learning and their academic outcomes—the more that students identify as a consumer, the worse their level of academic performance. This seems to be because they are more likely to adopt a surface, rather than deep approach to learning. Academic staff similarly see students engaging in some consumer behaviours some of the time and are conscious of the negative impact of this on students' attitudes towards learning.

Conclusions

Given that students now bear the major costs of their university education in England and Wales, as is the case in several other countries, it is right that they receive an excellent university experience. But students, unlike customers on the high street, play a vital role in shaping that experience and have a responsibility to engage with teaching and learning. When the policy and media rhetoric, as well as national evaluations of HE, focus strongly on the customer experience and consumer satisfaction, it is unsurprising that students experience conflict about what their role should be. It is clear that universities are listening to and responding to a student consumer voice, but acting as if 'the customer is always right' may be sacrificing academic standards. Teaching staff should continue to provide students with an intellectually stimulating and challenging learning environment, and work in partnership with students to ensure that universities can continue to fulfil their role of producing graduates capable of the highest levels of critical and creative thinking. This will support not only the development of individual students but also the development of wider society. In this regard, perhaps students could use their voices to resist the notion of the student consumer.

Notes

1. This is not a literal transaction, rather, an income contingent loan, which students pay back once they start earning above a certain threshold, currently £25,000.
2. A consumer is someone who uses products or services whereas a customer is someone who purchases a product. Students can, therefore, be considered both consumers and customers of their HEI.
3. That is, as an outcome that is referenced primarily, if not entirely, with reference to its economic benefit (Shumar, 1997).
4. Performance was measured with respect to students' self-reported percentage mark of their most recent assessed piece of work.

References

Biggs, J., Kember, D., & Leung, D. (2001). The revised two-factor study process questionnaire: R-SPQ-2F. *British Journal of Educational Psychology, 71*(1), 133–149.

Boyd, C. (2018). *A beginner's guide to the Office for Students*. Retrieved from https://wonkhe.com/blogs/a-beginners-guide-to-the-office-for-students/.

Bunce, L., Baird, A., & Jones, S. E. (2017). The student-as-consumer approach in higher education and its effects on academic performance. *Studies in Higher Education, 43*(11), 1958–1978.

Bunce, L., & Bennett, M. (in press). A degree of studying? Approaches to learning and academic performance among student 'consumers'. *Active Learning in Higher Education*.

Cardoso, S., Carvalho, T., & Santiago, R. (2011). From students to consumers: Reflections on the marketisation of Portuguese higher education. *European Journal of Education, 46*(2), 271–284.

Delucchi, M., & Korgen, K. (2002). "We're the customer—We pay the tuition": Student consumerism among undergraduate sociology majors. *Teaching Sociology, 30*(1), 100–107.

Department for Education and Skills (DfES). (2003). *The future of higher education*. Norwich: HMSO.

Diseth, Å., & Martinsen, Ø. (2003). Approaches to learning, cognitive style, and motives as predictors of academic achievement. *Educational Psychology, 23*(2), 195–207.

Duff, A., Boyle, E., Dunleavy, K., & Ferguson, J. (2004). The relationship between personality, approach to learning and academic performance. *Personality and Individual Differences, 36*(8), 1907–1920.

Ek, A. C., Ideland, M., Jönsson, S., & Malmberg, C. (2013). The tension between marketisation and academisation in higher education. *Studies in Higher Education, 38*(9), 1305–1318.

Eley, M. G. (1992). Differential adoption of study approaches within individual students. *Higher Education, 23*, 231–254.

Espinoza, J. (2015, November 24). University students in England 'pay the highest tuition fees in the world'. *The Telegraph*. Retrieved from https://www.telegraph.co.uk/education/universityeducation/12013303/University-students-in-England-pay-the-highest-tuition-fees-in-the-world.html.

Finney, T., & Finney, R. (2010). Are students their universities' customers? An exploratory study. *Education and Training, 52*(4), 276–291.

Greatrix, P. (2011). University isn't just a business—And the student isn't always right. *The Guardian*. Retrieved from https://www.theguardian.com/higher-education-network/higher-education-network-blog/2011/mar/14/students-as-consumers.

Higher Education Funding Council for England (HEFCE). (2011). *National Student Survey*. Retrieved from http://www.hefce.ac.uk/learning/nss/.

Higher Education Statistics Agency (HESA). (2017). *What do graduates do and earn? Starting salaries*. Retrieved from https://www.thecompleteuniversityguide.co.uk/careers/what-do-graduates-do-and-earn/starting-salaries-%E2%80%93-do-graduates-earn-more/.

Jones-Devitt, S., & Samiei, C. (2010). From Accrington Stanley to academia? The use of league tables and student surveys to determine 'quality' in higher education. In M. Molesworth, R. Scullion, & E. Nixon (Eds.), *The marketisation of higher education* (pp. 86–100). Oxon: Routledge.

King, N., & Bunce, L. (under review). A degree of consumerism? Academics' perceptions of motivation in undergraduate student 'consumers'. Manuscript submitted for publication.

Koris, R., & Nokelainen, P. (2015). The student-customer orientation questionnaire (SCOQ): Application of customer metaphor to higher education. *International Journal of Educational Management, 29*(1), 115–138.

Koris, R., Örtenblad, A., Kerem, K., & Ojala, T. (2015). Student-customer orientation at a higher education institution: The perspective of undergraduate business students. *Journal of Marketing for Higher Education, 25*(1), 29–44.

Lomas, L. (2007). Are students consumers? Perceptions of academic staff. *Quality in Higher Education, 13*(1), 31–44.

Marton, F., & Säljö, R. (1976). On qualitative differences in learning: I—Outcome and process. *British Journal of Educational Psychology, 46*(1), 4–11.

Marton, F., & Säljö, R. (1984). Approaches to learning. In F. Marton, D. J. Hounsell, & N. J. Entwistle (Eds.), *The experience of learning* (pp. 36–55). Edinburgh: Scottish Academic Press.

McMahon, W. W. (2009). *Higher learning, greater good: The private and social benefits of higher education.* Baltimore: Johns Hopkins University Press.

Molesworth, M., Nixon, E., & Scullion, R. (2009). Having, being and higher education: The marketisation of the university and the transformation of the student into consumer. *Teaching in Higher Education, 14*(3), 277–287.

Naidoo, R., & Jamieson, I. (2005). Empowering participants or corroding learning? Towards a research agenda on the impact of student consumerism in higher education. *Journal of Education Policy, 20*(3), 267–281.

National Committee of Inquiry into Higher Education (NCIHE). (1997). *Higher education in the learning society.* London: Department for Education.

Newman, J. H. (1959). *The idea of a university.* New York: Image Books (Original 1852).

Pitman, T. (2000). Perceptions of academics and students as customers: A survey of administrative staff in higher education. *Journal of Higher Education Policy and Management, 22*(2), 165–175.

Saunders, D. B. (2014). They do not buy it: Exploring the extent to which entering first-year students view themselves as customers. *Journal of Marketing for Higher Education, 25*, 5–28.

Shumar, W. (1997). *College for sale: A critique of the commodification of higher education.* London: Falmer Press.

Todd, S., Barnoff, L., Moffatt, K., Panitch, M., Parada, H., & Strumm, B. (2017). A social work re-reading of students as consumers. *Social Work Education, 36*(5), 542–556.

Tomlinson, M. (2014). *Exploring the impacts of policy changes on student approaches and attitudes to learning in contemporary higher education: Implications for student learning engagement.* Retrieved from https://www.heacademy.ac.uk/system/files/resources/exploring_the_impact_of_policy_changes_student_experience.pdf/.

Tomlinson, M. (2017). Student perceptions of themselves as 'consumers' of higher education. *British Journal of Sociology of Education, 38*(4), 450–467.

White, N. R. (2007). 'The customer is always right?': Student discourse about higher education in Australia. *Higher Education, 54*(4), 593–604.

Williams, J. (2011). Constructing consumption: What media representations reveal about today's students. In M. Molesworth, R. Scullion, & E. Nixon (Eds.), *The marketisation of higher education* (pp. 170–182). Oxon: Routledge.

Williams, J. (2013). *Consuming higher education: Why learning can't be bought.* London: Bloomsbury.

Woodall, T., Hiller, A., & Resnick, S. (2014). Making sense of higher education: Students as consumers and the value of the university experience. *Studies in Higher Education, 39*(1), 48–67.

5

International Student Voice(s)—Where and What Are They?

Anesa Hosein and Namrata Rao

Listening and responding to the student voice have gained increasing prominence in higher education institutions (HEIs) with the progressive marketisation of higher education (HE) (Tomlinson, 2017). For the purposes of this chapter, we refer to student voice as avenues via which students' opinions and needs are taken into consideration within universities. These avenues could provide opportunities for either *passive-assumed* or *active-formal* participation and/or representation of student concerns and opinions (sensu Bragg, 2007; Cook-Sather, 2006). Passive-assumed participation is where university staff recognise the need to incorporate policies or activities to meet the perceived needs of diversity in the student body, owing to their presence in the system. These policies and activities are shaped by guidance documents provided by third sector organisations

A. Hosein (✉)
Department of Higher Education, University of Surrey, Guildford, UK
e-mail: a.hosein@surrey.ac.uk

N. Rao
Faculty of Liberal Arts, Education and Social Science,
Liverpool Hope University, Liverpool, UK

© The Author(s) 2019
S. Lygo-Baker et al. (eds.), *Engaging Student Voices in Higher Education*,
https://doi.org/10.1007/978-3-030-20824-0_5

(e.g. Universities UK) and by initiatives and practices occuring in other universities. The student voice is thus an amalgamation of the various student voices across the HE sector and not particular to one university. For example, universities may decide to create centralised mathematics support centres to meet the needs of students with weaker mathematics knowledge because other universities are doing so. Elsewhere, these initiatives may be a response to written student feedback (that is the student voice) such as through course evaluations. In this way, the student voice is passively "heard" or considered within the current university. In this model, the students within the current university are not change agents and have limited power in the university-student partnership (Dunne & Zandstra, 2011). On the other hand, active-formal participation involves providing students with a forum to voice their concerns, needs, or provide insights to university staff and to the HE sector in general. Such formal structured opportunities are designed to foster the notion of students-as-partners or co-creators to allow for authentic opportunities to inform practices in HEIs such as curriculum design or in the dissemination of knowledge (Bovill Cook-Sather, & Felten, 2011; Hill, Blackler, Chellew, Ha, & Lendrum, 2013). The student voice is also expected to be heard through representation on student union and university committees. However, an important limitation of these active-formal spaces remains that the voice of the few student representatives is assumed to be the voice of the whole student body and may not necessarily be inclusive of the diverse voices of students.

This diversity of the student voice could refer to diverse voices representing gender, ethnicity, religion, ideology and nationality. In this chapter, we discuss the diverse voices of the international student body, using the UK as a case study to explore the extent to which their voices are heard in active-formal and passive-assumed ways.

UK universities have the second highest number of international students as well as the second highest ratio of international to Home students in the world (Walker, 2014) who come from a range of countries. There is a danger that use of the terminology "international student body" may lead to university staff treating them as a homogenous group or entity who are perceived as having the same voice and needs, even though they may come from very diverse cultures, nationalities and languages (see

Welikala, 2015). For example, when the first author started her PhD as an international student in the UK, she was automatically signed up for a course on Academic English that was intended for international students who were studying in a Foreign Language. Although she came from an English-speaking country (Trinidad and Tobago), this was not taken into consideration and hence she often had to respond to comments from her fellow students on the course such as "Ohhh ....Your English is very good".

Even when the international student body is considered to be heterogeneous by UK HEIs, this is largely for the purposes of ascertaining course fees wherein a student is categorised using geopolitical boundaries into either a Home (UK), European Union (EU) or non-EU student. Currently, Home and EU students pay the same tuition fees though it is likely this will change in the post-Brexit era (i.e. when the UK leaves the European Union). In this chapter, we have used the Home, EU and non-EU nomenclature as a starting point for exploring the diversity of the international student body. However, we do recognise the multiplicity of the student voices within each of these groups, which include a range of different students coming from countries with very diverse cultures, values, expectations and experiences which are likely to have an impact on their educational perceptions and outcomes.

Diversity in origin often leads to diversity in student support needs. However, the multiple and diverse voices of international students and the diversity in their support needs are often lost due to them being considered as a homogenous group. The issues and challenges faced by one set of international students are often considered to be the norm for all other international students even when this is not always likely to be the case. As already highlighted, some international students struggle with writing in the English Language; however, this is unlikely to be an issue for international students coming from English-speaking countries or for those who had English as a medium of instruction in their previous education. Hence, the multiplicity of international student voices needs to be recognised in framing policies and actions that intend to make a genuine attempt to enhance the student experience that aligns to individual needs.

To give greater recognition to the voices within the diverse international student body and with the view to highlight the multiplicity of their needs, this chapter will first examine the heterogeneity of the international student body within the UK. Second, the chapter will consider the spaces which currently exist for international students to share their voices and examine the extent to which these spaces recognise and privilege the diversity in their voices. We will use higher education statistics to examine the origins of these multiple voices of the international student in the UK HEIs and how these differ depending on the UK region they study in and the subjects they study. Through this, we will establish which international student voice(s) is/are likely to have dominance within the HE landscape. We will then use a case study approach to examine the actions and behaviours of two groups of international students (EU and non-EU) using primary and grey literature, which represents their level of dominance in UK HE. The intention of the chapter is to highlight the dominance of certain voices in a relatively diverse student body which often may marginalise the voices and needs of those in minority. Further recommendations to HEIs to allow for a more inclusive approach which recognises the heterogeneity of the international student body will be discussed.

The Landscape of International Students' Voices

In Chapter 2, Kinchin and Kinchin made reference to the dominant groups who are often considered the privileged majority and described the case of Alexander. Alexander's voice and needs may be less likely to be heard or catered for either through passive-assumed or active-formal avenues because he fails to be a member of a recognised marginalised group whose voices may be heard in various quarters. In examining the international student body, and their representation in various fora, in this chapter we highlight that even within particular groups (the international student body in this case), the voices of the dominant groups (those who predominate in numbers) may marginalise the voices of the less populous and less represented individuals in the group.

A Brief History of International Students in the UK

International students have historically been part of the UK HEIs since medieval times (such as Emo of Freisland who studied at Oxford University in 1190), through to the British Empire era (such as the Indian activist Mohandas Gandhi in the late 1800s and the Nobel Prize Literature writer V. S. Naipaul in the mid-1900s) until the present day. Over the last 20 years, the proportion of international students in the UK student population has increased from 11% (HESA 1996/1997 statistics) to 19% (HESA 2015/2016 statistics), alongside a more general rise in the numbers of students accessing higher education in UK universities (18% more Home students in 2015/2016 than in 1996/1997). This has been driven, in part, by the creation of a number of new universities through the Further and Higher Education Act in 1992, with the aim of increasing access to higher education for Home students, particularly those coming from non-traditional backgrounds, often being the first in their families accessing higher education.

Amongst international students, there has been a threefold rise in the number of non-EU students during this 20-year period whilst the number of EU students has increased by one-and-a-half times. This is perhaps in response to government policies that required universities to fund themselves which created a marketised approach to student recruitment. UK universities began courting non-EU students as a source for much-needed funding as they were often required to pay up to three times the tuition fees in comparison with EU and Home students.

This is not surprising, as in many other Western countries where the higher education sector has been pushed into adopting a marketised approach (such as the USA, Canada and Australia), the key to increasing their income has largely been through an increase in international students numbers for whom they charge higher tuition fees. Often these countries provide incentives to lure the international students to increase their market share of international students. For example, Canada provides a visa incentive that allows international students to work there after graduation for at least 2 years which has likely contributed to the sizeable increase in their international student body (Esses et al. 2018).

The Composition of the International Student Body Across the UK

From the perspective of UK HEIs, the voices of those international students that are heard most or likely to be respected may be those of the non-EU students, as they are not only the largest part of the international student body but they also bring in the most funds. One assumption is that the diversity of international students is consistent across the UK. Examining the international student body across the four constituent countries that make up the UK, we notice that the proportion and type of international students are not consistent across the countries (Fig. 5.1). Northern Ireland as a whole has the least number of international students, and in general, the proportion of EU and non-EU students is comparable. Wales, England and Scotland generally have more non-EU students than EU students. However, Scotland had the most EU students which perhaps reflects Scotland's policy of charging both EU and Home students £3000 tuition fees per annum as opposed to the other three countries where the tuition fees for EU and Home students were raised to £9000 per annum following the Browne Review (2010) in 2012. Governmental policies such as those around visas (as in the case of Canada) and student fees (as in the case of Scotland with lower tuition fees) appear to exercise a significant influence on the number and composition of the international student body. This may suggest that in the regions of England and Wales, the voices of non-EU students may be more prominent than those from EU countries, whilst EU students' voices may be less prominent across the UK because of the lower representation of their voices in the international student body.

The Composition of the International Student Body by Discipline

Looking further into how international students are distributed based on disciplines, there are higher numbers of international students pursuing a degree in the Arts & Social Sciences than in the Sciences (26% vs. 20%). Hence, the voices of Arts & Social Sciences international students may be

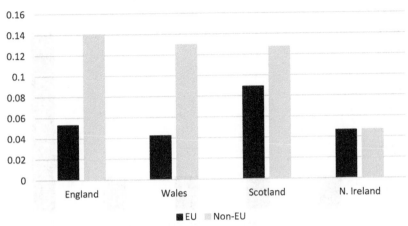

Fig. 5.1 Non-UK students' distribution across the constituent countries (HESA 2015/2016 dataset)

the dominant group within the international student body. These data, of course, are a broad generalisation across the disciplines, and there will be variability in the disciplines within Arts and Humanities and across different universities.

The Composition of the International Student Body by Level of Study

Further analysis shows that the distribution of international students varies with the level of study. The postgraduate student body has a larger percentage of international students than the undergraduate student body (38% vs. 14%). Therefore, the data suggest that the voices of postgraduate international students may be more likely heard and taken into account when addressing the needs of international students, particularly, as often the needs of undergraduate and postgraduate students are handled by two separate groups of personnel in most universities.

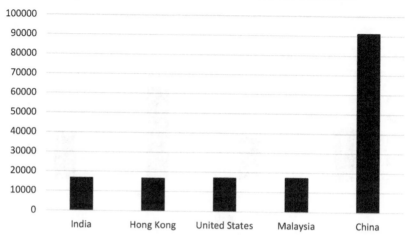

Fig. 5.2 Number of UK international students from the top 5 countries (HESA 2015/2016 dataset)

The Composition of the International Student Body by Country

So far, we have discussed international students as being either EU or non-EU. Disaggregating this further, the UK international student body is primarily dominated by Chinese students (21%) with only about 4% each from the other major countries (India, Hong Kong, USA and Malaysia) constituting the international student body (see Fig. 5.2).

The top five countries do not include any EU countries, but the major EU contenders are Germany, France and Italy who have about 3% share each. Therefore, looking at Fig. 5.2, it is likely that the voices of Chinese students would dominate due to their higher numbers. Further, within the Chinese student population the needs of the students coming from a relatively progressive area such as Shanghai might be very different to those students coming from relatively rural parts of China. Therefore, the needs of a seemingly homogenous Chinese international student body can also be very diverse.

Representation of International Student Voices in Research

The previous section noted that on the basis of statistical data, non-EU voices (particularly Chinese students), those of international students from the Arts & Social Sciences, and those who are studying at the postgraduate level, are most likely taken into account through passive-assumed avenues because of their dominance (by numbers). This section looks at whether the dominance of particular groups on a statistical basis is also mirrored in the published research. This can be important as often the published literature is likely to inform the activities and policies that are developed for international students based largely on the needs of international students who are discussed to a greater extent in literature.

We investigated the literature on international students by looking at two country case studies: one EU (Germany) and one non-EU (China). This is not intended to be a detailed or systematic review of the literature but rather a way of providing an indication of whether there is a dominance of student voices from particular countries within the research literature. We limited our search to the Web of Science publications in 2017 in the field of Education and Educational Research. We used the student keyword of "Chinese students" and geographic keywords of "British, UK, Scotland, England, Wales or Northern Ireland". To narrow the research to HE, the following keywords were used: higher education, undergraduate, postgraduate, university or doctoral. This was repeated with the keyword "German students". In our search, we found, for this period (2017), 8 articles relating to the Chinese students within UK universities and none for the German students. A similar search with "Indian students" was completed and also resulted in no articles. The literature for the Chinese students (see Table 5.1) mainly covered aspects such as preparation for studying overseas and recruitment of students (3 articles), language writing and preparation (3), experiences in international classrooms including the use of language and cultural shock (1) and engaging students in the classroom (1). In 7 out of the 8 articles, the research was undertaken in English universities; the other article was based in China. Further, two studies were in the Arts and Social Sciences and 1 in the Sciences and the

Table 5.1 Review of literature on Chinese international students with reference to the UK

Citation	Research area	Discipline	Geographical area	Level
(Cheng, Fan, & Liu, 2017)	Preparation and recruitment of students	Generic	China	UG
(Cowley, Sun, & Smith, 2017)	Engaging students in the classroom	Generic	England	UG and PG
(Halenko & Jones, 2017)	Preparation and recruitment of students	Generic	England	UG
(Huo et al., 2017)	Experiences in international classrooms	Arts & Social Sciences	England	Generic
(Leedham & Fernandez-Parra, 2017)	Language writing and preparation	Sciences	England	UG
(Lomer, 2017)	Preparation and recruitment of students	Generic	England	UG and PG
(Simpson, 2017)	Language writing and preparation	Generic	England	UG and PG
(Smith & Keng, 2017)	Language writing and preparation	Arts & Social Sciences	England	UG

rest were generic non-discipline specific studies. The majority of studies were at the undergraduate level.

This small review of the literature illustrates that the needs of the dominant groups within the international student body are being put to the forefront due to greater research emphasis on international students coming from certain countries over others. Within the research community, the non-EU student voices are being privileged, particularly the Chinese voices within England in the disciplines of Arts & Social Sciences.

Representation of International Student Voices in Practice

Our analysis suggests that when other researchers or practitioners take into account the international passive-assumed student voice from research, the student voice may be representative of the strongest voice (by numbers), that of the Chinese students within English universities. This may lead to universities creating environments that suit largely Chinese students (see Hou, Montgomery, & McDowell, 2011). Therefore, we turn our attention to the implications of this for the representation of the diverse student voices (active-informed) in different parts of universities, namely student unions, curriculum, panels/committees and societies.

Student Union

Student unions are pivotal for representation of student voices within the university, and universities often ensure that there is a representative for international students within student unions. However, often the international representation in such unions and even nationally in the National Union of Students (NUS) comes by way of an international officer. This single international officer is entrusted with voicing the diverse concerns of international students from different countries, disciplines and with very diverse needs.

Further, as international students often limit their engagement with the student union (see, e.g., Erichsen & Bolliger, 2011), hearing pluralistic voices is likely to be challenging. One office cannot represent the multiplicity of student voices, and this may lead to dominant voices being heard. Therefore, a committee of international students comprising of representation from the various international societies who can provide feedback to the international officer on diverse student issues may be a more appropriate model.

Curriculum

Whilst in recent years there has been a move to incorporate students-as-partners in the curriculum design process (Bovill, 2013), these initiatives rarely make deliberate efforts to engage international students (see, e.g., Bovill et al., 2011). Universities need to ensure the representation of international student voices in their curriculum development processes if they aspire to have a globally and culturally responsive, and inclusive curriculum.

With the current calls to decolonise the curriculum (see, e.g., Le Grange, 2016) to promote other voices rather than just the British or Westernised voice, programme leaders also need to be mindful of not letting a particular international voice dominate over the others during the curriculum design process. Instead, learning outcomes should be devised to be responsive and flexible to be able to draw on the experiences of all the international students on a course. For example, in the study of international business, the curriculum should allow the flexibility to focus on case studies from various countries. Inevitably, as English is the lingua franca of the UK classroom, the diverse content may be skewed to particular countries that have made their content available in English, which may marginalise some student voices in the classroom. Therefore, meeting the needs and engaging all the voices of the diverse student body may sometimes be more aspirational than practical.

Panels/Committees

Committees and panels such as staff-student liaison committees often do not have an international student representative due to their low numbers.

Further, in those committees where international students are present, their voices may be taken to be a representation of all the international voices rather than their own or of a smaller group of international students (Cook-Sather, 2006). Therefore, members of the panels/committees need to be aware of unconscious biases in using lone international voices as representations of a voice for all international students. Instead, committees should ensure that they are aware of the perhaps limited context from which the international student is drawing their experience. Committees need to build mechanisms to ensure more international student voices are included; for example, personal tutors and international staff may be able to represent multiple voices.

University Societies

Within universities, international societies often represent an amalgamation of all nationalities or one particular nationality or region of nationalities. These may often be the only societies representing the interests of the diverse international student body, with primary focus on encouraging socialising amongst international students to limit their feelings of isolation. However, they can sometimes act as a way of secluding international students, by creating their own ecological international student environment. Their voices may be heard by other international students, but these voices may not go beyond this environment. Therefore, this environmental seclusion of international students, whilst it may appear to make the international students feel safe, may in fact suppress their voice within the institution as they may not use another avenue to voice their concerns or work with others.

Conclusion: Limitations and Implications

This chapter examined international student voices within the UK, based on statistics and the research literature (passive-assumed) and the implications for the representation of international students' active-formal voices on panels, committees and student unions. We deconstructed international voices into EU and non-EU; however, by using this approach, we recognise that we have homogenised these voices into these two groups, when their different cultures, religion, ethnicity and gender may mean that they have different experiences and priorities. Crenshaw (1991) argues in her intersectionality theory that it is the combination of multiple identities such as culture, nationality, ethnicity and gender which makes experiences distinct. Whilst we recognise this to be true, by placing the spotlight on international voices, it ensures that we understand the larger landscape within which international students live and study. Therefore, the conclusions and implications from this chapter need to be understood within the context that they represent only the identity of students based on their countries of origin and not their other multiple identities which may also have significant implications.

The findings have shown that the international student voice is not homogenous and that the high proportion of Chinese students may consequently dominate the international student voice both in practice and in research. Further, these Chinese voices themselves are not homogenous and therefore, any authentic engagement with international student voices will be a complex phenomenon. Therefore, when administrators, committee members and academics think of the international student voice, they need to consider carefully whether they are considering all international student voices or student voices representative of a particular region to which the dominant more populous group belongs. Further, changes in policies and practices that are made in response to the needs of international students can often be more appropriate for a particular university or a particular region of the country. For example, the needs of students in London may be very different from those in Liverpool.

Also, international student voices are likely to be heard more in the Arts and Social Sciences disciplines than in the Sciences, and hence, international student policies and practices may often be informed by these voices and may not always be suitable for all disciplines. Therefore, universities should ensure prior to implementation of any policies and practices that consultation is achieved (not only sought) from across all disciplines. The needs of international students at the postgraduate level may be different from that at the undergraduate level. Whilst the various policies drivers may emphasise the need for listening to undergraduate international voices (based on the brief research literature review), the policies and practices enacted for undergraduate international students may not always meet the needs of postgraduate international students who may have additional and different responsibilities such as employment and family.

Our analytical approach presents a dilemma. On the one hand, we have dissected the international student voice into different student voices based on their group membership determined by their countries of origin, but there is a danger that we have now created one international student voice per group. As Cook-Sather (2006, pp. 367–368) notes "those who assert the importance of students' voice as a uniform and united entity run the risk of overlooking essential differences among students, their perspectives, and their needs". Yet, on the other, we are putting forward the idea that each student is an individual, and we need to give attention to the plurality of international student voices.

Grouping students and their voices together makes the analysis of trends in international student voices easier at the macro-level. Whilst these trends might be used to represent the average student, they can also be used as a starting point to find the often marginalised voices who get overlooked in the macro-level analysis. In other words, we must go out and find those who do not fit the norm. As university staff, we need to constantly monitor trends, to determine which student fits, who does not fit and why they do not fit. We acknowledge that finding the lone or different student voice in ever-increasing student cohort sizes is difficult. Hence, we task the academic and research community to create less resource and time intensive solutions for academics with ever-increasing responsibilities, such that they know each student as a person; not as a trend or a number (Hosein, 2017).

References

Bovill, C. (2013). Students and staff co-creating curricula: An example of good practice in higher education? In E. Dunne & D. Owen (Eds.), *The student engagement handbook: Practice in higher education* (pp. 461–476). Bingley, UK: Emerald.

Bovill, C., Cook-Sather, A., & Felten, P. (2011). Students as co-creators of teaching approaches, course design, and curricula: Implications for academic developers. *International Journal for Academic Development, 16*(2), 133–145.

Bragg, S. (2007). "Student voice" and governmentality: The production of enterprising subjects? *Discourse: Studies in the Cultural Politics of Education, 28*(3), 343–358.

Cheng, B., Fan, A., & Liu, M. (2017). Chinese high school students' plans in studying overseas: Who and why. *Frontiers of Education in China, 12*(3), 367–393.

Cook-Sather, A. (2006). Sound, presence, and power: "Student voice" in educational research and reform. *Curriculum Inquiry, 36*(4), 359–390.

Cowley, P., Sun, S., & Smith, M. (2017). Enhancing international students' engagement via social media—A case study of Wechat and Chinese students at a UK university. In L. G. Chova, A. L. Martinez, & I. C. Torres (Eds.), *Inted2017: 11th international technology, education and development conference* (pp. 7047–7057).

Crenshaw, K. (1991). Mapping the margins: Intersectionality, identity politics, and violence against women of color. *Stanford Law Review, 43*(6), 1241–1299.

Dunne, E., & Zandstra, R. (2011). *Students as change agents: New ways of engaging with learning and teaching in higher education.* Bristol: ESCalate Higher Education Academy Subject Centre for Education/University of Exeter.

Erichsen, E. A., & Bolliger, D. U. (2011). Towards understanding international graduate student isolation in traditional and online environments. *Educational Technology Research and Development, 59*(3), 309–326.

Esses, V., Sutter, A., Ortiz, A., Luo, N., Cui, J., & Deacon, L. (2018). *Retaining international students in canada post-graduation: Understanding the motivations and drivers of the decision to stay.* Retrieved from https://cbie.ca/wp-content/uploads/2018/06/Intl-students-post-graduation-RiB-8-EN-1.pdf.

Halenko, N., & Jones, C. (2017). Explicit instruction of spoken requests: An examination of pre-departure instruction and the study abroad environment. *System, 68,* 26–37.

Hill, J., Blackler, V., Chellew, R., Ha, L., & Lendrum, S. (2013). From researched to researcher: Student experiences of becoming co-producers and co-disseminators of knowledge. *Planet, 27*(1), 35–41.

Hosein, A. (2017). Pedagogic frailty and the research-teaching nexus. In I. M. Kinchin & N. E. Winstone (Eds.), *Pedagogic frailty and resilience in the university* (pp. 135–149). Rotterdam: Sense Publishers.

Hou, J., Montgomery, C., & McDowell, L. (2011). Transition in Chinese-British higher education articulation programmes: Closing the gap between east and west? In J. Ryan (Ed.), *China's higher education reform and internationalisation* (pp. 122–138). London: Routledge.

Huo, C.-Y., Middleton, C., Li, S.-J., Xu, H.-S., Wang, J.-J., & Zhang, Z.-Y. (2017). A study on countermeasures to culture shock. *International conference on advanced education and management science* (pp. 105–110).

Le Grange, L. (2016). Decolonising the university curriculum: Leading article. *South African Journal of Higher Education, 30*(2), 1–12.

Leedham, M., & Fernandez-Parra, M. (2017). Recounting and reflecting: The use of first person pronouns in Chinese, Greek and British students' assignments in engineering. *Journal of English for Academic Purposes, 26,* 66–77.

Lomer, S. (2017). Introduction. In S. Lomer (Ed.), *Recruiting international students in higher education: Representations and rationales in British policy* (pp. 1–24). Cham: Palgrave.

Simpson, C. (2017). Language, relationships and skills in mixed-nationality active learning classrooms. *Studies in Higher Education, 42*(4), 611–622.

Smith, S., & Keng, N. (2017). A business writing oil (online international learning): A Finland/UK case study. *International Journal of Computer-Assisted Language Learning and Teaching, 7*(4), 33–43.

Tomlinson, M. (2017). Student perceptions of themselves as 'consumers' of higher education. *British Journal of Sociology of Education, 38*(4), 450–467.

Walker, P. (2014). International student policies in UK higher education from colonialism to the coalition. *Journal of Studies in International Education, 18*(4), 325–344.

Welikala, T. (2015, 3 July). Universities don't understand how international students learn. *The Guardian.* Retrieved from https://www.theguardian.com/higher-education-network/2015/jul/03/universities-dont-understand-how-international-students-learn.

6

Developing Oracy Skills for Student Voice Work

Marion Heron and David M. Palfreyman

'Change based on what students say' (Brooman, Darwent, & Pimor, 2015, p. 663) has become a central feature of student voice in higher education in Anglophone contexts. The active participation of students in curriculum design can challenge assumptions about how students learn and how they want to be taught. Some of the benefits for students resulting from this new dynamic are engagement and empowerment (Bovill, Bulley, & Morss, 2011a); development of metacognitive skills through deeper understanding of learning; greater motivation and enthusiasm; and more collaborative relationships with staff (Bovill, Cook-Sather, & Felten, 2011b). The curriculum can also be enriched through a re-focus on relevant issues and a representation of diverse perspectives. However, student participation in such activities is not without challenges. Potential tensions arguably include ensuring equitable participation and opportunities for all. Alexan-

M. Heron (✉)
Department of Higher Education, University of Surrey, Guildford, UK
e-mail: m.heron@surrey.ac.uk

D. M. Palfreyman
College of Education, Zayed University, Dubai, United Arab Emirates

© The Author(s) 2019
S. Lygo-Baker et al. (eds.), *Engaging Student Voices in Higher Education*,
https://doi.org/10.1007/978-3-030-20824-0_6

89

der's account in Chapter 2 reminds us that the few students who are consulted are seen to represent the student 'voice', denying the fact that there are multiple and diverse voices, some of which are rarely heard. In the same way, critics have contested the purpose of student voice work, demonstrating that student participation may be paid lip service only (Carey, 2013), with no authentic engagement in the learning process.

Students' participation in curriculum design manifests itself in a variety of ways and with varying degrees of responsibility and accountability (Bovill & Bulley, 2011; Bovill et al., 2011b). Levels of participation range from attending class or giving feedback, to proposing course topics and assessments. The enactment of these different types of participation depends on pragmatic issues such as size of cohort, context, tutor/student time and student readiness. It has been argued that dialogue is central to all forms of student engagement (Fielding, 2004; Lodge, 2005; Rodgers, 2006), since it is through dialogue that both tutors and students challenge assumptions and gain greater insight into teaching and learning processes (Brooman et al., 2015). However, few studies identify what dialogue involves, and what skills students need in order to engage in effective dialogue.

The literature on student voice recognises that greater student participation and collaboration requires the provision of 'equivalent support and guidance' (Bovill & Bulley, 2011, p. 8), although few studies explore what this support might look like in practice. As well as confidence (Bovill et al., 2011a), students need the metacognitive skills 'required to undertake constructive negotiation' (Clarke, 1991, p. 24). Although scholars challenge assumptions of who speaks and why they speak, there is little exploration of *how* they speak. In other words, what skills and resources do students need to be able to participate and share their voices effectively? We believe that student voice and participation in dialogue are underpinned by and dependent upon students' ability to use appropriate linguistic and non-linguistic resources required for effective communication. Without these skills, there is a danger that these voices will not be heard or recognised. Therefore, in this chapter we problematise the assumption that students have the prerequisite oracy skills to engage in effective dialogue and thus to participate in student voice work. We argue that students need a set of oracy skills associated with the physical, linguistic, cognitive, and social dimensions of effective communication (Mercer, Warwick, & Ahmed, 2017).

Student Voice and Dialogue

Definitions of student voice are hard to find. At a fundamental level, Taylor and Robinson (2009) state that it is 'an ethical and moral practice which aims to give students the right of democratic participation in school processes' (p. 161). It has been argued by Seale (2009) that student voice work involves the following activities:

- Asking questions about student experiences;
- Seeing and understanding the student perspective;
- Reflecting on implications for practice; and
- Hearing or listening to previously inaudible or ignored voices.

However, this explanation is framed from the educator's perspective and describes what the educator does, neglecting student agency. On the other hand, Brooman et al.'s (2015, p. 664) description gives students active engagement in curriculum design through 'becoming involved with, and having better control over, the learning process'. Student voice work requires active participation and engagement through a variety of different activities, all requiring strong communication skills. This can be seen in the discourse on student voice, which is rich in language emphasising student empowerment through 'discussion', 'communication', 'consultation', and 'collaboration'. Central to most discussions on student voice is 'dialogue'. Robinson and Taylor (2007, p. 5) cite dialogue as one of the four core values that should underpin 'student voice work' to fully reflect its ethical and moral practice. Segal, Pollak, and Lefstein (2017, p. 7) outline the four conditions for student voice as (a) the opportunity to speak, (b) expressing one's own ideas, (c) on one's own terms, and (d) being heeded by others. Spoken skills are crucial to the achievement of these conditions. Lodge (2005) argues that dialogue is the vehicle for active student participation: dialogue is 'about engagement with others through talk to arrive at a point one would not get to alone' (p. 134). Dialogue has been assigned the role of developing an awareness of learning amongst students and teachers and ultimately developing the school as a learning community (Lodge, 2005). Fielding (2004) describes student voice as being enacted through a process in which teacher-led dialogue becomes student-led dialogue. However, despite the aspirations of such student involvement through dialogue and communication, there is little thought for the extent to which students possess these skills. Dialogue, and particularly student-led dialogue, places high communicative demands on students.

The Challenges for Students

The ability to engage in consultation with staff and other students assumes a degree of social confidence and linguistic competence that not all students possess (Rudduck & Fielding, 2006). There is a growing recognition that young people need to be able to use talk effectively for social and democratic engagement (Mercer et al., 2017) whilst Doherty, Kettle, May, and Caukill (2011) argue that due to the focus on employability expectations (see Chapter 8) and graduate attributes (see Chapter 14), oral communication skills are becoming the new cultural capital. It is important to note, however, that not all students come to university with the prerequisite communication skills (Doherty et al., 2011). Walker (2007) claims that 'non-traditional students are less likely to enter higher education equipped with the cultural and linguistic capital which higher education pedagogies assume' (p. 133).

If a repertoire of effective spoken skills is at the heart of what Coultas (2010) calls democratic pedagogy, then only those students who possess the appropriate linguistic and cultural capital required for effective engagement in educational contexts are the ones who speak the language of the institution (Robinson & Taylor, 2007). These are the students whose voice is heard, masking the plurality of voices which may well exist in the background (see Chapter 2). Heath (2004) describes how many young people do not have the linguistic experience from school or home to engage in educational and academic discussions about curriculum planning.

She argues that only through an intervention of specific linguistic resources (in this case, vocabulary) can students fully participate and thus be heard. Suggestions include encouraging the use of verbs such as *think, consider, suppose* and the use of formulaic expressions such as *If we do this then…*, or *How about…?* (p. 55).

Student Voice: The Challenges of Communication

The challenges students face in verbally participating in higher education processes have been well documented (Engin, 2017; Fejes, Johansson, & Dahlgren, 2005; Mack, 2012). There are a myriad of sociocultural factors which result in a reluctance to participate and communicate, such as lack of linguistic resources (grammar, vocabulary, pronunciation) (Hennebry, Lo, & Macaro, 2012), lack of content (Teo, 2013), cultural reasons (Remedios, Clarke, & Hawthorne, 2008), and unfamiliarity with the patterns of participation and discourse event (Fejes et al., 2005). Participation in dialogue about curriculum issues may present English as a second language (ESL) and international students with further difficulties and anxieties in Anglophone HE institutions. Numerous studies outline the challenges that ESL students experience in participating in educational events such as seminars and lectures (Aguilar, 2016; Basturkmen, 2016; Engin, 2017). Students may fear losing face (Nakane, 2006) resulting in silent participants (Engin, 2017). Lecturers' attitudes to international students and assumptions about their cultural background also impact on the extent to which international students' voices are heard. In particular, academics often equate language proficiency with academic ability, resulting in a lack of opportunity for the international student voice (Ryan & Viete, 2009). Linguistic competence as part of communication skills is therefore essential for student voice (Sneddon, 2011).

If students find directed and guided learning events, such as seminars, difficult to navigate in terms of participation, then the expectation that they will confidently engage in dialogue on curriculum design or other aspects of educational improvement is misguided and naïve. Student voice is, therefore, predicated on the ability to express one's ideas, and only the loudest, most articulate and confident voices are legitimised. Burbules (2006) describes how what might seem to be an opportunity for all to engage in dialogue actually involves considerable gate-keeping and access to the 'appropriate' linguistic capital:

> The danger of dialogue, which represents itself as an open conversation in which anyone can speak and any topic can be broached, is not only that certain people may not be speaking, certain things may not be spoken (or may not even be speakable in the terms tacitly valorized by the dialogue), but that precisely because the surface level of the engagement is so apparently reasonable, inclusive and well intentioned, what gets left out, or who gets left out, remains not only hidden but is subtly denigrated. If you cannot (or will not) express yourself in this manner, the fault lies with you. (Burbules, 2006, p. 108)

The point that Burbules is making is that the power of the discourse lies in the hands of those who control the discourse. Whilst we believe that this is a point to be contested, we also argue that we have a moral and ethical responsibility to provide opportunities for students to *develop* appropriate communication skills, not just to be able to engage in voice work, but to have equitable participation in other communicative events not only in the higher education context but beyond into employment (see Chapter 8). In the next section, we outline how we can develop the communicative skills students need to express their voices, which includes some of the notions above, such as words (lexis) and pronunciation, but also other aspects of communicative competence such as register, organisation, grammar, and appropriacy.

Student Voice and Communication Skills

Returning to the notion of student voice as engagement and participation in student-led dialogue, it is useful to identify the skills such dialogic interactions require. In the employability context, it has been argued that the term 'communication' is too broad to serve as a useful pedagogic goal

(Jackson, 2014) and as a result many students graduate with inadequate skills. In the same way, using terms such as 'dialogic' and 'dialogue' may fail to portray the rich and diverse linguistic and sociolinguistic skills necessary for student participation. Therefore, since dialogue is viewed as central to student voice work, it is worth considering the meaning of dialogue, or dialogic interaction, and the requisite skills for this type of active participation.

In a compulsory education context, scholars have identified the type of talk and skills required for effective communication and more equitable participation. Alexander (2013) argues that dialogic interaction is characterised by the following features:

- Collective: participants address tasks together;
- Reciprocal: participants listen to each other and share ideas;
- Supportive: participants articulate ideas freely with no fear of embarrassment;
- Cumulative: participants build on each other's ideas; and
- Purposeful: the talk is planned and purposeful with a specific goal in mind.

Mercer (2000) uses the term 'exploratory talk' to describe classroom interaction in which 'partners engage critically but constructively with each other's ideas… Knowledge is made publicly accountable and reasoning is visible in the talk' (p. 98). Participants are expected to listen, challenge each other, justify ideas, and present arguments. A further conceptual framework of dialogic interaction is offered by Michaels, O'Connor, and Resnick (2008). They argue that for talk to be considered to be dialogic, it must be accountable in the following ways:

- Accountable to the community: participants listen to each other and respect each other;
- Accountable to reasoning: participants explain their ideas, challenge each other, and justify opinion; and
- Accountable to knowledge: participants use evidence to support their ideas.

More recently, the term *oracy* has been reintroduced into the educational literature to describe effective oral communication skills. The term oracy was coined by Wilkinson (1965) to distinguish the skills of speaking and listening from literacy skills (reading and writing). Literacy skills have been recognised as crucial to effective learning in higher education (Hathaway, 2015), and recent developments have promoted the embedding of literacy skills into the higher education curriculum (Wingate, Andon, & Cogo, 2011). We believe that oracy skills deserve the same attention, as a focus on developing effective communication skills would give students more communicative competence to be able to participate equitably in discussions around their learning.

Oracy skills development in schools in the UK has been found to provide students with the communication skills to engage in discussion and, in particular, to be able to reason, defend ideas, challenge others, and present arguments (Mercer & Littleton, 2007). These are all crucial skills for engagement in student voice work.

Developing the Student Voice: The Oracy Skills Framework

The Oracy Skills Framework was developed by Mercer, Warwick, and Ahmed (2017) and is based on the identification of the communication skills involved in using talk in a variety of different social contexts. It is one of the few comprehensive tools which identifies the features of effective communication skills and as such provides a useful resource for both developing and assessing oracy skills. Although developed for the compulsory school context, it is clear that such a framework is equally relevant to HE. Mercer et al. (2017) also recognise the need for students to be able to communicate effectively outside the formal educational context in order to participate in democratic engagement. A further strength of the framework is that the features of effective communication identified are relevant to a range of educational and social communicative events in arenas where the student voice is elicited, both in and outside the HE classroom. Fundamentally, the framework strives to ensure equitable participation for all students regardless of linguistic, cultural, and educational

Table 6.1 Oracy skills framework (Mercer et al. 2017)

Dimension of oracy	Skills
Physical	• voice
	• body language
Linguistic	• vocabulary
	• language variety
	• structure
	• rhetorical techniques
Cognitive	• content
	• clarifying and summarising
	• self-regulation
	• reasoning
	• audience awareness
Social and emotional	• working with others
	• listening and responding
	• confidence in speaking

background and recognising that not all students enter education (either school or post-18) with the same set of skills.

The Oracy Skills Framework was developed from theories of second language acquisition and in particular the theory of communicative competence. Communicative competence comprises the following sets of skills: linguistic competence (accurate and effective use of grammar, syntax, vocabulary, phonology), discourse competence (coherence, cohesion, organisation), sociolinguistic competence (appropriacy, register), and strategic competence (overcoming difficulties in communication) (Canale & Swain, 1980), as well as formulaic competence (ability to use set phrases and formulaic phrases, e.g. 'in my opinion') and interactional competence (turn-taking skills) (Celce-Murcia, 2008). These features of communicative competence are reflected in the four dimensions of oracy as outlined below. Two key aspects of the framework are its accessibility and practical application due to the incorporation of teacher and student-friendly language (Mercer et al., 2017). Table 6.1 outlines the four dimensions of oracy with their sub-skills.

In school contexts, the framework is used as a set of rubrics for oral assessments, but it is equally a central design tool for assessments, classroom activities, and resources. Below we outline several practical suggestions for using the framework to develop student voices.

Firstly, if we return to the expectations of students involved in voice work outlined at the beginning of this chapter, such as to engage in student-led dialogue (Fielding, 2004) on areas of the curriculum, we can begin to see the types of talk repertoires which students must master to be effective communicators. The list below is derived from the work of Alexander (2013), Mercer (1995), and Resnick, Michaels, and O'Connor (2010). Students need to be able to:

- explain;
- ask different types of questions;
- speculate and imagine;
- analyse and solve problems;
- explore and evaluate ideas;
- discuss;
- argue, reason and justify; and
- challenge.

Secondly, the Oracy Skills Framework (above) can be incorporated into rubrics for oral presentations. Studies have highlighted the dominance of oral assessment practices in higher education (Huxham, Campbell, & Westwood, 2012), yet the literature on oral assessment rubrics is scant, and a study by Doherty et al. (2011) has highlighted the lack of explicit focus on the rubrics as part of pedagogy and as part of formative feedback. Reference to the Oracy Skills Framework would provide a common language to talk about talk in a dialogic context and would emphasise the four dimensions of oracy for effective communication in a variety of different contexts. Students would be encouraged not just to develop the content of their talk, but also their confidence, language, and body language.

Student Voice in English as a Medium of Instruction (EMI) Contexts

'EMI' institutions or programmes are typically placed in non-Anglophone countries or regions, sometimes on branch campuses of institutions based in Anglophone countries, and often employing local as well as expatriate staff. Local students will bring or face similar issues mentioned above for (non-)traditional or international students. They may have limited experience in secondary education of expressing their views and limited skills for dialogue around unfamiliar subject matter and learning approaches. Some will be 'traditional' students and some 'non-traditional'; however, what is 'traditional' in the local context may not be what is considered 'traditional' in the UK or other Anglophone countries.

Voice is often considered as expressing the already-existing perspective of an individual (e.g. a student) or group (a cohort or student body); however, like any communication, voice is a co-operative endeavour (Canagarajah, 2014). Students may need to *develop* a voice, using elements of their own experience and background; until they do so, they may not be able to articulate their own perspective. Furthermore, this voice needs to be heard and understood by others from different backgrounds. Canagarajah's work is situated within the context of a written communication course, where fostering a student's *personal* voice (in engagement with the voices of authors cited) is an aim of the course. Voice work more broadly involves the articulation of a range of perspectives, from groups as well as individuals. This is achieved within a context—an 'ecology' (Canagarajah, 2014) which affords various resources and constraints regarding what can be said, understood, and built upon, about what and in what ways. Student voices emerge from individual experiences and from shared, ongoing cultural conversations, which can shape, amplify, or silence the voices of particular groups and individuals.

Within the voice work framework described by Seale (2009), it is hoped that students will give meaningful and thoughtful responses about their experiences; contribute to understanding of the student perspective; and exercise voice in contexts where they have previously been inaudible or ignored. This requires some social confidence and linguistic competence even in one's first language. Like many international students in Anglophone countries, students in an EMI context may have difficulty using their English in unfamiliar ways, including voice work.

On the other hand, EMI students are typically studying in their own country, within their own local context, with which lecturers may be unfamiliar. Students in such contexts can sometimes call on different bases of language, content, genre, familiarity, and social influence (Holliday, 2009). For example, in the context of a state university in the United Arab Emirates, a local student unsure whether she has understood a point in the course may check in Arabic with her classmate; also, students may express concerns not in the classroom but with their families, which form extended social networks, or to the university administration, many of whom are from the same community as the students. Voice work can benefit from engaging with and building on these local resources. The students' shared background may also bring some local inequalities, such as a greater confidence in English amongst students from English-medium private schools compared with those from Arabic-medium state schools (O'Neill, 2016).

In this context, voice work requires cultural responsiveness by tutors to support dialogue. That is, teachers also need to work on their communicative skills to work with student voices: to provide spaces for student perspectives; to check that their own understanding of students' reference points; and to help reconcile different perspectives in pursuit of higher education goals. Ryan and Viete (2009) recommend that in an academic environment, teacher and students should value diversity (rather than only conformity), interact respectfully ("actively search for meaning in what others say", p. 311), and focus on growth (rather than deficit). Student voice can 'transform the familiar' (Seale, 2009), that is, bring to life from the student perspective issues which may be familiar to tutors in abstract terms—but only if tutors engage with it.

Ashencaen Crabtree (2010) reports on a culturally responsive pedagogy in the UAE, including assignments requiring students to report and reflect on family and gender issues within their own lives. Making such connections between students' experiences and the curriculum can support student voice in powerful ways; however, as Wortham (2006) points out, students whose voice is less often heard may not benefit from these connections if their contributions are treated (by tutors and even by fellow students) as marginal or disruptive. The value of student voices depends partly on who hears and responds to them and in what ways. As a holder of considerable power, the tutor is an important audience for student voices, and her/his response is crucial. There may also be space for voice work between different groups of students (e.g. the less and more privileged). The voicing student herself may benefit from reflecting and articulating her experience and understanding, for example in self-assessment practices.

Further Research

Further research into students' linguistic experiences of voice work would be a timely contribution to the literature on student-staff partnership projects. This is a growing feature of higher education activities, yet is underpinned by similar tensions to those outlined in this chapter, and indeed in this book. How are students chosen to work with staff on collaborative research projects, and aside from the necessary research skills, what communication skills can afford students a voice and active role in this process? A further step in research would be to explore what happens when staff and students engage in dialogue about curriculum design. How are voices enacted, allowed, and valued? Research which uses the lenses of conversational analysis and discourse analysis can help to focus on the actual talk and how talk work is done (Stokoe, 2000).

Conclusion

If students possess the necessary communication skills to be able to engage in talk (dialogue), then they are more likely to have a voice. A student who does not possess these skills does not and cannot engage in dialogue and therefore becomes a silenced participant. With a clearer understanding of what dialogue entails, we can consider how to support students in verbalising their thoughts and how to ensure more equitable participation and democratic inclusivity in student voice work. The power to be heard rests upon the ability of the speaker to be linguistically proficient in the talk repertoires described above. Explicit recognition of this and explicit teaching of these skills are crucial to ensure equitable participation. Oracy skills are the vehicle to ensure that all voices are heard, not just the loudest (Robinson & Taylor, 2007).

References

Aguilar, M. (2016). Seminars. In K. Hyland & P. Shaw (Eds.), *The Routledge handbook of English for academic purposes* (pp. 335–347). Oxon: Routledge.

Alexander, R. (2013). *Essays on pedagogy*. London: Routledge.

Ashencaen Crabtree, S. (2010). Engaging students from the United Arab Emirates in culturally responsive education. *Innovations in Education and Teaching International, 47*(1), 85–94.

Başturkmen, H. (2016). Dialogic interaction. In K. Hyland & P. Shaw (Eds.), *The Routledge handbook of English for academic purposes* (pp. 152–164). Oxon: Routledge.

Bovill, C., & Bulley, C. J. (2011). A model of active student participation in curriculum design: Exploring desirability and possibility. In C. Rust (Ed.), *Improving Student Learning (ISL) 18: Global theories and local practices: Institutional, disciplinary and cultural variations* (pp. 176–188). Oxford Centre for Staff and Learning Development: Oxford Brookes University.

Bovill, C., Bulley, C. J., & Morss, K. (2011a). Engaging and empowering first-year students through curriculum design: Perspectives from the literature. *Teaching in Higher Education, 16*(2), 197–209.

Bovill, C., Cook-Sather, A., & Felten, P. (2011b). Students as co-creators of teaching approaches, course design, and curricula: Implications for academic developers. *International Journal for Academic Development, 16*(2), 133–145.

Brooman, S., Darwent, S., & Pimor, A. (2015). The student voice in higher education curriculum design: Is there value in listening? *Innovations in Education and Teaching International, 52*(6), 663–674.

Burbules, N. C. (2006). Rethinking dialogue in networked spaces. *Cultural Studies? Critical Methodologies, 6*(1), 107–122.

Canagarajah, A. S. (2014). "Blessed in my own way": Pedagogical affordances for dialogical voice construction in multilingual student writing. *Journal of Second Language Writing, 27*, 122–139.

Canale, M., & Swain, M. (1980). Theoretical bases of communicative approaches to second language teaching and testing. *Applied Linguistics, 1*(1), 1–47.

Carey, P. (2013). Student as co-producer in a marketised higher education system: A case study of students' experience of participation in curriculum design. *Innovations in Education and Teaching International, 50*(3), 250–260.

Celce-Murcia, M. (2008). Rethinking the role of communicative competence in language teaching. In A. A. Soler & M. P. S. Jorda (Eds.), *Intercultural language use and language learning* (pp. 41–57). Dordrecht: Springer.

Clarke, D. F. (1991). The negotiated syllabus: What is it and how is it likely to work? *Applied Linguistics, 12*(1), 13–28.

Coultas, V. (2010). A revival of talk: The challenge for oracy in schools now. *English Drama Media, 16*, 15–18.

Doherty, C., Kettle, M., May, L., & Caukill, E. (2011). Talking the talk: Oracy demands in first year university assessment tasks. *Assessment in Education: Principles, Policy & Practice, 18*(1), 27–39.

Engin, M. (2017). Contributions and silence in academic talk: Exploring learner experiences of dialogic interaction. *Learning, Culture and Social Interaction, 12*, 78–86.

Fejes, A., Johansson, K., & Dahlgren, M. A. (2005). Learning to play the seminar game: Students' initial encounters with a basic working form in higher education. *Teaching in Higher Education, 10*(1), 29–41.

Fielding, M. (2004). Transformative approaches to student voice: Theoretical underpinnings, recalcitrant realities. *British Educational Research Journal, 30*(2), 295–311.

Hathaway, J. (2015). Developing that voice: Locating academic writing tuition in the mainstream of higher education. *Teaching in Higher Education, 20*(5), 506–517.

Heath, S. B. (2004). Risks, rules and roles. In A. Perret-Clermont, C. Pontecorvo, L. B. Resnick, T. Zittoun, & Burge, B. (Eds.), *Joining society: Social interaction and learning in adolescence and youth* (pp. 41–70). Cambridge: Cambridge University Press.

Hennebry, M., Lo, Y. Y., & Macaro, E. (2012). Differing perspectives of non-native speaker students' linguistic experiences on higher degree courses. *Oxford Review of Education, 38*(2), 209–230.

Holliday, A. (2009). The role of culture in English language education: Key challenges. *Language and intercultural communication, 9*(3), 144–155.

Huxham, M., Campbell, F., & Westwood, J. (2012). Oral versus written assessments: A test of student performance and attitudes. *Assessment and Evaluation in Higher Education, 37*(1), 125–136.

Jackson, D. (2014). Business graduate performance in oral communication skills and strategies for improvement. *The International Journal of Management Education, 12*(1), 22–34.

Lodge, C. (2005). From hearing voices to engaging in dialogue: Problematising student participation in school improvement. *Journal of Educational Change, 6*(2), 125–146.

Mack, L. (2012). Does every student have a voice? Critical action research on equitable classroom participation practices. *Language Teaching Research, 16*(3), 417–434.

Michaels, S., O'Connor, C., & Resnick, L. B. (2008). Deliberative discourse idealized and realized: Accountable talk in the classroom and in civic life. *Studies in Philosophy and Education, 27*(4), 283–297.

Mercer, N. (1995). *The guided construction of knowledge: Talk amongst teachers and learners.* Clevedon: Multilingual Matters.

Mercer, N. (2000). *Words and minds: How we use language to think together.* Oxon: Psychology Press.

Mercer, N., & Littleton, K. (2007). *Dialogue and the development of children's thinking: A sociocultural approach.* London: Routledge.

Mercer, N., Warwick, P., & Ahmed, A. (2017). An oracy assessment toolkit: Linking research and development in the assessment of students' spoken language skills at age 11–12. *Learning and Instruction, 48,* 51–60.

Nakane, I. (2006). Silence and politeness in intercultural communication in university seminars. *Journal of Pragmatics, 38*(11), 1811–1835.

O'Neill, G. T. (2016). Heritage, heteroglossia and home: Multilingualism in Emirati families. In L. Buckingham (Ed.), *Language, identity and education on the Arabian Peninsula: Bilingual policies in a multilingual context* (pp. 13–38). Bristol: Multilingual Matters.

Remedios, L., Clarke, D., & Hawthorne, L. (2008). The silent participant in small group collaborative learning contexts. *Active Learning in Higher Education, 9*(3), 201–216.

Resnick, L. B., Michaels, S., & O'Connor, C. (2010). How (well-structured) talk builds the mind. In D. D. Preiss & R. J. Sternberg (Eds.), *Innovations in educational psychology: Perspectives on learning, teaching and human development* (pp. 163–194). New York: Springer.

Robinson, C., & Taylor, C. (2007). Theorizing student voice: Values and perspectives. *Improving Schools, 10*(1), 5–17.

Rodgers, C. R. (2006). Attending to student voice: The impact of descriptive feedback on learning and teaching. *Curriculum Inquiry, 36*(2), 209–237.

Rudduck, J., & Fielding, M. (2006). Student voice and the perils of popularity. *Educational Review, 58*(2), 219–231.

Ryan, J., & Viete, R. (2009). Respectful interactions: Learning with international students in the English-speaking academy. *Teaching in Higher Education, 14*(3), 303–314.

Seale, J. (2009). Doing student voice work in higher education: An exploration of the value of participatory methods. *British Educational Research Journal, 36*(6), 995–1015.

Segal, A., Pollak, I., & Lefstein, A. (2017). Democracy, voice and dialogic pedagogy: The struggle to be heard and heeded. *Language and Education, 31*(1), 6–25.

Sneddon, R. (2011). Two languages, two voices: Magda and Albana become authors. In G. Czerniawski & W. Kidd (Eds.), *The student voice handbook: Bridging the academic/practitioner divide* (pp. 351–362). Bingley, UK: Emerald.

Stokoe, E. H. (2000). Constructing topicality in university students' small-group discussion: A conversation analytic approach. *Language and Education, 14*(3), 184–203.

Teo, P. (2013). 'Stretch your answers': Opening the dialogic space in teaching and learning. *Learning, Culture and Social Interaction, 2*(2), 91–101.

Taylor, C., & Robinson, C. (2009). Student voice: Theorising power and participation. *Pedagogy, Culture & Society, 17*(2), 161–175.

Walker, M. (2007). Widening participation in higher education: Lifelong learning as capability. In D. N. Aspin (Ed.), *Philosophical perspectives on lifelong learning* (pp. 131–147). Dordrecht: Springer.

Wilkinson, A. (1965). The concept of oracy. *Educational Review, 17*(4), 11–15.

Wingate, U., Andon, N., & Cogo, A. (2011). Embedding academic writing instruction into subject teaching: A case study. *Active Learning in Higher Education, 12*(1), 69–81.

Wortham, S. (2006). *Learning identity: The joint emergence of social identification and academic learning.* New York: Cambridge University Press.

Part II

From Voice to Voices:
Engaging Student Voices
Beyond Metrics

7

Developing Assessment Feedback: From Occasional Survey to Everyday Practice

Naomi E. Winstone and David Boud

In contemporary discourse surrounding Higher Education, the student 'voice' is raised loudly in dissatisfaction with assessment and feedback, as measured by institutional surveys of the student experience, as well as national metrics such as the National Student Survey (NSS) in the UK and the Course Experience Questionnaire (CEQ) in Australia. Based on findings that assessment and feedback consistently emerge as the area of their experience with which students are least satisfied, 'sectoral concern' and 'shock' have been expressed (Williams & Kane, 2009, pp. 264 and

N. E. Winstone (✉)
Department of Higher Education, University of Surrey,
Guildford, UK
e-mail: n.winstone@surrey.ac.uk

D. Boud
Centre for Research in Assessment and Digital Learning,
Deakin University, Geelong, VIC, Australia

Faculty of Arts and Social Sciences, University of Technology Sydney, Ultimo,
NSW, Australia

Work and Learning Research Centre, Middlesex University, London, UK

© The Author(s) 2019
S. Lygo-Baker et al. (eds.), *Engaging Student Voices in Higher Education,*
https://doi.org/10.1007/978-3-030-20824-0_7

265), with this area of student experience being described as the sector's 'Achilles' Heel' in terms of academic quality (Knight, 2002, p. 107).

The overarching student 'voice' expresses concern regarding the promptness, quality, and utility of feedback (Williams & Kane, 2008). This has resulted in a cascade of efforts to improve the student experience, resulting in rapid growth of quality assurance regimes worldwide (Jarvis, 2014). Despite the instigation of policies and practices targeted at improving the student experience of feedback, many educators feel despondent about whether assessment and feedback will cease to be problematic areas of students' experience (Rand, 2017). But how authentic and homogenous is this student 'voice'?

The NSS is described as 'a misleading snap shot' by Williams and Kane (2009, p. 265), perhaps because 'generic questionnaires provide little substantive feedback to academics about what needs to improve, how or why, or what works well for some students and not others' (Blackmore, 2009, p. 866). In fact, several studies demonstrate that student satisfaction with assessment and feedback, as measured by the NSS, is a weak predictor of overall satisfaction with their educational experience (Bell & Brooks, 2018; Burgess, Senior, & Moores, 2018; Fielding, Dunleavy, & Langan, 2010). Some have argued that metrics such as the NSS are not focused on students, instead focused primarily on providing information for managers that can be used for internal planning and decision making (Williams & Cappuccini-Ansfield, 2007; Williams & Kane, 2009), serving more of an accountability and marketing purpose than a pedagogic one (Blackmore, 2009). In this sense, evaluation based on such metrics can unproductively become 'the tail that wags curriculum and pedagogy' (Blackmore, 2009, p. 865).

In this chapter, we first consider why metrics, such as student satisfaction surveys, provide limited information to inform assessment and feedback practices. We then look beyond satisfaction surveys to consider more meaningful ways by which student voices might be engaged to inform practice. We conclude with the importance of reciprocity and partnership between students and educators for a learning-focused approach to feedback.

Satisfaction Metrics: A Singular Student Voice?

Whilst it is possible to explore NSS data according to different student characteristics, the findings that most commonly make headlines are on a global, generalist level, where 'students' are taken to be a homogenous grouping. However, student experiences are far from homogenous. For example, an analysis of student responses to satisfaction surveys between 1996 and 2007 (Williams & Kane, 2009) showed that mature students are not as dissatisfied as younger students with the promptness and usefulness of feedback; Black and Chinese students are more satisfied than other ethnic groups; and females are generally more satisfied with assessment and feedback than males. These findings are important in showing that broad-brush statements about students' dissatisfaction with feedback are likely to be inaccurate. Such groupings may facilitate categorisation, but are not helpful in understanding students' responses to feedback.

A further risk with seeking to respond to apparent dissatisfaction with assessment and feedback as measured by satisfaction surveys is that such instruments tap into just a small dimension of students' experiences in this area, so many action plans seek to improve students' satisfaction on these measures, rather than their learning. In particular, a narrow focus on the usefulness or promptness of feedback in satisfaction surveys (Williams & Cappuccini-Ansfield, 2007) places educators, rather than students, at the centre of the feedback process.

Boud and Molloy (2013, p. 3) caution against the application of 'instrumental "band aid" solutions'; simplistic changes to different elements of practice, rather than a more systemic approach to enhancing practice through sustainable change. For example, students' dissatisfaction with assessment and feedback is often interpreted as representing their limited awareness of the myriad ways through which they can access feedback information. As a result, a common response is for educators to constantly flag up when students are 'receiving' feedback. Again, this solution may minimise attempts to uncover where and how feedback is having limited impact on students learning, as cautioned by Boud and Molloy (2013, p. 2):

The 'let's increase our signposting of feedback' response interprets negative student ratings as a lack of awareness of feedback on their part – that is, a learner deficit, not a problem of teaching and courses...The quick fix misses the underlying problems.

This is a crucial point, as when we really listen to students, we find that issues such as how prompt or detailed the information received is, do not hold as much importance as the extent to which students can develop and improve on the basis of it (Winstone, Nash, Rowntree, & Menezes, 2016), yet the metrics from which the dominant student 'voice' emerge focus on the former. These findings were echoed in a recent large-scale survey of over 4000 students from two Australian universities, where only a very small number of students cited prompt turnaround of feedback as a feature of effective feedback (Dawson et al., 2019). Furthermore, students' self-reported engagement with their courses also influences the extent to which they see different elements of the assessment and feedback experience as important. For example, students with high levels of engagement ascribed less importance to the promptness of feedback, and more to the extent to which feedback helped them to clarify things they did not understand (Bennett & Kane, 2014).

Satisfaction Metrics: Timely Feedback?

One of the common items assessing student satisfaction with their experience of assessment and feedback asks students to rate the extent to which they received timely feedback on their work. It is therefore perhaps ironic that the feedback students provide is itself not timely, being received by educators far too late for them to be able to act on those comments in a way that will benefit the students who provided them. A key feature of timely feedback is that it is received at a time where the recipient has opportunity to act upon the advice. In this sense, then, the feedback that institutions receive from student satisfaction surveys models the least useful form of feedback from a pedagogic perspective: it is purely summative, received at the end of the course, with no opportunity to take direct action to remedy issues within the current academic cycle.

A further issue with using a high stakes survey at a single time point, rather than gathering regular feedback information to inform practice, is that individual 'landmark' events can influence students' overall scoring (Gee, 2017). Such events are significant experiences or incidents which, whilst they may be out of line with a student's general experiences, colour their perceptions. In this way, student satisfaction surveys can be used as a 'weapon of revenge' against institutions, where what is perceived to be a poor experience in one area can spill over to poor ratings in other, unrelated areas (Bell & Brooks, 2018, p. 125).

Satisfaction Metrics: Unambiguous Items?

Empirical work demonstrates that ascribing weight to the results of student satisfaction surveys is misplaced, as the wording of items assessing satisfaction with assessment and feedback is open to multiple and varying interpretations (Bennett & Kane, 2014; Eley, 2001). Thus, hiding under cohort averages are likely to be wildly different perceptions and experiences (Bennett & Kane, 2014), which is a significant issue where institutional efforts to improve pedagogic practices are so heavily influenced by the 'student voice'.

For example, the 'promptness' of feedback will mean different things to different students (Bennett & Kane, 2014), and perceptions of what makes feedback 'useful' are also likely to differ. Useful feedback might be represented by very detailed comments for some students or short summaries for others, and the utility of feedback might also differ according to the modality through which it is delivered, such as written feedback or face-to-face feedback (Bennett & Kane, 2014).

Beyond the wording of the items themselves, it is also likely that perceptions of quality are largely subjective. Bennett and Kane (2014) report that when reflecting on whether an aspect of their course had been 'good', students showed that they consulted their 'internal metrics' to consider what 'good' looks like, leading to very different interpretations of quality. Similarly, some students may respond to items on the basis of an initial 'gut reaction'; a different response may be reached on the basis of more mindful consideration of their experience (Bennett & Kane, 2014).

There are also affective influences on students' responses to satisfaction surveys; more positive evaluations are given by students if they are performing well in their course (Bell & Brooks, 2018), and students are more likely to rate their experience positively if strong personal relationships have been built with course staff (Bennett & Kane, 2014). Indeed, it is likely that 'satisfaction' with feedback represents whether or not it was positive and reassuring, not whether it was timely or useful (Boehler et al., 2006). It is clear that satisfaction surveys result in assumptions being made by those giving and those receiving course evaluations, hence it is difficult to determine meaningful actions that might be taken.

Satisfaction Metrics: Implicit Messages

For many educators who may be promoting learning-focused feedback practices, it can be disheartening to see that these efforts do not pay off when students complete evaluation surveys. This may not be because students do not appreciate these efforts; rather, they are not given any opportunity to evaluate them in typical satisfaction surveys, and the questions asked in such surveys may distract students from a more meaningful focus on what it is that makes feedback effective. Back in 2010, David Nicol argued that the NSS items focus on the delivery of feedback, thus representing a transmission-focused, rather than learning-focused, feedback paradigm (Nicol, 2010). The NSS items were revised in 2017, with minimal tweaks that failed to shift the dominant paradigm of feedback away from a focus on transmission (Nash & Winstone, 2017; see Table 7.1).

There are several potential unintended outcomes of framing the questions in this way. First, it is likely to lead institutions to focus their efforts

Table 7.1 Assessment and feedback items in the 2017 UK National Student Survey (NSS)

1.	The criteria used in marking have been clear in advance
2.	Marking and assessment has been fair
3.	Feedback on my work has been timely
4.	I have received helpful comments on my work

on improving the *transmission* of feedback (Nicol, 2010), such as reducing the turnaround time or providing guidance to markers regarding the type of language they should use in their comments. It has long been argued in the field of organisational performance management that metrics drive efforts to maximise performance solely in the area appraised by that metric (e.g. Ariely, 2010), whilst in the field of educational assessment, the warning that we should measure what is valued, or else come to value what is measured, is well-rehearsed (Hargreaves, Boyle, & Harris, 2014). Thus, it is possible that coming to value the transmission-focused approach to assessment and feedback that is conceptualised within the NSS items has been partly responsible for feedback practice in the UK being 'stubbornly resistant to change' (Ferrell, 2012, p. 21). By failing to value learning-focused approaches to feedback by placing them at the centre of approaches to evaluation, there is little incentive for educators seeking to work in learning-focused ways.

Perhaps a more concerning outcome of the framing of satisfaction items in this way is that it may well reinforce students' positions as passive receivers, rather than active seekers, of feedback. As argued by Winstone and Pitt (2017), why shouldn't students believe that this is the model of feedback that is valued by their educators, if this is the way in which they are asked to assess its quality? We could send a powerful message about the importance of student agency in the feedback process by asking them not to rate the utility of feedback they have *received*, but rather the extent to which they have been enabled to gather or use feedback to support their learning.

Engaging Student Voices in Everyday Practice

What, then, might we attend to if we are to take on this more active focus on students in examining the efficacy of feedback? How can we promote a more learning-focused view of feedback and thus hear student voices when and where they are able to make a real difference to the feedback they experience? We now turn to consideration of how educators can learn about students' experiences of feedback, not at the end of module/unit or programme of study, but during the module/unit itself. We argue that such an approach stands to provide educators with more useful information about how students actually experience assessment and feedback than could be provided by a single survey, and at a time when educators can act upon what students are telling them.

Our starting point is consideration of what feedback is for and how it operates to pursue these ends. The shift in thinking which has led to a more student-focused paradigm is characterised in a recent definition, where 'feedback is defined as a process through which learners make sense of information from various sources and use it to enhance their work or learning strategies' (Carless & Boud, 2018, p. 1315). Student voices are of central importance here, because feedback is a process only they can ultimately enact. Teachers contribute to and foster the process, but students conduct it.

The first implication of this approach is that educators must listen to what students need, not weeks and months after the process has been initiated (e.g. after an assignment, at the end of semester), but at the time it occurs, and thus at a time when it can still be influenced. The simplest manifestation of this, and perhaps the most powerful in making the shift, is to invite students to request feedback on specific skills or elements of their work on an assignment coversheet when they submit their work (see Bloxham & Campbell, 2010; Wakefield, Adie, Pitt, & Owens, 2014). Of course, if such a suggestion were to be introduced without a compelling rationale (and perhaps examples to illustrate it), it would be seen as an unfamiliar activity and most students would write nothing, or simply ask for whatever the marker wants to give. Instead, this practice should be introduced very early in a course and reinforced and encouraged over a sequence of assignments if it is to be seen as a new norm in the process of submitting work.

This approach provides an opening to begin the process of introducing students to the idea of developing their feedback literacy, that is, an appreciation of how feedback works and how they can make feedback effective (Carless & Boud, 2018). It allows educators to listen directly to what students regard as being helpful comments for them as an individual learner. Rather than 'second-guessing' what helpful or useful feedback might look like, this approach places students in control and recognises that what is considered 'helpful' to one student may not be so to another. Thus, by asking students to request specific feedback on their work, educators can provide tailored information for each individual, with the added benefit that this practice may make the marking process more time-efficient for educators. Rather than waiting until the end of the module/unit or course to find out whether students have perceived the feedback they have received to be useful, this approach enables students to voice their preferences at a time where educators can act promptly.

The second implication is that feedback should be introduced as a dialogue, not a monologue (Nicol, 2010). Giving students the opportunity to request specific feedback positions feedback as a dialogic activity (Ajjawi & Boud, 2017; Yang & Carless, 2013), where the provider of comments enters into a process that students have initiated, and which students conclude by demonstrating their response in subsequent work. The use of the metaphor of dialogue is not to imply a continuing to and fro between student and tutor; that may be unrealistic. It does, however, suggest the disposition of student and tutor to the process of producing better work: heavy judgement is out and respectful interaction becomes the norm. In this way of thinking, it is important that marking and giving feedback are not treated as one and the same, where comments become part of the obligation of the educator to justify their mark. A conceptual distinction is needed between marking and mark justification on the one hand (which is the responsibility of the staff member), and on the other, the continuation of the process of learning and demonstration of that learning (which is the responsibility of the student, aided rather than controlled by the educator). By moving beyond feedback as part of the process of justifying a grade, and instead of engaging in dialogue with students about their work, the process of assessing students' work can become more transparent and open, which may go some way to minimising students' dissatisfaction with the 'fairness' of marking procedures.

The third implication is that if feedback is about contributing to the enhancement of what a student can do, then some response from them should be expected. This could be a response which shows what they can do in subsequent work, or some intermediate indication of the direction in which they are moving. The response might be observable in the form of their next assignment with a brief commentary on how they have used the inputs of others to make changes to their approach, if this follows on soon from the previous one. Or, when the module/unit is not designed to allow this to happen, it might take the form of a statement by the student of what they will take forward into their future work from their experience of the first assignment, the comments they have received on it from others and their own reflections on the process. Depending on the nature of the course, this could be returned to the tutor, discussed in a peer group, or lodged as part of their ongoing learning portfolio in the learning management system/virtual learning environment, to be readily accessed by themselves or anyone aiding them in their learning.

There is perhaps no better evidence for an educator regarding the efficacy and quality of their assessment design and the feedback information they have provided for their students than seeing what students do (or do not do) with that information. If students do not appear to be engaging with or applying it from one assignment to the next, this provides powerful knowledge to educators about how useful students perceive that information to be. It should also encourage educators to look critically at the assessment design in their module/unit and at the programme level, to ensure that they have provided students with sufficient opportunities to enact feedback. Evaluating the 'timeliness' of feedback in this way is arguably more important than focusing on a specific turnaround time for the receipt of comments. Thus, rather than waiting until the end of a student's programme of study to find out that they have not found feedback helpful, directly observing students' behaviours in response to feedback can enable educators to make changes to their practice at a time where such changes can have a direct impact on students' learning.

These are straightforward implications that assume that the direction of travel for the learner is clear. However, this is commonly not the case. Criteria for how an assignment is to be judged might be made available in advance in the form of learning outcomes to be achieved or a rubric indicating standards of performance. However, these both take for granted that they are transparent and can be readily understood. In Chapter 2, we saw how Alexander received a single session on grading criteria in the second year of his programme. A 'bolt-on' session such as this is likely to have limited impact on students' ability to take the perspective of a marker. It is not the mere provision of criteria or expected standards in advance that facilitates students' learning through feedback, but rather a process of dialogue that provides opportunities for clarification and concerns of interpretation to be voiced (Balloo, Evans, Hughes, Zhu, & Winstone, 2018). Crucially, these activities enable educators to know, in advance of work being submitted, whether the criteria have been understood and form an opportunity to provide further clarification at a time where it is most beneficial to student learning.

If students are not to become overly dependent on their educators, then producing work and discussing its quality is part of a wider enterprise than feedback alone. Feedback has been positioned as part of the broader process of learning in what has been termed 'developing evaluative judgement' (Tai, Ajjawi, Boud, Dawson, & Panadero, 2017). Students not only need to produce good work that meets appropriate standards and takes account of suitable criteria, they need also to develop the capacity to judge for themselves whether their own work and that of others meets these standards. Feedback for developing evaluative judgement requires learners to discern what constitutes good work of a particular kind and utilise ways of noticing whether their own work and that of others is fit for this purpose (Boud, Dawson, Tai, & Ajjawi, 2018). Developing evaluative judgement does not occur simply by waiting for others to offer their comments, but involves an active process of feedback-seeking. That is, identifying what is needed from others to help refine one's own judgements, enabling them to provide helpful information, and acting upon it. This is important in the context of students' perceptions of assessment and feedback, as perceptions of unfairness in the process most readily occur when students' expectations of the grade their work will likely receive contrast greatly with the judgements of their educators. Thus, supporting students to develop evaluative judgement stands to give students superior access to the mindset of a marker and also enables educators to clarify and recalibrate students' expectations where they may be founded on limited understanding of standards and criteria.

Shifting the emphasis away from survey measures after assessment and feedback cycles have taken place, to engaging in meaningful dialogue with students before work is submitted, provides educators with useful information about students' experience of feedback at a time where this information can be used to enhance practice.

A Partnership Approach to Assessment and Feedback

Whilst there needs to be a systemic shift from understanding feedback as an educator-driven to a student-driven process, this does not absolve educators from playing a vital role (Nash & Winstone, 2017). Instead, this approach is one of partnership, where educators design assessment such that students can apply new understandings to subsequent work. It is also about establishing feedback as a dialogic process where students work to develop an understanding of quality work. It involves positioning feedback as something to be solicited by the person who will benefit from it, rather than having information thrust upon them as an adjunct to grading.

Placing students in control of seeking feedback that they perceive will be most beneficial to them enables us to engage in dialogic feedback processes with individual students and also conveys an important message that students' own role in the feedback process is essential. Furthermore, rather than seeking students' views on their experience of feedback after the event, we have argued that pre-submission activities, such as engaging in dialogue around standards, criteria, and exemplars, enables students to access the perspective of markers, and enables educators to take steps to ensure that criteria are understood and internalised.

Crucially, the approach that we have outlined places students' voices centre stage in understanding how assessment and feedback processes support their learning, but does so as part of what Telio, Ajjawi, and Regehr (2015) in medical education call the educational alliance, wherein students, teachers, and others such as clinical mentors co-construct learning in a mutually constituted context of trust and candour. Students' voices contribute to the shaping of practice, rather than students merely being on the receiving end of practices that they evaluate at a later date. Furthermore, if, as educators, we are able to take meaningful action on students' feedback at a time where they can see the impact, then we are directly modelling feedback literacy by engaging with, and acting upon, their feedback.

Attention to students' voices is as important as ever in a learning-focused model of feedback, but it is essential to distinguish between students commenting on a system in which they have been disempowered through transmission-focused rhetoric, and student voices in a context where feedback is established as a core feature of the curriculum, designed to improve understanding and generate high-quality work that is owned by students. This will help shift the voices we hear from plaintiff cries about a poorly designed curriculum in which students are marginalised, to legitimate analysis for improving a curriculum in which students have agency and ownership.

References

Ajjawi, R., & Boud, D. (2017). Researching feedback dialogue: An interactional analysis approach. *Assessment and Evaluation in Higher Education, 42*(2), 252–265.

Ariely, D. (2010). You are what you measure. *Harvard Business Review, 88*(6), 38.

Balloo, K., Evans, C., Hughes, A., Zhu, X., & Winstone, N. (2018). Transparency isn't spoon-feeding: How a transformative approach to the use of explicit assessment criteria can support student self-regulation. *Frontiers in Education, 3*(Article 69).

Bell, A. R., & Brooks, C. (2018). What makes students satisfied? A discussion and analysis of the UK's national student survey. *Journal of Further and Higher Education, 42*(8), 1118–1142.

Bennett, R., & Kane, S. (2014). Students' interpretations of the meanings of questionnaire items in the National Student Survey. *Quality in Higher Education, 20*, 129–164.

Blackmore, J. (2009). Academic pedagogies, quality logics and performative universities: Evaluating teaching and what students want. *Studies in Higher Education, 34*(8), 857–872.

Bloxham, S., & Campbell, L. (2010). Generating dialogue in assessment feedback: Exploring the use of interactive cover sheets. *Assessment and Evaluation in Higher Education, 35*(3), 291–300.

Boehler, M. L., Rogers, D. A., Schwind, C. J., Mayforth, R., Quin, J., Williams, R. G., & Dunnington, G. (2006). An investigation of medical student reactions to feedback: A randomised controlled trial. *Medical Education, 40*(8), 746–749.

Boud, D., Dawson, P., Tai, J., & Ajjawi, R. (2018). Creating an agenda for developing students' evaluative judgement. In D. Boud, R. Ajjawi, P. Dawson, & J. Tai (Eds.), *Developing evaluative judgement in higher education: Assessment for knowing and producing quality work* (pp. 186–195). London: Routledge.

Boud, D., & Molloy, E. (Eds.). (2013). *Feedback in higher and professional education: understanding it and doing it well.* London: Routledge.

Burgess, A., Senior, C., & Moores, E. (2018). A 10-year case study on the changing determinants of university student satisfaction in the UK. *PLoS ONE, 13*(2), 1–15.

Carless, D., & Boud, D. (2018). The development of student feedback literacy: Enabling uptake of feedback. *Assessment and Evaluation in Higher Education, 43*(8), 1315–1325.

Dawson, P., Henderson, M., Mahoney, P., Phillips, M., Ryan, T., Boud, D., et al. (2019). What makes for effective feedback: Staff and student perspectives. *Assessment and Evaluation in Higher Education, 44*(1), 25–36.

Eley, M. (2001). The course experience questionnaire: Altering question format and phrasing could improve the CEQ's effectiveness. *Higher Education Research and Development, 20*(3), 293–312.

Ferrell, G. (2012). *A view of the Assessment and Feedback Landscape: Baseline analysis of policy and practice from the JISC Assessment & Feedback programme.* Retrieved from http://jiscdesignstudio.pbworks.com/w/file/fetch/61260239/JISC%20AF%20Baseline%20Report%20May%202012.pdf.

Fielding, A., Dunleavy, P. J., & Langan, M. (2010). Interpreting context to the UK's national student (satisfaction) survey data for science subjects. *Journal of Further and Higher Education, 34*(3), 347–368.

Gee, N. (2017). A study of student completion strategies in a Likert-type course evaluation survey. *Journal of Further and Higher Education, 41*(3), 340–350.

Hargreaves, A., Boyle, A., & Harris, A. (2014). *Uplifting leadership: How organizations, teams, and communities raise performance.* Hoboken, NJ: Wiley.

Jarvis, D. S. L. (2014). Regulating higher education: Quality assurance and neo-liberal managerialism in higher education—A critical introduction. *Policy and Society, 33*(3), 155–166.

Knight, P. T. (2002). The Achilles heel of quality: The assessment of student learning. *Quality in Higher Education, 81,* 107–115.

Nash, R. A., & Winstone, N. E. (2017). Responsibility sharing in the giving and receiving of assessment feedback. *Frontiers in Psychology, 8,* 1519.

Nicol, D. (2010). From monologue to dialogue: Improving written feedback processes in mass higher education. *Assessment & Evaluation in Higher Education, 35*(5), 501–517.

Rand, J. (2017). Misunderstandings and mismatches: The collective disillusionment of written summative assessment feedback. *Research in Education, 97*(1), 33–48.

Tai, J., Ajjawi, R., Boud, D., Dawson, P., & Panadero, E. (2017). Developing evaluative judgement: Enabling students to make decisions about the quality of work. *Higher Education, 76,* 467–481.

Telio, S., Ajjawi, R., & Regehr, G. (2015). The "educational alliance" as a framework for reconceptualizing feedback in medical education. *Academic Medicine, 90*(5), 609–614.

Wakefield, C., Adie, J., Pitt, E., & Owens, T. (2014). Feeding forward from summative assessment: The essay feedback checklist as a learning tool. *Assessment and Evaluation in Higher Education, 39*(2), 253–262.

Williams, J., & Cappuccini-Ansfield, G. (2007). Fitness for purpose? National and institution approaches to publicising the student voice. *Quality in Higher Education, 13*(2), 159–172.

Williams, J., & Kane, D. (2008). *Exploring the national student survey: Assessment and feedback issues.* York, UK: Higher Education Academy.

Williams, J., & Kane, D. (2009). Assessment and feedback: Institutional experiences of student feedback, 1996 to 2007. *Higher Education Quarterly, 63,* 264–286.

Winstone, N., Nash, R., Rowntree, J., & Menezes, R. (2016). What do students want most from feedback information? Distinguishing necessities from luxuries using a budgeting methodology. *Assessment and Evaluation in Higher Education, 41*(8), 1237–1253.

Winstone, N., & Pitt, E. (2017). Feedback is a two-way street, so why does the NSS only look one way? *Times Higher Education, 2332,* 30.

Yang, M., & Carless, D. (2013). The feedback triangle and the enhancement of dialogic feedback processes. *Teaching in Higher Education, 18*(3), 285–297.

8

What Happens After What Happens Next? The Single Voice of DLHE and Its Distortions on the Student Learning Journey

Keith Herrmann

Increasingly, universities are competing for students on the basis that they are the best for graduate employment. Universities that can trumpet the outcomes of the Destinations of Leavers from Higher Education (DLHE) Survey to prospective students and their parents do so to encourage students to take their courses. This message resonates increasingly with young people, their parents and employers. With tuition fees in England increasingly driving subject and university choice on the back of how many graduates secure employment from their courses, it is no surprise that the 'employability' narrative is a key element of the conversation universities

The Higher Education Statistics Agency (HESA) has delivered a survey of graduates since 1994/95 under the name of Destination of Leavers from Higher Education (DLHE). The DLHE survey captured the 'destinations' of graduates, i.e. employment and/or further study, travel, other activities etc. six months after graduation. In 2016, HESA carried out a full review and as a result, created a new Graduate Outcomes survey. This new survey extends the survey period to 15 months after graduation, asks additional questions and includes a change to the survey methodology. The new Graduate Outcomes survey only returns its first results in Spring 2020. Hence this article continues to refer to it as the DLHE survey. For more information see www.graduateoutcomes.ac. uk.

K. Herrmann (✉)
University of Surrey, Guildford, UK

© The Author(s) 2019
S. Lygo-Baker et al. (eds.), *Engaging Student Voices in Higher Education*,
https://doi.org/10.1007/978-3-030-20824-0_8

125

have with students (prospective and current). The DLHE data also drive university performance in national league tables (Guardian, The Times and Sunday Times, The Good University Guide) and international league tables (QS World University Rankings) and grading (Gold, Silver, Bronze) for the Teaching Excellence Framework (TEF) governed by the Office for Students (OfS). These can have a significant impact on university reputation and their consequent ability to recruit students.

The challenge, however, is developing the employability narrative beyond a single number; the value of any degree programme cannot be captured in a single figure for graduate employment. Students naturally have many motivations for going to university (Kniveton, 2004), but more recently these very personal drivers have been coloured by the pressures of increased university tuition fees and hence a more instrumentalist view on the value of higher education and its outcomes (Holmes, 2006; see Chapter 4).

Typically, these are captured in the single figure of the percentage of graduates in graduate-level employment and/or further study six months after graduation. These messages are accentuated by employers talking about graduates being 'unemployable' and not meeting the needs of employers (CBI & Pearson, 2016; Minocha, Hristov, & Reynolds, 2017). Hence, employability has currency in universities, having permeated the discourse of senior managers. Yet, there are issues about whose voice is determining what employability means for students, with the distinction often lost between graduates in employment (the DLHE number) and how employable graduates actually are (Rich, 2015). There is also often little thought given to what this means for defining what a university is and its purpose in the twenty-first century (Boulton & Lucas, 2011; Collini, 2012; Chertkovskaya, Watt, Tramer, & Spoelstra, 2013).

By contrast with the singular voice of employers and the dominance of the DLHE figures in determining what employability means in universities, it will be argued that a wider range of voices are needed to inform how we better prepare our students for future employment. This wider collective of voices, very much predicated on including students, academics and employers, will help acknowledge that employability in universities is about more than a single number. Naturally, acknowledging many voices makes it more difficult to distil meaning and have clarity of purpose for what employability means in the student learning journey, but the concatenation of multiple voices brings richness of perspective. Engaging with multiple voices can better contextualise employability in the subject discipline and in the lived student experience, rather than the meaninglessness of a single figure representing graduate employment.

The Context for Employability in Universities

There is much literature about universities and employability, with many different definitions. This is not only a national issue, but also a global one. The Smith Report (Smith, Bell, Bennett, & McAlpine, 2018) scrutinised employability from a practitioner perspective, but also noted the external influences and pressures on universities to ensure that employability as voiced by employers is a key driving force in curriculum design and delivery, with examples from Australia, Canada, Germany, Ireland, Netherlands, South Africa, the UK and the United States.

The neoliberal mantra about the purposive contribution of universities to economic growth and global competitiveness has allowed the state to take control of the employability agenda in universities (Boden & Nedeva, 2010). These authors argue that the state now determines what it means, how it is measured and to some extent even dictates to universities what they will do to meet the state's objectives with regard to employability. As Gordon Brown, then Chancellor of the Exchequer, said:

> Given the substantial public investment in university students, it is particularly important that they are employable upon graduation. (HEFCE, 1999, p. 27)

The Forging Futures report (UKCES & UUK, 2014) positions employability as being about skills and the role for universities is to respond to the requirements of business in relation to their higher-level skills needs. The report posits the view that it is through more active and strategic collaboration between universities and employers that skills shortages can be met. It is taken as given that this is good for universities, employers and students. It reinforces the economic value of universities and how the employability work of universities should be responsive to the needs of the labour market. This performative function means that universities are about 'producing workers so that we can compete in the global knowledge economy' (Boden & Nedeva, 2010, p. 37). By contrast, the needs, voices and interests of students and academics are considered secondary, as subservient to the needs of business. This utilitarian view of universities is also noted in other research (Department for Business, Innovation and Skills, 2011; Holmes, 2006; Jorre de St Jorre & Oliver, 2018; Shah, Pell, & Brooke, 2004; Smith et al., 2018).

The Discursive Nature of Employability

As much as there is currency to employability in the university setting, it also has the potentially perverse impact of distorting what employability means, whose voices determine how it is implemented in universities and whose benefit it serves. Given that there is not an agreed definition of employability (Boden & Nedeva, 2010; Cole & Tibby, 2013; Holmes, 2013; Knight & Yorke, 2003; Yorke, 2004), this means that it can be subject to a wide range of interpretations (Knight, 2001). Boden and Nedeva (2010) argue that by ceding to the power of funding levers in higher education, by framing the role of universities in the form of its contribution to the economy and having the voice of employers determine what they think constitutes an employable graduate, has in effect involved a transition of authority over employability away from higher education to the state. No surprise therefore that the discourse on employability is about graduate outcomes in the narrow sense, that is, the results of the DLHE survey and that the needs of employers are what matters.

Very little consideration is given to the voices of students. Instead, the student voice is purportedly framed in employability terms in the form of the DLHE survey which captures the employment outcomes of graduates nationally, by institution and by subject. This offers a positional stance on employability (Holmes, 2013); graduates are economic assets, described as being in a graduate role, a non-graduate role or unemployed. There is no dialogic device through which graduates can present their voices on employability. The discourse on employability is expressed as an impassive single voice—that of the data on graduates in employment nationally.

Smith et al. (2018) offer an alternative perspective on defining employability, viewed not as an instrumentalist function of the university as institution, but more as a device through which learning can be better framed as part of the student journey. Taking on Holmes' (2013) model of employability as processual and not outcomes-driven, they argue that employability can be a blend of learning, knowledge, career development and technical or discipline-based knowledge and skills. Of course, this view of employability also remains closely associated with the possessional view, that is, a list of graduate attributes, skills and competencies, which remains continually contested (Holmes, 2013; see Chapter 14). Nonetheless, by positioning employability as being about learning (process) rather than outcome, there is the opportunity to wrestle back the ownership of employability from the state and employers. However, deep and meaningful partnership between academics and students remains the challenge (see Chapter 18). Students are often too accepting of the knowledge of academics (Jackson, 2017; Jorre de St Jorre & Oliver, 2018; Shah et al., 2004), and academics by return are often fearful of engaging students in a discourse about employability involving co-creation of meaning, subject-level context and the voices of employers (Minocha et al., 2017). Hence, the maintenance of a single voice appears more comfortable than recognising and adding to the complexity of the different voices that are available.

The Distorting Voice of the DLHE and Student Choices

The focus on the DLHE survey as a proxy for what is considered a good university education epitomises an outcomes-oriented view of employability. When graduate outcomes are used as a proxy for employability, then very easily the context of employability and its meaning in the journey of the student is narrowed to focus on employment outcomes. By contrast, a processual model (Holmes, 2013) for employability shares ownership and engagement with employability across a wider range of internal and external stakeholders, including students, academics, professional careers services staff, senior university leadership and externally with employers, professional bodies and the state (Smith et al., 2018).

This focus on employment outcomes has been further augmented by the recent publication of the Longitudinal Earnings Outcome (LEO) data which link graduates to their personal employment, benefits and earnings information (Department for Education, 2016). The LEO data link HMRC's tax records and other sources to education data to provide a longer-term view on individual graduate earnings. The data show the average earnings for graduates by university and by subject discipline over time. This takes the marketisation of the student experience to the extreme, under the pretence that it will help students make more informed choices. What this approach fails to appreciate is that these data are only one of many factors that inform student choice about which course to study and where. Furthermore, it frames employment as the single most important outcome from university education. The DLHE survey is an instrument of performativity (Boden & Nedeva, 2010). It is about measuring and ranking universities in terms of the employment outcomes of their graduates. It is also a gauge of how responsive and how well-matched degree programmes are to the labour market.

Few studies have considered that employability is about students and graduates, about their voices as well, not just those of employers or the state or the economy. A qualitative study from Bournemouth University surveyed graduates to assess their journeys post-graduation. This showed that the journey to graduate employment is sometimes longer than expected and that the types of roles and jobs obtained are not always in the subjects studied. From an employability skills point of view, the findings were positive, with most graduates indicating that their course had developed the skills they needed in the workplace after graduation (Shah et al., 2004). It also found, however, that the employability skills provided in their courses could have been improved further. The graduate respondents felt that the university could have made industry skills more explicit in course delivery and to illustrate their relevance in the workplace. The vagaries and competitiveness of the labour market are evident in the large percentage initially taking non-graduate jobs and often jobs unrelated to the industry sector they wished to be in.

As a search for professional identity, the DLHE outcomes are positive at a national level (HESA, 2018). Some 71.3% of employed graduates were in a professional-level job. More generally, the findings are positive:

- 74.2% of graduates were in employment six months after graduating.
- Only 5.3% were unemployed—the lowest rate since 1989.
- 21% of graduates went on to full- or part-time further study.
- The average graduate salary in the UK was £21,776.

So why the despair? Why the concern about the distorting vagaries of the DLHE data on how employability is understood and measured? It is argued that the distorting voice of the data on earnings and employment outcome places the purpose of a university at risk if scholarship, research excellence and the learning journey are subjugated to the chase for the 'best results' on graduate employment and earnings outcomes rather than what is right for the individual student. As outlined above, it reinforces the neoliberal hegemony of employability as meeting the needs of the state and the economy, not those of individual graduates. It belittles the voices of students in determining what it means for them and ignores how their voices could bring new meaning to the student learning journey in shaping both curricular and co-curricular experiences. The subjugation of the individual to learning a set of technical skills rather than the development of the mind distorts what universities are for and negates their broader contribution to society as enlightening, discovering and progressing knowledge (Boden & Nedeva, 2010).

The growing emphasis on long-term earnings and career trajectories is disconcerting as it is not plausible to make the connection between what a university does for its students and their long-term employment outcomes—there are just too many factors and intervening variables to make any of these data useful. For that matter, it does not recognise the agency that graduates themselves possess to control their own futures, to decide on their early career pathways and their long-term futures. As we saw in Chapter 2, Alexander is forced to become an outsider, to find an identity outside of the conventional identities assumed by students studying engineering. His story shows that there is no consideration given to students crafting their own journeys, identities and understanding of what it means to be employable through their experience of university education.

The plethora of metrics of university performance is supposedly about informing student choice, whether choice of institution, of subject, of career and of graduate outcome. Here Rose (1989) offers a powerful insight, by arguing 'that such "choice" is a chimera because we do not do the choosing in circumstances of our making or indeed choosing' (Boden & Nedeva, 2010, p. 39). In the case of the student choices outlined above, the data to inform choice are chosen by the state. As an imposition on universities, employability in the form of the DLHE survey is used as a blunt instrument to inform students about the performance of a university or a particularly course in the labour market. Little consideration is given to the context within which the information should be understood and used. It subjugates the student to consumer rather than learner (see Chapter 4). However, the data from the DLHE survey have many uses, some of which are informative for students—the HECSU 'What do Graduates Do' annual report, for example, provides both analysis of graduate employment by subject as well as offering students and graduates useful insights into a career-planning perspective.

In summary, key government reports on higher education all emphasise the role of universities in supporting graduate employability (Browne, 2010; Dearing, 1997; Leitch, 2006; Roberts, 2002; Wilson, 2012). The framing of employability as being about graduate employment outcomes (DLHE) provides a dominant veneer over what is a more complex endeavour. It discounts the value of careers education and the importance of using data within the context of independent career guidance that can help students make informed choices (based on their interests, skills and career ambitions) and find their own voices as a counterbalance to the more instrumentalist and utilitarian view of what is an employable graduate (Holmes, 2006).

Furthermore, it does not give adequate recognition to the importance of pre-professional identity for students (Jackson, 2017), nor to student and graduate capability for self-authoring (Holland, Lachicotte, Skinner, & Cain, 2001), nor their social, family and educational background or habitus (Bourdieu & Passeron, 1977), nor to the liminal spaces (Turner, 1969) within which students find themselves as they navigate their way into university, transition through and out on graduating into employment. Instead, it frames employability as being about skills, attributes, behaviours and competencies that employers need, thus diminishing the power of the university as a diverse community of multiple voices.

Employer Voices in Framing Course Design to Enhance Employability

The third dimension to the employability challenge in universities is the voices of employers and how these are understood and interpreted in course design. The new industrial strategy (HM Government, 2017) references the importance of universities producing graduates that meet the needs of employers. Many universities already have degree programmes accredited by professional bodies, trade associations and employer groups. The interaction between these bodies and universities aims to ensure that courses are designed to equip students with the knowledge, professional skills and personal qualities to succeed in the workplace. However, it could be argued that the needs of employers are often situated in the here and now, the present—many of the reports on skills gaps and shortages highlight the urgency of addressing the immediate concerns employers have (CBI & Pearson, 2016; UKCES & UUK, 2014). However, in this time of the fourth industrial revolution (Schwab, 2015) when the race against (with) the machines will be the single defining feature of the future workforce, it is important that we design the student learning journey so that it equips our graduates to be adaptable, and not just for the graduate job that is secured within six months of graduation.

Graduates will face a world of work 'mechanised' by artificial intelligence where even graduate-level jobs will be replaced by machines. The fusion of technologies that are blurring the lines between the physical, digital and biological spheres means that being human is about more than knowledge, it is about more than economic and social value. It is about graduates being creative, adaptive, innovative and connected. The student learning journey ought to enable students to develop and use higher-order graduate attributes to deal with the volatility, uncertainty, complexity and ambiguity that they will face in the workplace. This will be the distinguishing feature of graduate success and the impact of universities in the future.

Universities need to recognise, embrace and cultivate a wider range of voices which shape the student learning journey and enrich the classroom experience with professional practice, but in a way that relies on the interplay between academic, student and employer and not subjugating the one voice to the other. Universities can listen to a wider range of voices to bring subject-level context to employability in the classroom. Alongside the contributions of industrial advisory boards to curriculum design, speakers from industry in the classroom, students working on live company projects and student-staff liaison committees, there is the broader challenge of how universities go about enabling student authorship of their learning experiences. Many universities use employability awards as a way of providing students with a platform to author their own narrative about their university experiences, to find and express their own voices about who they are. This recognises that students have voices that are unique to themselves, that have value and that need to be heard by both academics and employers alike. Employability awards also help stretch the meaning of employability beyond a single number, a single voice, but in many ways, as outlined below, they are often framed using the language of employers.

The academic and business literature on employability is often framed with reference to lists of employability skills. Starting with the lists from the ESECT project (Yorke, 2004) through to the framework developed by the Higher Education Academy (Cole & Tibby, 2013), the conceptualisations of employability are numerous and subjectively configured, but all essentially grounded in the view that it is about individual acquisition of capability framed around meeting the needs of employers. The much cited ESECT definition, for example, is:

a set of achievements – skills, understandings and personal attributes – that makes graduates more likely to gain employment and be successful in their chosen occupations, which benefits themselves, the workforce, the community and the economy. (Yorke, 2004, p. 8)

This way of thinking about employability is echoed in how employers articulate their needs for graduate talent (AGR, 1995; Department for

Business, Innovation and Skills, 2015), and in the policy domain, this further legitimises the discourse that 'the major role of universities is the production of an appropriately trained workforce that fits employers' needs' (Boden & Nedeva, 2010, p. 38). However, it is the sweeping changes to industries, economies and societies noted above that ought to encourage us to pause, to explore ways of re-appropriating what employability means. It needs to better capture the voices of a broader cast of stakeholders, including students. We need to move away from confusing employability as an institutional feature of universities (i.e. what we expect universities to deliver) with individual ability to gain employment (Harvey, 2001).

This requires us to move beyond the employer discourse on employability towards engagement with multiple rather than singular voices. As regards involving student voices, we need to reframe how we engage with students, especially where they have work experience as part of their degree programme and/or access to work experience outside of their studies. Outlined below is a short illustration of how academics could leverage the knowledge and experiences that year-long placement students have to contribute to a refresh of the curriculum as a lived experience:

1. The learning and teaching framework could require academics to work with their returning placement students to look anew at the final-year curriculum at the start of the academic year and explore how they enable student voices to connect the curriculum with the lived knowledge and experiences from their placement year.
2. Academic staff could then collaborate with their students to reframe the curriculum in working practice to ensure it responds to the voiced wisdom of the placement students. Elements of the curriculum would be replaced with contributions from the students themselves based on their up-to-date knowledge from industry practice, thus keeping the curriculum alive and relevant, stretching both students and academics.
3. Finally, academic staff could use a graduate attributes framework as a reflective device to help students connect the classroom with the world of work. Rather than just focusing narrowly on how the attributes developed in their studies alone, students could think more laterally about how their degree equips them for a multitude of career opportunities

within and beyond their subject domain. This is particularly important given that many graduate recruiters do not recruit according to subject and many graduates do not follow linear career pathways towards clearly defined professional identities (Purcell et al., 2012). This would give freedom to students seeking to explore career options beyond their subject discipline.

Making the definition of employability part of students' learning journeys brings authenticity to the experience that no lecture from an employer can mimic. It counters the view that employability is often a bolt on and thus disarticulated from learning and teaching. It also allows students to learn, use and share the language of their subject discipline as it is applied in practice. Bringing the world of work into the classroom via students themselves enables students to bring authenticity to the curriculum through their own lived experiences rather than through a textbook, an online video, or employer talk. We can see what happens when this is not achieved—in Alexander's case, the 'intensely oral culture' of engineering (Darling & Dannels, 2003) was missing from his experience of the subject altogether and thus further dislocated him from his studies.

We cannot afford the neoliberal imposition of 'oven-ready' graduates as the key outcome, as this will only equip our graduates to address the short-term needs of employers. A longer-term view can re-install the trust we previously had in the academy. Alongside this, we should explore how we can reconceptualise the domain of the university and the role that students have in it. Notwithstanding the dominance of the National Student Survey, the DLHE survey and other performance metrics such as the TEF, universities should actively engage student views on their experiences of their learning journeys, of their career aspirations and of their graduate employment ambitions to garner insights about how employability could be framed (Higdon, 2016). The voices of students can be used to redefine employability (Higdon & Stevens, 2017) and to inform both curriculum design and delivery.

The Higdon and Stevens (2017) study looked at the voices of dance students to map their career journeys into dance, through university and onwards into employment. Albeit a small sample, it offers some useful qualitative insights into the student lifeworld and how they define and experience the development of employability skills. Recognising the protean nature of artists' career journeys, the research found students seeking to self-author, to establish their own identity notwithstanding the difficulties of the labour market in dance. These externalities were taken as a given but did not usurp the students of their identity and agency in seeking a sense of purpose in career. While their articulation of the meaning of employability for them used simple phrases like 'how are you going to make money', their grounded and internally developed views are askance with the formulaic approaches of the academic literature with endless lists of employability skills that don't resonate with students.

Regarding the plurality of students' voices, the challenge remains to break out of the current framing of employability. While the dominant personal attributes and skills frameworks used to define employability have their uses in terms of shaping the curriculum and establishing links with industry, we must ask searching questions of ourselves about the nature of student identity and how we enable students to bring their voices to give meaning to employability and its relevance in their learning journeys. Engaging meaningfully with multiple and diverse student voices to guide our understanding of employability means that the university itself has to move beyond proselytising the single voice of the DLHE data and of the employer view on employability. Universities should instead seek to celebrate the diversity of outcomes from its graduates in value-driven stories which capture the breadth of voices about the experiences students have at university as well as beyond. They need to give currency to the individual and to the distinctiveness of their personal stories (see Chapter 2). Having the DLHE number as a proxy for employability is only an indicative articulation of what the average outcome may be. It can't inspire, it can't offer insight, it can't determine the future for students. Ultimately, it is the co-created journey of a conversation between students, academics and employers and the kaleidoscope of voices and perspectives that they all contribute which bring meaning to what employability is.

To finish and to return to the observations in this chapter about the future world of work:

Ultimately though, in the context of automation, the challenge for the universities of 2040 will be finding ways to enable individuals to embrace a world where 'to be employed is to be at risk [and] to be employable is to be secure' (Hawkins, 1999), yet recognising at the same time that any such notion of 'security' is unachievable. (Costea, et al., 2007, cited in Herrmann, 2018, p. 132)

References

Association of Graduate Recruiters. (1995). *Skills for graduates in the 21st century.* Cambridge: Association of Graduate Recruiters.

Boden, R., & Nedeva, M. (2010). Employing discourse: Universities and graduate 'employability'. *Journal of Education Policy, 25*(1), 37–54.

Boulton, G., & Lucas, C. (2011). What are universities for? *Chinese Science Bulletin, 56*(23), 2506–2517.

Bourdieu, P., & Passeron, J.-C. (1977). *Reproduction in education, society and culture.* London: Sage.

Browne, J. (2010). *Securing a sustainable future for higher education: Independent review of higher education and student finance in England.* London: Department for Business, Innovation and Skills.

CBI & Pearson. (2016). *The right combination: CBI and Pearson education and skills survey.* Retrieved from https://www.voced.edu.au/content/ngv:73692.

Chertskovskaya, E., Watt, P., Tramer, S., & Spoelstra, S. (2013). Giving notice to employability. *Ephemera: Theory and Politics in Organization, 13*(4), 701–716.

Cole, D., & Tibby, M. (2013). *Defining and developing your approach to employability—A framework for higher education institutions.* York, UK: Higher Education Academy.

Collini, S. (2012). *What are universities for?* London: Penguin.

Darling, A. L., & Dannels, D. P. (2003). Practicing engineers talk about the importance of talk: A report on the role of oral communication in the workplace. *Communication Education, 52*(1), 1–16.

Dearing, R. (1997). *The Dearing report, higher education in the learning society.* London: The National Committee of Inquiry into Higher Education. Retrieved from http://www.educationengland.org.uk/documents/dearing1997/dearing1997.html.

Department for Business, Innovation and Skills. (2011). *Higher education: Students at the heart of the system.* London: BIS.

Department for Business, Innovation and Skills. (2015). *Understanding employers' graduate recruitment and selection practices* (BIS Research Paper No. 231).

Department for Education. (2016). *Employment and earnings outcomes of higher education graduates: Experimental data from the longitudinal education outcomes (LEO) dataset.* London: DfE.

Harvey, L. (2001). Defining and measuring employability. *Quality in Higher Education, 7*(2), 97–109.

Hawkins, P. (1999). *The art of building windmills: Career tactics for the 21st century.* Liverpool, UK: University of Liverpool Graduate into Employment Unit.

Higher Education Funding Council for England (HEFCE). (1999). *Performance indicators in higher education.* Bristol: HEFCE.

Herrmann, K. (2018). Universities inside out: Situating university-business co-operation at the centre of the student learning journey. In T. Davey, A. Meerman, B. Orazbayeva, M. Riedel, V. Galán-Muros, C. Plewa, & N. Eckert (Eds.), *The future of universities thoughtbook.* Retrieved from http://futureuniversities.com/.

Higdon, R. (2016). Employability: The missing voice—How student and graduate views could be used to develop future higher education policy and inform curricula. *Power and Education, 8*(2), 176–195.

Higdon, R., & Stevens, R. (2017). Redefining employability: student voices mapping their dance journeys and futures. *Research in Dance Education, 18*(3), 301–320.

Higher Education Statistics Agency. (2018). *Destinations of leavers from higher education institutions, 2016/17.* Cheltenham, UK: Higher Education Statistics Agency.

HM Government. (2017). *Industrial strategy: Building a Britain fit for the future.* Retrieved from https://www.gov.uk/government/publications/industrial-strategy-building-a-britain-fit-for-the-future.

Holland, D., Lachicotte, W., Skinner, D., & Cain, C. (2001). *Identity and agency in cultural worlds.* Cambridge, MA: Harvard University Press.

Holmes, L. (2006). *Reconsidering graduate employability: Beyond possessive-instrumentalism.* Paper presented at the Seventh International Conference on HRD Research and Practice Across Europe, University of Tilburg.

Holmes, L. (2013). Competing perspectives on graduate employability: Possession, position or process? *Studies in Higher Education, 38*(4), 538–554.

Jackson, D. (2017). Developing pre-professional identity in undergraduates through work-integrated learning. *Higher Education, 74,* 833–853.

Jorre de St Jorre, T., & Oliver, B. (2018). Want students to engage? Contextualise graduate learning outcomes and assess for employability. *Higher Education Research and Development, 37*(1), 44–57.

Knight, P. (2001). Editorial: Employability and quality. *Quality in Higher Education, 7*(2), 93–95.

Knight, P., & Yorke, M. (2003). *Assessment, learning and employability.* Maidenhead, UK: Open University Press.

Kniveton, B. H. (2004). The influences and motivations on which students base their choice of career. *Research in Education, 72*(1), 47–59.

Leitch, S. (2006). *Prosperity for all in the global economy: World class skills.* Final Report of the Leitch Review of Skills. London: HM Treasury. Retrieved from http://www.hm-treasury.gov.uk/leitch_review_index.htm.

Minocha, S., Hristov, D., & Reynolds, M. (2017). From graduate employability to employment: Policy and practice in UK higher education. *International Journal of Training and Development, 21*(3), 235–248.

Purcell, K., Elias, P., Atfield, G., Behle, H., Ellison, R., Luchinskaya, D., … Tzanakou, C. (2012). *Futuretrack Stage 4 Full Report: Transitions into employment, further study and other outcomes.* Retrieved from https://hecsu.ac.uk/assets/assets/documents/Futuretrack_Stage_4_Final_report_6th_Nov_2012.pdf.

Rich, J. (2015). *Employability: Degrees of value—Occasional paper 1.* Oxford: HEPI.

Roberts, G. (2002). *SET for success: The supply of people with science, technology, engineering and mathematics skills.* London: HM Treasury.

Rose, N. (1989). *Governing the soul: The shaping of the private self.* London: Free Association Books.

Schwab, K. (2015). *The Fourth Industrial Revolution: What it means, how to respond.* Retrieved from https://www.weforum.org/agenda/2016/01/the-fourth-industrial-revolution-what-it-means-and-how-to-respond/.

Shah, A., Pell, K., & Brooke, P. (2004). Beyond first destinations: Graduate employability survey. *Active Learning in Higher Education, 5*(1), 9–26.

Smith, M., Bell, K., Bennett, D., & McAlpine, A. (2018). *Employability in a global context: Evolving policy and practice in employability, work integrated learning, and career development learning.* Wollongong, Australia: Graduate Careers Australia.

Turner, V. (1969). *The ritual process.* London: Penguin.

UKCES & UUK. (2014). *Forging futures: building higher level skills through university and employer collaboration.* Retrieved from https://www.gov.

uk/government/publications/forging-futures-building-higher-level-skills-through-university-and-employer-collaboration.

Wilson, T. (2012). *A review of business: University collaboration.* London: Department for Business, Innovation and Skills.

Yorke, M. (2004). *Employability and higher education: What it is—And what it is not.* York, UK: Higher Education Academy.

9

Mechanisms to Represent the Doctoral Researcher Voice

Shane Dowle, Sam Hopkins and Carol Spencely

Whose Voice?

The 'postgraduate voice' is a problematic concept to work with since it would be impossible, and mistaken, to try to reduce it to a singular entity. Indeed, the term 'postgraduate' includes a wide range of students who are studying for different qualifications, with the only commonality being that, generally, there is a requirement for an undergraduate level degree to enter the programme of study. Furthermore, postgraduate qualifications vary between countries and educational systems. To address some of these variabilities, in 1999 the Bologna Process created the European Higher Education Area in which parity in standards of higher education qualifications was agreed. For postgraduate education, the Bologna Process defined two different educational levels: Master's (second cycle Bologna) and doctoral research (third cycle Bologna; European Higher Education Area, 2005).

S. Dowle (✉) · S. Hopkins · C. Spencely
University of Surrey, Guildford, UK
e-mail: s.dowle@surrey.ac.uk

© The Author(s) 2019
S. Lygo-Baker et al. (eds.), *Engaging Student Voices in Higher Education*,
https://doi.org/10.1007/978-3-030-20824-0_9

Here, we will narrow the discussion to include only postgraduate education in the UK, but there is still huge heterogeneity in the form these degrees take. Qualifications include certificates, diplomas, Master's degrees, and doctorates. This chapter will further narrow the focus to the voice of doctoral researchers studying for a doctoral qualification. However, there is still a wide variety of doctoral qualifications: PhD, DPhil, DBA, EngD, DClinPsy, EdD, all of which add to the challenge of defining a doctoral student voice.

Doctoral qualifications vary, and the doctoral student body is also defined by its diversity. HESA data show that in 2016–2017, there were 100,085 doctoral research students registered in the UK. Individuals come to the doctorate at different stages of their life: 44% of doctoral researchers are over 30 years of age, suggesting that a significant proportion of students have followed other routes, outside of academia, prior to their postgraduate research. Motivation to pursue a doctorate comes from intrinsic and extrinsic factors, with many of the extrinsic factors reported to be career-related (Vitae, 2018). A large proportion (83%) of those studying a doctoral research programme part-time are over the age of 30, with researchers looking to deepen their knowledge for professional advancement or to enhance their career options (Higher Education Statistics Agency, 2018).

Doctoral researchers contribute to making academic research an international community and market. They come from various cultural and educational backgrounds, they have access to different levels of funding, and there are disparate working patterns across research disciplines and between institutions. Students may be working in teams or working alone; their studies may be practice-based, lab-based, theoretical, computer-based, and so on. Indeed, all doctoral researchers will be researching something that is uniquely different from any other project. This calls into question the possibility of a single harmonious 'postgraduate voice'. However, this 'voice' will be different to that of undergraduate students and must be considered separately and with an understanding of its complexities.

The Voice in Context

In order to capture some of the complexities intrinsic to the postgraduate researcher voice, it is helpful to consider how the nature of doctoral qualifications in the UK has evolved over time and to consider the impact of these changes on the audibility of the doctoral researcher voice. We contend that the collective and individual voices of doctoral researchers were silent, muted, or muffled during the majority of Bogle's (2017) first three stages of the doctorate spanning from 1917 to early 1990s. Nevertheless, policy interventions from the 1990s onwards have given doctoral researchers a platform from which their voices can be projected.

In contrast to our European and trans-Atlantic neighbours, the doctorate was late to arrive in the UK (Simpson, 1983). The first registration for a UK PhD did not take place until 1917 at the University of Oxford. The model of doctoral education adopted in the UK was strongly influenced by the German, Humboldtian approach (Simpson, 1983; Taylor, 2012). In other words, the doctorate was framed as a qualification rooted in the quest for pure knowledge that would carry academic disciplines forward (Park, 2005). The esoteric ideals of the doctorate were underpinned by a very simple support structure: the doctoral researcher would be responsible for carrying out a research project under the tutelage of an academic expert, the supervisor.[1] The researcher's work would culminate in the production of a written output—the thesis—that would be examined *viva voce* by a panel of acknowledged experts. As others have pointed out, this model was left untouched for decades and still forms the spine of the contemporary doctoral experience (Hancock & Walsh, 2014; McAlpine, 2017).

The focus of this early incarnation of the doctorate was the generation of substantive knowledge by members of the academic discipline *for* the academic discipline. The idea of a doctoral researcher voice would have been an alien concept to those who supervised doctoral researchers. Indeed, the individual and collective needs of doctoral researchers were rarely vocalised and even more rarely heard during this period. It was assumed that all doctoral researchers were 'stewards of the discipline' (Jackson, 2003) who wanted to pursue an academic career. It was also taken for granted that the master-apprentice model, whereby the doctoral researcher tacitly learns the tricks of the trade from their supervisor, was the most suitable method for training new researchers (Delamont, Atkinson, & Parry, 2000). The doctoral experience was mysterious, opaque, and obscured from view, which Park (2005) has likened to a 'secret garden'.

Under this mode of delivery, the doctoral researcher was overly dependent on their supervisor. If the relationship between them was difficult, then the doctoral researcher had few, if any, avenues for voicing their concerns and seeking help. Indeed, doctoral researchers were benignly neglected by their institutions, and the business of doing research was left solely in the hands of the supervisor and doctoral researcher (Denicolo, 2003). The voices of doctoral researchers were, at best, muffled and, at worst, completely silenced by the pervading structure.

From the 1990s, however, the way in which doctoral education was structured and delivered changed in response to the burgeoning of the knowledge-based economy. The New Labour government at the time outlined a vision to secure the UK's competitive capability in global markets by prioritising innovation and encouraging partnerships between knowledge producers and industry (Hancock, Hughes, & Walsh, 2017). This marked the start of a new trend of external policy interventions as the ears of government became attuned to the value of both doctoral research and doctoral researchers to the national economy.

As commented upon by Duke and Denicolo (2017) and John and Denicolo (2013), a flurry of policy interventions ensued that both challenged and radically altered the delivery of doctoral education so that it could better serve the knowledge economy. The *laissez-faire* approach that had endured hitherto was no longer tenable as the government (and, by proxy, the taxpayer), businesses, and industry became important stakeholders in doctoral education. New demands were placed on doctoral education, which had the effect of ripping it from its unfettered, hidden state and reshaping for the needs of the knowledge economy.

The 'Roberts Report' (Roberts, 2002), for example, drew attention to the narrowness of the PhD and brought about an increase in investment to support doctoral researchers in developing a broader pallet of skills for career trajectories beyond academia. In other developments, commercial and public funders (including Research Councils) moved to introduce greater accountability into doctoral education in an attempt to drive up efficiency. They wanted to see a more timely return on their investment, and so the days of lengthy degree registrations and high attrition rates were no longer considered acceptable (Collinson & Hockey, 1995). The Research Councils have played a critical role in accelerating the doctoral process via enacting a policy of institutional financial sanctions for low submission rates (Wright & Cochrane, 2000) and, latterly, to fund a cohort-based approach through Centres for Doctoral Training (CDTs) and Doctoral Training Partnerships (DTPs). Complementary to the actions of the Research Councils was a push from regulators to make the delivery of doctorates more organised within institutions. The Quality Assurance Agency (QAA), for example, established a set of standards and protocols against which universities had to align in order to be able to award research degrees. The drive for better organisation and structural coherence for doctoral education is further evidenced by the contemporary phenomenon of Graduate Schools and Doctoral Colleges, which, inter alia, are responsible for maintaining oversight of and accountability for doctoral education (Smith McGloin & Wynne, 2015).

Whilst these developments were primarily driven by the exigencies of the knowledge economy, they have fuelled changes to the audibility and status of the doctoral researcher voice. The doctorate is no longer a private affair involving just the researcher and supervisor. Instead, doctoral researchers are now more likely to be a part of multiple cohorts; they will have at least two supervisors; their projects and progress are likely to be overseen by a Graduate School or Doctoral College; and institutions are required to have mechanisms in place to hear and act upon their feedback. Doctoral education is now more out in the open than it had been previously. This has created a number of platforms for doctoral researchers to articulate views of their experience, both collectively and individually.

In the sections that follow, we consider the mechanisms most universities have in place to listen and respond to doctoral researcher feedback. Whilst these mechanisms have turned up the volume of the doctoral researcher voice, we problematise some of the common approaches and argue that within the cacophony, individual researchers' voices remain muffled or lost.

Mechanisms to Represent the Doctoral Researcher 'Voice'

What Mechanisms Are There?

Universities and teams within universities have myriad mechanisms for hearing the cacophony of the doctoral researcher voice—how well this voice is heard and then acted upon is a matter for discussion. The predominant voice comes from the postgraduate research experience survey (PRES) conducted by 117 UK institutions nationwide which gathered the views of over 57,000 doctoral researchers in 2017 (Slight, 2017). The PRES questionnaire tool is comprised of a series of scales that examine how satisfied a doctoral researcher is with certain aspects of their experience during their doctoral study. The questions range from topics such as supervision and research culture to the facilities and working space provided. These results can then be divided and compared using a number of grouping factors such as year of study or discipline. Nevertheless, the PRES survey has limitations. Indeed, the 2017 PRES report recognises that it only captures a partial sample of the overall doctoral researcher population (Slight, 2017), perhaps as a consequence of universities volunteering to opt into the survey and then experiencing challenges in convincing doctoral researchers to complete the survey. Even though the creators of the survey recognise that it is only a partial sample of the doctoral researcher voice, it is often taken by universities to represent the homogenous student voice. During the 2017 administration of the survey, the PRES sample did not correspond with overall doctoral researcher population demographics in areas such as gender, registration status (full-time or part-time), and residence (Slight, 2017).

In addition to PRES, there are further mechanisms set up to hear the postgraduate researcher voice within universities. These include, but are not limited to, fora, representative committees and representation on committees within the university governance structure. Typically, these mechanisms ask one or more doctoral researchers to represent their department, school, or faculty to either sit on a university committee or to attend a representative meeting where they act as a conduit between their area and the higher faculty or the central services. Whilst these mechanisms are created with the good intention to establish dialogue with the students and capture some of the voices within the group, it is often only the loudest or most concerning voices that are heard.

One of the most important avenues for doctoral researchers to have their voices heard is through their supervisors. The relationship between the supervisor and student is crucial and a vital way that a doctoral researcher can get their voice heard. When this relationship works, then the doctoral researcher may feel that they do not need another outlet for voicing their concerns and opinions about their experience. However, doctoral researchers may not feel it appropriate to voice their concerns or challenge their supervisor and, therefore, need to seek out other options. This is never more important than when the reason for concern is the supervisory relationship.

There are also informal methods, perhaps richer in harmonics, of hearing the voices of doctoral researchers. These range from blogs such as 'Academics Anonymous' and '23 Things for Research' to Twitter and other social media outlets where many doctoral researchers feel they are able to speak freely and perhaps without the expectation of being heard by their university. There are advantages and disadvantages to these more informal methods. Firstly, doctoral researchers can talk freely and immediately about their situation. The informal nature of social media can create a network of support amongst doctoral researchers; for example, a part-time and distance learning Facebook group that is used by students to communicate with their peers for support and information as well as congratulations for achievements. The disadvantages include an indelible digital footprint and the quick and instant nature of social media meaning that things can be said in the heat of the moment, later to be regretted. The doctoral researchers are giving and getting feedback from their peers and their voice is being heard, but not necessarily by the institution.

How Are They Heard?

The question of who is doing the listening is an interesting one, and there is a whole host of lateral communication that goes on where doctoral researchers give voice and are heard individually, leading to a richer sound.

This latter voice is often peer to peer, through mentoring or with staff members who are not at a level to act on the feedback they are receiving. A peer mentoring scheme will allow two-way communication between students, but there is also a level of trust built up between the mentors and the person managing the programme. This means that if there is ever a problem or issue that the university should know about, but that the doctoral researcher is not confident enough to voice themselves, the mentor will be able to raise the matter with a member of staff for further action. The culture of an organisation is paramount to fostering these relationships by recognising their value and allowing time to let them develop. Perhaps if we captured these voices more carefully, we would get a fuller chorus of information, rather than just the skilled solo artists who articulate their voice through the conventional channels. Then the 'silencing of the individual' that occurs through survey approaches, such as PRES, would be counterbalanced with a richer sound.

How Are They Acted Upon?

Naturally, the response from institutions to the information given by doctoral researchers varies; however, the importance of the PRES survey when compared to the undergraduate National Student Survey (NSS) which filters into the Teaching Excellence Framework (TEF) raises the question of whether or not institutions are compelled to judge this feedback with the same gravitas. However, this may not necessarily be a bad thing; as mentioned above, the PRES captures a homogenous perspective and headline set of scores that do not really address the individual issues of many students.

What doctoral researchers say and to whom can be vital in determining what happens as a result. Doctoral researchers will happily give their opinion in confidential surveys until they feel that nothing is being done no matter how many questionnaires are distributed and completed. Doctoral researchers are likely to become questionnaire-fatigued and stop responding if they do not see or feel change. Indeed, the PRES report 2017 has a question 'My institution values and responds to feedback from research degree students' and the UK-resident students reported low satisfaction against this variable—only 58% said that they agreed with the statement (Slight, 2017). Agreement with this statement was also found to alter in relation to time registered on the doctoral programme: the percentage agreeing to the statement decreased in line with years of study. It is possible that these scores reflect what the doctoral researchers expect from their doctoral programme based on their past experience with higher education. Some universities have tried to address this through a 'you said, we did' approach where the response of the university is posted somewhere for all to see. This is incumbent on the student to find where these responses are being posted, but the most engaged will see that changes are being made in response to their feedback or at least reasons for a lack of change. However, even this approach can have its pitfalls, and doctoral researchers may see that the issues raised by a few vocal students are addressed whilst they feel largely ignored.

Surveys and 'Representation'

PRES data are sometimes used by university management teams to provide evidence of impact of initiatives or demonstrate a need for change. However, with the wide range of doctoral programmes, doctoral researchers, and forms of research undertaken, this quantitative survey cannot possibly represent the whole doctoral researcher population. One might ask: Do these data and analytics equate to a student voice at all? As we have already discussed earlier in this chapter, we think not. Warnings about equating student data to the student voice have been explored by Spanner (2018) in an online blog. She asks pertinent questions of student data such as: Who benefits? Who decides? What is it for?

If we adopt the definition of student voice as 'giving students the ability to influence learning to include policies, programs, contexts and principles' (Harper, 2003), then we need to make doctoral researchers true partners in the decision-making processes. We also need to acknowledge that there are multiple and diverse doctoral researcher voices rather than a single voice such as that which emerges through the PRES. Not only do multiple doctoral researcher voices need to be heard, but they need to be listened to and need to see change take place as a result. It is crucial that we empower all doctoral researchers to have a voice to make changes that will benefit themselves and their peers in both the immediate and longer term, through shaping policy, processes, and the working environment. So, how can we facilitate this?

Firstly, we suggest that there needs to be a recognition from those that influence institutional policy at all levels that surveys and service evaluation methods struggle to capture and represent doctoral researcher voices in their totality. Survey data such as these do provide value and might help to improve the experience of doctoral researchers, but the associated limitations must be recognised.

Secondly, we need to create safe spaces where doctoral researchers talk openly about the doctoral researcher experience which leads to a tailored and supportive experience for each individual. For example, unhappily in all institutions there will likely be a known research supervisor whose working practices are 'toxic' (Grove, 2016). But often due to power dynamics and politics, doctoral researchers will only come forward once a threshold of tolerance has been crossed, which is often when the situation is reaching a crisis point for the student. Equally, there are examples of fabulous and collegiate working practices that enhance the working environment for all in the research department including the research students. For example, a table tennis table in the common room to relieve stress during thesis writing, regular coffee meetings, or a local programme of research student-centred professional development events. Ideas to address and share these experiences and make doctoral researcher voices heard include developing a 'good practice case studies' document to share across the institution, having regular drop-in sessions with trusted colleagues from Graduate Schools or equivalent, peer-to-peer mentoring or buddy schemes across departments; such initiatives all help to build a nurturing and supportive environment for doctoral researchers.

Our third suggestion relates to encouraging transparent and open working practices. We need to make sure that we are not selectively listening to the doctoral researcher voices we like to hear or that are in tune with the prevailing orthodoxy. As previously discussed, this requires being open to capturing opinions and doctoral researcher voices through social media channels, through mentoring schemes, through informal meetings and activities, whilst concurrently being mindful of invading these protected spaces and ensuring anonymity of the research students.

Fourthly, we should make the effort to communicate and evidence changes made in response to feedback from doctoral researchers. This will help to address the survey-fatigue that all students (and staff!) complain of by showing that not only are doctoral researchers' voices heard but that they are listened to and acted upon. We therefore advocate for inclusive approaches that listen to the plurality of doctoral researcher voices, resulting in the adoption of mechanisms that promote positive changes in the behaviours and agency of doctoral students.

Note

1. Note we use the term 'supervisor' throughout this chapter which is common in the UK to refer to academic staff with a responsibility for overseeing doctoral candidature.

References

Bogle, D. (2017). *100 years of the PhD in the UK.* Retrieved from https://www.vitae.ac.uk/news/vitae-blog/100-years-of-the-phd-by-prof-david-bogle.

Collinson, J., & Hockey, J. (1995). Sanctions and savings: Some reflections on ESRC doctoral policy. *Higher Education Review, 27*(3), 56–63.

Delamont, S., Atkinson, P., & Parry, O. (2000). *The doctoral experience: Success and failure in graduate school.* London: Falmer Press.

Denicolo, P. (2003). Assessing the PhD: A constructive view of criteria. *Quality Assurance in Education, 11*(2), 84–91.

Duke, D. C., & Denicolo, P. M. (2017). What supervisors and universities can do to enhance doctoral student experience (and how they can help themselves). *FEMS Microbiology Letters, 364*(9), fnx090.

European Higher Education Area. (2005). *The framework of qualifications.* Retrieved from http://www.ehea.info/pid34260/tools.html.

Grove, J. (2016). PhDs: 'Toxic' supervisors and 'students from hell'. *Times Higher Education Supplement*. Retrieved from https://www.timeshighereducation.com/news/phds-toxic-supervisors-and-students-from-hell.

Hancock, S., Hughes, G., & Walsh, E. (2017). Purist or pragmatist? UK doctoral scientists' moral positions on the knowledge economy. *Studies in Higher Education, 42*(7), 1244–1258.

Hancock, S., & Walsh, E. (2014). Beyond knowledge and skills: Rethinking the development of professional identity during the STEM doctorate. *Studies in Higher Education, 41*(1), 37–50.

Harper, D. (2003). Students as change agents: The generation Y model. In M. Swe Khine & D. Fisher (Eds.), *Technology-rich learning environments: A future perspective* (pp. 307–329). New Jersey: World Scientific.

Higher Education Statistics Agency. (2018). *Higher education student data.* Retrieved from https://www.hesa.ac.uk/data-and-analysis/students.

Jackson, A. (2003). Carnegie initiative on the doctorate. *Notices of the AMS, 50*(5), 566–568.

John, T., & Denicolo, P. (2013). Doctoral education: A review of the literature monitoring the doctoral student experience in selected OECD countries (Mainly UK). *Springer Science Reviews, 1*(1–2), 41–49.

McAlpine, L. (2017). Building on success? Future challenges for doctoral education globally. *Studies in Graduate and Postdoctoral Education, 8*(2), 66–77.

Park, C. (2005). New Variant PhD: The changing nature of the doctorate in the UK. *Journal of Higher Education Policy and Management, 27*(2), 189–207.

Roberts, G. G. (2002). *SET for success: The supply of people with science, technology, engineering and mathematics skills: The report of Sir Gareth Roberts' review.* London: HM Treasury.

Simpson, R. (1983). *How the PhD came to Britain: A century of struggle for postgraduate education.* Guildford: Society for Research into Higher Education.

Slight, C. (2017). *Postgraduate research experience survey 2017: Experiences and personal outlook of postgraduate researchers.* Retrieved from https://www.heacademy.ac.uk/system/files/hub/download/pres_2017_report_0.pdf.

Smith McGloin, R., & Wynne, C. (2015). *Structural changes in doctoral education in the UK: A review of graduate schools and the development of doctoral colleges.* Retrieved from http://www.ukcge.ac.uk/article/report-released-structural-changes-in-doctoral-education-in-the-278.aspx.

Spanner, L. (2018). *When student data isn't student voice.* Retrieved from https://wonkhe.com/blogs/when-student-data-isnt-student-voice/.

Taylor, S. E. (2012). Changes in doctoral education: Implications for supervisors in developing early career researchers. *International Journal for Researcher Development, 3*(2), 118–138.

Vitae. (2018). https://www.vitae.ac.uk/doing-research/are-you-thinking-of-doing-a-phd/why-do-a-doctoral-degree.

Wright, T., & Cochrane, R. (2000). Factors influencing successful submission of PhD theses. *Studies in Higher Education, 25*(2), 181–195. https://doi.org/10.1080/713696139.

Part III

**Engaging Student Voices Across
the Higher Education Experience**

10

'Duck to Water' or 'Fish Out of Water'? Diversity in the Experience of Negotiating the Transition to University

Naomi E. Winstone and Julie A. Hulme

Educational transitions remain at the forefront of policy and practice in education worldwide (e.g. Boyle, Grieshaber, & Petriwskyj, 2018; Hillman, 2005; Krause, Hartley, James, & McInnis, 2005). Educational transitions are not defined universally, with many accounts using 'taken-for-granted notions of transition' (Gale & Parker, 2014, p. 737) that draw on homogenised 'student voice' data. Thus, practitioners require deeper understandings of students' lived experiences; otherwise, they risk adopting a 'scattergun' approach to supporting students (Brooman & Darwent, 2014, p. 1523). Exploration of multiple student voices on educational transition is essential to developing a clear understanding of educational transitional processes.

N. E. Winstone (✉)
Department of Higher Education, University of Surrey, Guildford, UK
e-mail: n.winstone@surrey.ac.uk

J. A. Hulme
School of Psychology, Keele University, Keele, UK

© The Author(s) 2019
S. Lygo-Baker et al. (eds.), *Engaging Student Voices in Higher Education*,
https://doi.org/10.1007/978-3-030-20824-0_10

159

Hearing Different Voices on Transition

Supporting students in successful transitions from school or college to university is a key concern of practitioners, senior managers, and policy makers in Higher Education. Negotiating these transitions are often framed as a 'challenge' (Hulme & De Wilde, 2015) with 'potential for substantial problems' (Kirkpatrick & Mulligan, 2002, p. 75). A cursory review of the literature reveals a discourse that reinforces students' vulnerabilities and weaknesses, where students (particularly those from 'non-traditional' backgrounds) are described as 'lost in the crowd' (Scanlon, Rowling, & Weber, 2007, p. 223), as 'fish out of water' (Tranter, 2003, p. 1), and where transition is described as a 'challenging hurdle' (Lowe & Cook, 2003, p. 53) that creates 'special needs' (Nelson, Kift, Humphries, & Harper, 2006, p. 1). Likewise, an emphasis on developing the resilience, adaptability, emotional intelligence, or grit of students to help them to navigate transition (e.g. Holliman, Martin, & Collie, 2018; Pope, Roper, & Qualter, 2011) may be helpful in understanding the 'challenges', but implies a personal deficit in those students who find transition difficult.

Whilst such terminology raises awareness of the potential difficulties faced by new undergraduates, emphasising transitional challenges could narrow the focus of both practitioners and students to remediation of a problematic experience, rather than preparation for an important milestone. Problematising educational transitions, by focusing only on challenges, and on specific types of challenge, arguably ignores student diversity, assuming that transition is universally difficult, especially for those with 'vulnerable' characteristics. In reality, whilst early experiences of university can lead to many students feeling adrift, the notion of transition as a 'struggle' is a far cry from the experience of others. Some take to university like a 'duck to water'; the process of adjusting to university life can be positive, with exciting opportunities to make new friends, try new activities, and develop a new identity (Devlin & McKay, 2014). Even challenging early experiences of university can facilitate, rather than hinder, transition:

> ...transitions can lead to profound change and be an impetus for new learning, or they can be unsettling, difficult and unproductive. Yet, while certain

transitions are unsettling and difficult for some people, risk, challenge and even difficulty might also be important factors in successful transitions for others. (Ecclestone, Biesta, & Hughes, 2010, p. 2)

This is critical, as homogenising the transition experience as a difficult period in time where we need to protect students from negative emotions might dilute the impact of the transition period as a 'rite of passage' (see the seminal work of Tinto, 1988). A strong focus on 'bridging the gap' of transition might lead to ignorance of the possibility that the gap is important; it should be experienced and lived, rather than 'bridged'. Experiencing the disequilibrium of finding oneself adrift in an alien university environment (e.g. Jackson, 2003) may not be a problematic experience that we need to protect students against, but an essential part of their development and growing independence. Indeed, the concept of transition as a component of transformation and enhanced learning is well recognised within the higher education literature. Meyer and Land (2003, 2005) describe students' transition from a lack of understanding to a state of deep understanding via 'threshold concepts', by which they mean the process of acquisition of new and difficult knowledge. In making the transition from their previous state of learning (pre-university) to an advanced level of thinking about their discipline, Meyer and Land suggest that students pass through a 'liminal' or transitional space, which can be uncomfortable and troublesome, while they struggle to cross the threshold to their new, transformed state of understanding. The liminality and associated struggle are essential components of learning, akin to growing pains; without them, students' understanding cannot be transformed. The transition to university for some students may thus be framed as a watershed, transformative experience, rather than a problematic one.

Heterogeneity in students' experiences of transition undoubtedly arises from variability in students' backgrounds, expectations, and experiences:

Learning is not just about how students meet the requirements demanded of them at specific points in their academic career, but is embedded in the totality of their prior learning experiences. (Christie, Tett, Cree, & McCune, 2016, p. 480)

To explore the influence of prior learning experiences on the transition to university, we now report two approaches that draw upon students' voices as collected through our own research projects.

Students' Expectations of University

Many scholars have identified discrepancies between students' expectations of the university experience, and what they encounter during the initial stages of their undergraduate journey (e.g. Smith & Hopkins, 2005; Tranter, 2003), where 'experiencing a gap is the rule, not the exception' (Holmegaard, Madsen, & Ulriksen, 2016, p. 169). Unrealistic expectations may be problematic, as a discrepancy between expected and lived experiences of university can detrimentally affect academic engagement (Rowley, Hartley, & Larkin, 2008). Thus, we must consider individual expectations of university life, and how these personal beliefs relate to the lived experience of the transition.

Balloo (2018) used Q-methodology to explore differences in students' expectations of university, finding three distinct profiles: expecting to put in the hard work and be supported by tutors; expecting a different experience to high school; and expecting to strike a balance between university and everyday life. These profiles differed, for example, in terms of the expected direct scaffolding from tutors, and interest in the experience of being at university. Balloo concluded that 'there are distinct voices reflecting different profiles of students in terms of what they want from higher education' (p. 2259).

It is commonly argued that students from more traditional backgrounds, as a result of their social and cultural capital (Bourdieu & Passeron, 1977), may possess greater knowledge about university than their counterparts from non-traditional backgrounds (Scanlon et al., 2007). However, it is important to draw a distinction between 'knowledge about' university and 'knowledge of' university (Schutz, 1964, p. 93). The former represents generalist second-hand knowledge of a particular context, whilst the latter is contextualised knowledge based on first-hand experience, what we might term 'insider knowledge' (Schutz, 1964). Crucially, whilst some students may possess more 'knowledge about' university, most students are in the same situation with regard to 'knowledge of' university, regardless of their personal background or social and cultural capital (perhaps excepting those undertaking their second degree). Students' 'knowledge about' university, held at the start of the course, may then conflict with their lived experience.

The Theory of Met Expectations (Porter & Steers, 1973) predicts that congruence between expectations and lived experience leads to stronger adjustment to, and satisfaction with, the new environment. Winstone and Bretton (2013) drew upon this theoretical context to explore the expectation-reality gap in the experience of new Psychology undergraduate students. In a focus group, students discussed their first-year experience, revealing where and how their experience differed from their expectations. One salient area of misalignment related to students' expectations and experiences of independent learning at university. Through their discussions, students revealed that they expected greater explicit direction in teaching methods at university, and the requirement for self-regulated learning was unexpected. This is unsurprising, given that many students report that they expect teaching methods at university to be similar to those experienced at school (Lowe & Cook, 2003) and that they underestimate the amount of time spent in self-directed study (Cook & Leckey, 1999). In Winstone and Bretton's study, students expressed that whilst they knew they would learn in lectures at university, their expectations of lectures were different to their experience. For example, students discussed how lectures were more interactive than expected, but also that maintaining concentration in the lecture setting was harder than anticipated. In Chapter 2, Alexander articulated how it was only later in the course that it became clear how best to approach studying at university.

In their analysis, Winstone and Bretton (2013) discussed how students' academic self-concept can be damaged by the 'recalibration' of achievement expectations. For many students, in comparison with grades received at school or college, their early grades at university are perceived to be relatively low. Identities are formed in relation to perceptions of competence (Wenger, 1998), so even the most able students can feel that they are no longer competent as learners, due to the 'learning shock' of disappointment with early grades (Christie, Tett, Cree, Hounsell, & McCune, 2008, p. 570).

Jackson (2003) explores this change in learners' self-concept in terms of the 'Big-Fish-Little-Pond Effect' (BFLP; Marsh, 1987), whereby the transition to university involves adjustment from being a 'big fish' in a 'little pond' to being a 'little fish' in a 'big pond'. Jackson measured students' academic self-concept at the beginning and end of the first semester and found some evidence of the BFLP effect, whereby the academic self-concept of females, but not males, declined significantly over the course of the first semester.

In a heretofore unpublished study, we explored the BFLP effect by asking 91 Psychology undergraduates to rate on a scale from 1 (not at all confident) to 5 (very confident) their confidence in their ability across a range of academic skills at the start and end of their first year at university (see Fig. 10.1). We analysed these data using paired t-tests and, as shown in Fig. 10.1, students' confidence grew in several domains over the course of the year: note-taking, formatting citations and references according to APA style, avoiding plagiarism and searching for sources. However, the data also revealed areas where students' confidence decreased significantly, suggesting that students initially expected these skills to be easier than they were experienced to be in reality: maintaining attention in lectures, maintaining attendance at lectures, giving a presentation, and keeping up with course reading.

Through these data, students reveal significant misalignment between expectations and experience, particularly with regard to their own competence, which may influence their identities as learners.

Transitions as a Trajectory

As identity is crucial to understanding transition (Holmegaard et al., 2016), it stands to reason that there cannot be a homogenous student voice. Rather, individual characteristics interact with environmental characteristics to create a unique transition experience for each individual. In Chapter 2, we saw how Alexander gained his sense of belonging at University not from his academic peer group, but from his extra-curricular activities. A student-centred approach to transition is essential (e.g. Bowles, Fisher, McPhail, Rosenstreich, & Dobson, 2014), in part because students'

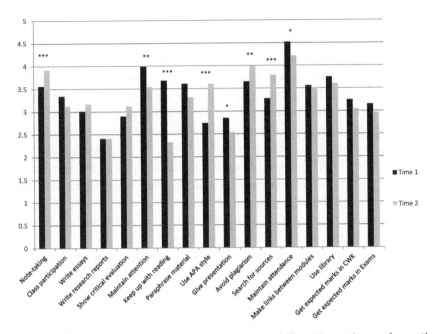

Fig. 10.1 Mean confidence ratings across academic skills at Time 1 (start of year 1) and Time 2 (end of year 1). Paired t-tests: * $p < 0.05$ ** $p < 0.01$ *** $p < 0.001$

prior experiences of transition periods can influence their approach to and experience of successive transitions. Whilst practitioners in HE seek to support students in making the specific transition to university, for students, this is the latest in a series of transitions that they have made/will make. In short, taking a lifespan approach, where the transitions within a student's educational journey form an individual 'trajectory', might illuminate important practices that can better support retention and success (Boyle et al., 2018; Hulme & De Wilde, 2015). The nature of this ongoing educational student journey is reflected in Gale and Parker's (2014, p. 734) definition of transition: 'change navigated by students in their movement within and through formal education'.

When considering the transition to university within a students' trajectory of educational transitions, students' expectations of transition are as important as their expectations of university. The Meleis Transition Theory (Meleis, Sawyer, Im, Messias, & Schumacher, 2000) argues that successive transitions share common features, such as the presence of new needs, the inefficacy of prior strategies in meeting these needs, and the mismatch between expectations and experience. Additionally, an important enabler of successful transition is a sense of mastery. Placing transitions within a trajectory affords the opportunity for prior experience of transitions to facilitate this sense of mastery during the subsequent transition. Thus, Meleis' theory suggests that it might be beneficial to link educational transitions sequentially. According to Kail (1990, p. 95), 'knowledge allows us to understand novel versions of familiar experiences'. Supporting students in reflecting on prior experience of transition when faced with a new transition period might help with the development of a transition 'roadmap' that can guide their behaviour (McMillan, 2013) and reduce anxiety by 'making the future familiar' (Spalding, 2003, p. 289).

Returning to our survey study with 91 Psychology undergraduates, we also asked them about their experience of the transition to university, within the context of the last major transition they made, from GCSE to A Level (in England, this represents the move from compulsory education at 16, to post-compulsory education, from 16 to 18). During their first week at university, we asked students to rate on a five-point scale (from extremely difficult to extremely easy) their experience of making the transition from GCSE to A Level study, and their expected ease of the transition to university. There was a strong positive correlation between these two ratings ($r = 0.45$, $p < 0.001$), suggesting that students who experienced a smoother transition from GCSE to A Level expected the transition to university to be easier. At the end of the academic year, we asked students two open-ended questions: 'How has your experience of the A Level to university transition been similar to your experience of the GCSE to A Level transition?', and 'What did you learn from the GCSE to A Level transition that has helped you make the transition to university?'. We coded students' responses thematically, and here, we report their most common responses to the questions.

When reflecting on the similarity between the transition to university and the GCSE to A Level transition, many students expressed that both transitions required adjustment to an increase in workload and an increase in the difficulty and level of academic work. The most common response was that both transitions required them to become more independent as learners. This latter point is particularly interesting given the research evidence discussed earlier, where many students perceive a misalignment between the level of independence required at university and their expectations (e.g. Cook & Leckey, 1999; Winstone & Bretton, 2013). Even though these aspects of higher education may be difficult for new students, by surfacing their prior experiences, individual students can see that they have previously navigated a similar process successfully and that there are lessons for each to learn from those experiences that can help them in the new environment.

When considering what they had learnt from the prior transition that helped them transition to university, many students again referenced the need to be more independent and take greater responsibility for their own learning. This suggests that by the end of the first year, students recognised that they were able to use their prior experience of successfully negotiating a transition period to help them in their latest educational transition. Many students also indicated that the transition to university was helped by their learning of time management and organisational skills during their previous transition. Students commonly reported that they had learnt from their previous transition that, although adapting to a new environment may seem difficult at first, perseverance is important because things get easier over time. This is a valuable reminder for students that adjusting to university is not the first time that they may have experienced difficulty within a new environment, but that they managed to adjust before, so can do so again. These findings suggest that new students may benefit from surfacing their experiences of an earlier transition, to remind them of their learning and the strategies that can be deployed within the latest transition period in their personal trajectory.

This might suggest that, rather than offering generalised advice to students on negotiating educational transitions, enabling individual students to recognise the value of previous experience, and to apply their own learning to the transition to university, may be beneficial. In this regard, students may be facilitated to navigate educational transitions based on their personal, historical 'voices', rather than from the institutional views of a homogenous 'student voice'.

Engaging Student Voices in Understanding Transition

In this chapter, we have explored common perceptions of transition as a problem to be overcome and have argued that such an approach can risk homogenising the experience as one that *all* students find difficult, in similar ways. Yet, the majority of students do not have contextualised knowledge of university, and their initial experiences may conflict with their expectations. We then examined the voices of students themselves, as they emerged through our research. Examining students' expectations in the context of their lived realities provides insight into important dimensions of the transition experience such as self-concept and confidence. Finally, we considered the possibility of placing the transition to university within the context of an ongoing trajectory of transitions. One of the greatest resources that students bring to the process of transition is their own experience of having negotiated prior transitions, and the personal resources and strategies that enabled them to do so. We conclude by offering some recommendations for engaging student voices in understanding transition experiences.

1. *Educational transition is a process, not an event.*

Within the literature, emphasis is placed on initial induction periods; equally important is to consider students' ongoing transitions through different stages of higher education (Christie et al., 2016; Nightingale et al., 2013). Engaging with student voices through longitudinal research is critical to this endeavour. For example, in their longitudinal analysis of the transition of non-traditional students into an 'elite' university, Christie et al. (2016) showed that developing a student identity is an ongoing process, where different struggles are experienced at different times in a university journey. There are also critical points in the university experience where we need to engage with student voices; for example, the transition to the second year of university, where marks typically begin to count towards degree outcomes, is another point where expectations can misalign with experience. This period is represented by the literature on the 'Sophomore

Slump' (referring to a similar period in the US educational experience; e.g. Whittle, 2018).

2. *A prime audience for student voices on transition should be the next cohort of students.*

Practitioners can learn much from engaging with student voices on transition experiences, but students' experiences of different stages of university provide crucial information for those about to embark upon the same journey. It is difficult to envisage what university is like until it is experienced (Briggs, Clark, & Hall, 2012), but sharing 'insider knowledge', reflecting the diversity of knowledge and experiences from different students, is a valuable practice. When we asked students for advice to pass on to the next cohort of students, these were some prominent examples:

- Be organised and develop your time management—buy a diary and actually use it.
- Don't expect super high percentages for marks like in school—it's different. 60s or 70s are GOOD!
- Don't panic about small stuff—if you don't know there is someone who does.
- Get involved- enjoy yourself—it's not just work. Be social.
- Don't compare yourself to other people.
- Don't leave assignments until the last minute.
- Do reading when it is set.
- Attend all lectures and tutorials.
- Don't be afraid to ask for help.

Some of these examples have the potential to counteract areas of misalignment between expectations and experience; for example, whilst lecturers may tell students that marks over 60% are considered good at university, this information is likely to mean more coming from students themselves.

3. The transition to university is one of many transition points.

Hulme and De Wilde (2015) argue that the literature focuses heavily on what universities do to support transition, whilst the question of preparatory efforts in pre-tertiary settings has received little interest. Crucially, a coordinated approach between pre-tertiary settings and universities is needed if students are to be supported in developing a strong identity as a university student (Briggs et al., 2012; Kitching & Hulme, 2013). Ineffective preparation before students arrive at university can prevent successful transition (Kift & Nelson, 2005), with preparation being seen by some as the 'foremost factor' influencing the success of transition (Ozga & Sukhnandan, 1998). A focus on the trajectory of transitions through which a student passes encourages collaboration between practitioners at successive transition points and supports students' reflection upon their own educational journey.

Perhaps the most important factor in engaging student voices in understanding transition is the uniqueness of each student's prior experience. Crucially, 'each student enters university with a specific and complex profile which entails specific adaptation to the academic world' (De Clercq, Galand, & Frenay, 2017, p. 41). Students' reports of their experiences may be the greatest source of support and information to enable successful transition. Such information is of value to students themselves, to other students, and to those working with students, to make university a fulfilling experience. We need to recognise that:

> …the normative and the universal discourses of transition do not capture the diversity of student lives, their experiences of university, or of universities themselves. (Gale & Parker, 2014, p. 745)

It is also crucial to involve students in research on transitions; for example, in line with the recent emphasis placed on staff–student partnerships in pedagogic development (e.g. Healey, Flint, & Harrington, 2016; see Chapters 3 and 18), students have been included as both researchers and co-authors in work on transitions (e.g. Maunder, Cunliffe, Galvin, Mjali, & Rogers, 2013). Whilst the transition to university may be a key stage of the university lifecycle, it is also one of the most complex, and finding ways to engage the uniqueness of student voices is key to understanding how to facilitate the process, rather than the event, of transition.

References

Balloo, K. (2018). In-depth profiles of the expectations of undergraduate students commencing university: A Q methodological analysis. *Studies in Higher Education, 43*(12), 2251–2262.

Bourdieu, P., & Passeron, J. C. (1977). *Reproduction in education, society and culture*. London: Sage.

Bowles, A., Fisher, R., McPhail, R., Rosenstreich, D., & Dobson, A. (2014). Staying the distance: Students' perceptions of enablers of transition to higher education. *Higher Education Research and Development, 33*(2), 212–225.

Boyle, T., Grieshaber, S., & Petriwskyj, A. (2018). An integrative review of transitions to school literature. *Educational Research Review, 24,* 170–180.

Briggs, A. R. J., Clark, J., & Hall, I. (2012). Building bridges: Understanding student transition to university. *Quality in Higher Education, 18*(1), 3–21.

Brooman, S., & Darwent, S. (2014). Measuring the beginning: A quantitative study of the transition to higher education. *Studies in Higher Education, 39*(9), 1523–1541.

Christie, H., Tett, L., Cree, V. E., Hounsell, J., & McCune, V. (2008). 'A real rollercoaster of confidence and emotions': Learning to be a university student. *Studies in Higher Education, 33*(5), 567–581.

Christie, H., Tett, L., Cree, V. E., & McCune, V. (2016). 'It all just clicked': A longitudinal perspective on transitions within university. *Studies in Higher Education, 41*(3), 478–490.

Cook, A., & Leckey, J. (1999). Do expectations meet reality? A survey of changes in first-year student opinion. *Journal of Further and Higher Education, 23*(2), 157–171.

De Clercq, M., Galand, B., & Frenay, M. (2017). Transition from high school to university: A person-centred approach to academic achievement. *European Journal of Psychology of Education, 32*(1), 39–59.

Devlin, M., & McKay, J. (2014). Reframing 'the problem': Students from low socioeconomic status backgrounds transitioning to university. In H. Brook, D. Fergie, M. Maeorg, & D. Michell (Eds.), *Universities in transition: Fore-*

grounding social contexts of knowledge in the first year experience (pp. 97–125). Adelaide: University of Adelaide Press.

Ecclestone, K., Biesta, G., & Hughes, M. (2010). Transitions in the lifecourse: The role of identity, agency and structure. In K. Ecclestone, G. Biesta, & M. Hughes (Eds.), *Transitions and learning through the lifecourse* (pp. 1–15). Abingdon, UK: Routledge.

Gale, T., & Parker, S. (2014). Navigating change: A typology of student transition in higher education. *Studies in Higher Education, 39*(5), 734–753.

Healey, M., Flint, A., & Harrington, K. (2016). Students as partners: Reflections on a conceptual model. *Teaching and Learning Inquiry, 4*(2), 1–13.

Hillman, K. (2005). *The first year experience: The transition from secondary school to university and TAFE in Australia* (LSAY Research Reports).

Holliman, A. J., Martin, A. J., & Collie, R. J. (2018). Adaptability, engagement and degree completion: A longitudinal investigation of university students. *Educational Psychology, 38*(6), 785–799.

Holmegaard, H. T., Madsen, L. M., & Ulriksen, L. (2016). Where is the engineering I applied for? A longitudinal study of students' transition into higher education engineering, and their considerations of staying or leaving. *European Journal of Engineering Education, 41*(2), 154–171.

Hulme, J. A., & De Wilde, J. (2015). *Tackling transition in STEM disciplines: Supporting the Science, Technology, Engineering and Mathematics student journey into higher education in England and Wales.* York, UK: Higher Education Academy.

Jackson, C. (2003). Transitions into higher education: Gendered implications for academic self-concept. *Oxford Review of Education, 29*(3), 331–346.

Kail, R. (1990). *The development of memory in children* (3rd ed.). New York: W. H. Freeman.

Kift, S., & Nelson, D. (2005, July). *Beyond curriculum reform: Embedding the transition experience.* Paper presented at the HERDSA conference, Sydney.

Kirkpatrick, A., & Mulligan, D. (2002). Cultures of learning: Critical reading in the social and applied sciences. *Australian Review of Applied Linguistics, 25*(2), 73–99.

Kitching, H. J., & Hulme, J. A. (2013). Bridging the gap: Facilitating students' transition from pre-tertiary to university psychology education. *Psychology Teaching Review, 19*(2), 15–30.

Krause, K. L., Hartley, R., James, R., & McInnis, C. (2005). *The first year experience in Australian universities: Findings from a decade of national studies.* Commonwealth of Australia.

Lowe, H., & Cook, A. (2003). Mind the gap: Are students prepared for higher education? *Journal of Further and Higher Education, 27*(1), 53–76.

Marsh, H. W. (1987). The big-fish-little-pond effect on academic self-concept. *Journal of Educational Psychology, 79*, 280–295.

Maunder, R. E., Cunliffe, M., Galvin, J., Mjali, S., & Rogers, J. (2013). Listening to student voices: Student researchers exploring undergraduate experiences of university transition. *Higher Education, 66*(2), 139–152.

McMillan, W. (2013). Transition to university: The role played by emotion. *European Journal of Dental Education, 17*, 169–176.

Meleis, A., Sawyer, L., Im, E.-O., Messias, D. K. H., & Schumacher, K. (2000). Experiencing transitions: An emerging middle-range theory. *Advances in Nursing Science, 23*(1), 12–28.

Meyer, J. H. F., & Land, R. (2003). Threshold concepts and troublesome knowledge: Linkages to ways of thinking and practising within the disciplines. In C. Rust (Ed.), *Improving student learning: Improving student learning theory and practice—10 years on.* Oxford, UK: Oxford Centre for Staff and Learning Development.

Meyer, J. H. F., & Land, R. (2005). Threshold concepts and troublesome knowledge (2): Epistemological considerations and a conceptual framework for learning and teaching. *Higher Education, 49*, 373–388.

Nelson, K. J., Kift, S. M., Humphreys, J. K., & Harper, W. E. (2006). A blueprint for enhanced transition: Taking an holistic approach to managing student transition into a large university. In *Proceedings First Year in Higher Education Conference*, Gold Coast, QLD.

Nightingale, S. M., Roberts, S., Tariq, V., Appleby, Y., Barnes, L., Harris, R. A., ... Qualter, P. (2013). Trajectories of university adjustment in the United Kingdom: Emotion management and emotional self-efficacy protect against initial poor adjustment. *Learning and Individual Differences, 27*, 174–181.

Ozga, J., & Sukhnandan, L. (1998). Undergraduate non-completion: Developing an explanatory model. *Higher Education Quarterly, 52*(3), 316–333.

Pope, D., Roper, C., & Qualter, P. (2011). The influence of emotional intelligence on academic progress and achievement in UK university students. *Assessment and Evaluation in Higher Education, 37*(8), 907–918.

Porter, L. W., & Steers, R. M. (1973). Organizational, work, and personal factors in employee turnover and absenteeism. *Psychological Bulletin, 80*(2), 151–176.

Rowley, M., Hartley, J., & Larkin, D. (2008). Learning from experience: The expectations and experiences of first-year undergraduate psychology students. *Journal of Further and Higher Education, 32*(4), 399–413.

Scanlon, L., Rowling, L., & Weber, Z. (2007). 'You don't have like an identity…
you are just lost in a crowd': Forming a student identity in the first-year
transition to university. *Journal of Youth Studies, 10*(2), 223–241.

Schutz, A. (1964). *Collected papers: Studies in social theory* (Vol. II). The Hague:
Martinus Nijhoff.

Smith, K., & Hopkins, C. (2005). Great expectations sixth-formers' perceptions
of teaching and learning in degree-level English. *Arts and Humanities in Higher
Education, 4*(3), 304–318.

Spalding, N. J. (2003). Reducing anxiety by pre-operative education: Make the
future familiar. *Occupational Therapy International, 10*(4), 278–293.

Tinto, V. (1988). Stages of student departure: Reflections on the longitudinal
character of student leaving. *The Journal of Higher Education, 59*, 438–455.

Tranter, D. (2003, July 17–18). *'Fish out of water': Students from disadvantaged
schools and the university experience*. Paper presented at Creating spaces: Inter-
disciplinary writings in the social sciences conference, Australian National
University, Canberra.

Wenger, E. (1998). *Communities of practice: Learning, meaning and identity*. Cambridge, UK: Cambridge University Press.

Whittle, S. R. (2018). The second-year slump–now you see it, now you don't:
Using DREEM-S to monitor changes in student perception of their educational environment. *Journal of Further and Higher Education, 42*(1), 92–101.

Winstone, N., & Bretton, H. (2013). Strengthening the transition to university by confronting the expectation-reality gap in psychology undergraduates.
Psychology Teaching Review, 19, 2–14.

11

Making Learning Happen: Students' Development of Academic and Information Literacies

Karen Gravett

This book considers who today's higher education students are: what do their voices, actions and behaviours inform us about being a university student? This chapter explores students' experiences as they develop their academic and information literacy skills. Arguably, the need for students to develop these literacies becomes ever greater as the interweaving issues of information quality and digital citizenship create new questions to be considered. While at the same time the increasing cultural, linguistic and social diversity of the student population may result in students requiring additional support when developing the skills required to engage with information and to write effectively at university. Students have suggested to us that working with professional learning development and library staff to make learning happen can be a 'safe' experience—where students seek help within a specialised support unit that is distinct from the subject area at a distance from disciplinary constraints (Barnett, 2018; Gravett & Kinchin, 2018). Moreover, students' voices and behaviours suggest that

K. Gravett (✉)
Department of Higher Education, University of Surrey, Guildford, UK
e-mail: k.gravett@surrey.ac.uk

© The Author(s) 2019
S. Lygo-Baker et al. (eds.), *Engaging Student Voices in Higher Education*,
https://doi.org/10.1007/978-3-030-20824-0_11

developing academic and information literacy skills can impact on not just their growth in this area, but also on their wider learning identity (Gravett & Kinchin, 2018).

However, within these learning experiences, it is evident that for some students literacy development is not without challenge; increasingly, students look for instruction and report feelings of being overwhelmed by perceived expectations (Barnett, 2018; Gravett & Kinchin, 2018). This chapter will explore some of the ways students might experience their learning and the relationship between the development of literacies and students' developing learner identities. With financial, social and external pressures increasingly reshaping students' experiences of university, this chapter will argue that the way we work both to make learning happen and also to promote well-being deserves re-examination as we look again at the voices and behaviours of students to inform our practice.

Exploring the Information and Academic Literacy Landscape

What academic and information skills might look like can be understood in a number of ways. Some definitions that can be usefully applied are offered here with the understanding that there is still further debate to be had about nomenclature, the overlap between terms, and even the concept of 'literacy' itself. Secker (2017) argues that the use of the word literacy 'signifies not the teaching of skills or competencies, but practices, attitudes and behaviours' (Secker, 2017, p. 6). Information literacy is a central concept in the work of information professionals and is defined by the Chartered Institute of Library and Information Professionals (CILIP) as 'the ability to think critically and make balanced judgements about any information we find and use' (CILIP, 2018). This definition from UNESCO goes further:

> Information literacy empowers people in all walks of life to seek, evaluate, use and create information effectively to achieve their personal, social, occupational and educational goals. It is a basic human right in a digital world. (UNESCO, 2005)

It can be argued that the need for students to develop information literacies has never been greater as technological growth has transformed the information landscape, resulting in a wealth of information being easier to access than ever before. Moreover, questions about the quality of information have become increasingly prominent due to the twin concerns over both the proliferation of information and also the difficulty of making informed judgements and determining the validity of a source (Secker & Coonan, 2013). In today's information-rich, post-truth society, many higher education professionals believe that it is critical that students be equipped with the appropriate skills to be able to manage information effectively (Secker & Coonan, 2013).

Further, parallels and overlaps for practitioners are with the debates surrounding the development of digital literacies. Digital literacies have been defined by the Joint Information Systems Committee (JISC) as 'the capabilities which fit someone for living, learning and working in a digital society' (JISC, 2015). Discussions about academic literacies also add richness to this debate. Academic literacies focus on students' writing and have been much theorised (Gourlay, 2009; Lea & Street, 1998, 2006; Lillis, 2010; Lillis & Tuck, 2016). There are significant parallels too with the concept of assessment literacy that is also increasing in prominence within the literature (Price, Rust, O'Donovan, & Handley, 2012). Reconciling different definitions is problematic, and clearly, there is further debate to be had; for example, Secker (2015, p. 1) asks: 'Do we need new literacies...does terminology matter?' Arguably, a plurality of interpretations can be enriching for practitioners opening up dialogues between professionals and across disciplines.

There is further diversity still regarding the practices institutions employ to promote literacy development. The learning developer role has expanded significantly over the past fifteen years and today is present in many institutions in different guises: within faculties or more commonly, as in the case of the author's institution, within a centralised service such as the library. Here, a learning development team includes student learning advisors and librarians. Students can approach learning developers via one-to-one tutorial sessions to discuss any aspect of their learning, and learning development staff also deliver embedded literacy development programmes. Differing service models reflect the debate that exists within the sector regarding the relationship of learning development and disciplinary programmes, with many supporting the view that literacy development within academic programmes is preferable to 'disembodied skills' programs (Keane, 2011, p. 714).

Furthermore, the integrated teaching of literacy development is important if institutions are to avoid a pedagogic deficit model. These narratives locate literacy problems as the responsibility of individuals, who simply require extra support in order to assimilate (see Scott et al., 2014). As a result, perhaps the most significant definition of academic literacies has been offered by Lea and Street (1998, 2006) who were among the first theorists to offer a positive, divergent, approach highlighting the complexity of writing practices as:

> Complex, dynamic, nuanced, situated, and involving both epistemological issues and social processes, including power relations among people, institutions, and social identities. (Lea & Street, 2006, p. 369)

Lea and Street's work has greatly influenced recent understandings of the epistemology of academic literacies, for example Lillis and Tuck (2016, p. 30) who describe literacies as 'ideologically shaped, reflecting institutional structures and relations of power', and Price et al. (2012, p. 15) who explain that 'in order to be successful students must understand the rules of the new game'.

Crucially, this articulation of literacy practices as ideologically shaped social processes transcends a simplistic notion of mechanical skills to be learnt; in fact, it disrupts entirely a 'skills paradigm' conceptualisation. Indeed, Bent (2013, p. 29) argues that our primary objective should be to recognise the greater value of literacies:

> Is information literacy just one of a range of academic literacies or as academic literacies deal with making meaning from information, should we view information literacy as the broader concept? In reality the distinction is merely semantic the value lying in the recognition that information literacy is not a simple transferable skill in which students can be 'trained'.

Rather than attempting to consolidate or to delimit interpretations, then, this chapter is instead concerned with an exploration of the holistic learning process of academic and information literacy development. Ultimately, these understandings destabilise mechanical constructions of skills development and instead position literacy development as something broader: practices that reflect institutional structures and power relations. It is this concept of literacies as social practices that will be explored in this chapter.

Challenges Within Students' Learning Development

In recent years, the literature has started to examine the difficulties some students' experience when transitioning into and through higher education (Crozier & Reay, 2011; Gale & Parker, 2012; Scanlon, Rowling, & Weber, 2007; Scott et al., 2014; Thomas & Quinn, 2007; See Chapter 10). Research has also begun to examine the relationship between transitions and literacy practices (Burke, 2012; Gourlay, 2009; Gravett & Kinchin, 2018; Hutchings, 2013). It has been observed that students recurrently use words such as 'stressful', 'overwhelmed' and 'anxious' about the development of academic and information literacies (Gravett & Kinchin, 2018). Students' emotions and how students *feel* as they experience higher education are only recently beginning to be prioritised in the literature (Gilmore & Anderson, 2016; Mazer, McKenna-Buchanan, Quinlan, & Titsworth, 2014; Quinlan, 2016a, 2016b). For example, Quinlan explains that:

> Higher education can evoke strong negative responses – anxiety, replete with beating hearts and sweaty palms; frustration, fear, guilt, shame…Yet these deeply felt experiences…are hardly discussed in the context of improving higher education. (Quinlan, 2016a, p. 1)

Students' self-reported anxiety relating to teaching and learning chimes with a wider backdrop of increased concern about student mental health (e.g. Ibrahim, Kelly, Adams, & Glazebrook, 2013; Macaskill, 2012). Today's higher education experience has been described as 'anxiety-provoking' (Bewick, Koutsopoulou, Miles, Slaa, & Barkham, 2010,

p. 643), where 'the mental health of university students is of increasing concern globally' (Macaskill, 2012, p. 426). Likewise, statistical data suggest significant annual increases in students' support-seeking behaviour from university well-being centres (Anthoney, Stead, & Turney, 2017).

Similarly, research suggests that students may experience uncertainty and lack agency. Gourlay and Deane (2012, p. 26) explain that support staff such as librarians frequently 'observe students to be in a state of confusion regarding writing requirements' and Tapp (2013, p. 237) reported students to be concerned that they would 'do it wrong' because of uncertainty about writing at university and the greater independence expected. In our work, we have witnessed a growing reliance on staff for direction and emotional support: individuals request help to check their work, to tell them are they 'on the right lines', and to provide reassurance. Many students report frustration at not understanding 'what is expected' of them (Barnett, 2018; Gravett & Kinchin, 2018). Thus, staff observations resonate with perspectives from the literature depicting students as struggling to grapple with expectations (Christie, Tett, Cree, Hounsell, & McCune, 2008; Gourlay & Deane, 2012; Smith, 2008; Thomas & Quinn, 2007).

However, it is also important to note that students' experiences are not homogenous. Indeed, Robinson and Taylor (2007, p. 6) remind us that the very word 'voice' causes concern as 'such a monolingual assumption is illusory'. Within any narrative of students' experiences will be those 'other' voices whom offer a variety of different perspectives and nuances to the debate. With this in mind, it is important to consider also those students who may not struggle with the development of academic literacies, or those students who may feel dislocated from the institution—as in the example of Alexander in Chapter 2—and whom may not make use of library services, or may not communicate their concerns. Thus, in seeking to understand how to support the needs of those we witness who do experience difficulties, it is also important to be mindful of the plurality of students' experiences and to seek to learn from and offer support to students who experience university differently.

However, while avoiding attempts to depict a 'monolingual' narrative of students' experiences, it is still of interest to unpack the tensions experienced within literacy development and to disrupt notions of this process as a straightforward experience of skills to be learnt. As Mann writes, as practitioners, it may be worthwhile for us to 'consider carefully our own role in the potentially alienated experience of learning of our students' (2001, p. 17). Thus, this chapter explores the possible factors influencing these perceived trends in behaviour—albeit with an awareness of the heterogeneity of students' experiences—and seeks to generate further discussion and opportunities for research.

Understanding Students' Difficulties

Recent narratives of the student experience, particularly within the media, tend to homogenise 'the student experience' and have tended to be unflinchingly negative. It is often argued that the marketisation of higher education means that students pursue an instrumental view of learning. They require 'spoon-feeding' (Grayling, 2009), or worse, are *snowflakes* who lack resilience, unlike previous more robust generations (Fischer, 2017). Widening participation and the massification of higher education are often given as reasons to explain students' behaviours, with 'non-traditional' students posited as outsiders who exist in opposition to institutional norms (Gulley, 2016). Indeed, even the very description of students as 'non-traditional' can be seen to interpellate individuals into a negative identity: a social group defined discursively by 'otherness'—in binary opposition to more legitimate, 'traditional', students. Of course, student populations are changing. As outreach initiatives expand access to higher education, today's student population has diversified. Likewise, financial concerns are certainly prevalent, with increasing instability occurring in the educational and professional landscape and greater pressure placed on graduates as they seek employment in a competitive workplace (see Chapter 8). But narratives that homogenise students' experiences or that describe students in deficit terms are unhelpful at best, and at worst insulting and even infantilising, as per the metaphor of spoon-feeding.

Rather, there are undoubtedly many other potential contributory forces. Arguably, one possible contributory factor leading towards an increase in the seeking of reassurance from learning development staff could be the changing nature of staff–student relations. For example, Scanlon et al.

(2007) explain that neoliberal forces have reduced the time lecturers have to support students:

> Students must be more independent...this has always been difficult for many students in their initial transition to university. What is new, however, is the contemporary university characterised by an economically driven agenda in which lecturers have less time with students and a student population far more diverse than ever before. (Scanlon et al., 2007, p. 233)

> Students highlighted interaction with lecturers as fundamental to their identity formation because it was through this interaction that they began to understand the university construct of being a student. (ibid., p. 237)

Here, students describe the interaction with university staff as crucial to their formation of a learner identity; however, Scanlon et al. report that lecturers have less time to engage with their students. Research has shown that students may rely on the reassurance of staff and require scaffolding in order to develop independent learning strategies (Hockings, Thomas, Ottaway, & Jones, 2017). Teaching groups are now larger, and it has been increasingly recognised that today's academic staff experience a highly pressured environment, with many competing demands (Murphy, 2011; Winstone, 2017). Thus, a social justice agenda and discourses of widening participation and inclusion operate in tension with economic realities. This may mean that universities risk losing sight of the value of human relations (Mann, 2008).

Whitchurch's research has recognised the increasing blurring of boundaries between academic and professional support within a 'third space' (2013). Perhaps, this blurring of boundaries means that students are taking more opportunities to utilise the expertise of professional staff to complement the support offered by their faculty tutors, or more frequently turning to these staff members to express their anxieties regarding academic practices. It seems possible then that further consideration of the optimal relationship between different staff roles, as well as further work to ensure the provision of clearer, structured, independent learning opportunities, may be important if we are to alleviate student anxiety.

Another possible cause for student apprehension appears related to uncertainty about assessment. Research has shown that often students have limited understanding of the standards expected of them, a lack of knowledge about university procedures, and that this can be deeply unsettling (Christie et al., 2008). Researchers have also used the work of Bernstein (1975) to demonstrate that some pedagogic practices can be *invisible* for students. This can be particularly the case for minority groups who may lack the required cultural capital (Bourdieu, 1984) to easily interpret the university experience (Crozier & Reay, 2011). Here, Mann explains the challenges students' experience with a powerful metaphor:

> Most students entering the new world of the academy are in an equivalent position to those crossing the borders of a new country—they have to deal with the bureaucracy of checkpoints, or matriculation, they may have limited knowledge of the local language and customs. (Mann, 2001, p. 11)

Mann's research has revealed students' sense of alienation to be driven by a lack of understanding of university 'customs'. Similarly, the literature has explored the difficulties some students experience when interpreting assessment feedback (e.g. Jönsson, 2013; Winstone, Nash, Rowntree, & Parker, 2017). Academic practices, then, can be mystifying; a lack of understanding regarding university assessment, and the lack of clarity of practices, may be a key cause for apprehension.

At the same time, this uncertainty about assessment practices can be seen to be compounded by increased concerns about issues relating to academic misconduct. The rise of plagiarism detection software such as Turnitin and the increased emphasis on academic misconduct within university discourses potentially exacerbate the anxieties students feel about grasping the processes of academia (e.g. Ashworth, Banister, & Thorne, 2006). And recently, researchers have questioned the impact of Turnitin (Thompsett & Ahluwalia, 2015; Walker, 2010).

However, central to an understanding of this area of literacy development is a consideration of its relationship to the construction of student identity. As we have seen, literacies are not simply mechanical skills to be acquired. Rather, the development of literacies can be understood as a 'threshold practice' in the very construction of student identity (Gourlay, 2009). This trope of the threshold evinces the transformative nature of literacy practices. Literacy development thus becomes inextricably linked with issues of identity formation. Moreover, issues of participation, and validation, are also important here—for example, Burke explains that:

> There are certain rules of the game that must be adhered to if a student is going to succeed in higher education. 'Other' bodies of knowledge that the student might bring to their work are often invalidated. (Burke, 2012, p. 147)

Developing literacies can thus be an unsettling process as students must 'unlearn' other pre-existing bodies of knowledge and master the 'rules of the game'. This learning environment can foster 'a sense of self-as-intruder in the new institution's space' (Hutchings, 2013, p. 313) as learning environments become no longer familiar or negotiable. Arguably, then, literacy development can be conceptualised as a threshold practice of both learning and unlearning.

Students have reported that when using learning development and library services, learning can happen in an environment where they feel safe, anonymous and empowered to share their concerns in a way that they may not feel comfortable doing with their faculty tutors (Gravett & Winstone, 2018). Likewise, while few students report that they would actually approach a member of academic staff to ask for clarification regarding their feedback (Carless, 2006), students may feel more content to seek advice from learning developers (Gravett & Winstone, 2018). Consequently, professional services staff may be in a unique position to observe students' difficulties with literacy development and to offer additional support.

Future Opportunities for Developing Students' Learning

It has been argued that some level of discomfort is a necessary part of learning if it is to be truly transformative (Land, 2017). It may be that we can understand this area of academic literacy as an area of 'troublesome knowledge' (Land, 2017, p. 180), where encounters with such troublesome knowledge potentially lead to 'a sense of frailty in response to being confronted with troublesome knowledge, or ideas that may be disturbing' (Land, 2017, p. 182). Similarly, Gilmore and Anderson (2016, p. 694) contest the view 'that anxiety is inexorably linked with the inhibition of learning and cognition or with a diminished sense of human agency'. However, clearly too much anxiety can be debilitating. And yet, this discussion does not seek to 'diminish' students as somehow less capable—as has been a critique of previous explorations of students' emotional wellbeing (Ecclestone, 2011). Rather, it seeks to open up a dialogue regarding institutional practices.

It would be of interest for further research to seek additional opportunities to listen to the multiplicity of student voices. In particular, this may include the voices of those who may feel disengaged from university, such as Alexander (Chapter 2), and may not seek help from university support services. One direction would be to explore how different minority and majority groups develop literacies and cope with some of the challenges considered in this chapter and to seek further opportunities to listen to individual stories of academic literacy development, for example via auto-ethnographic or narrative interview research methods. There is also further debate to be had regarding the importance of collaboration between academic and professional services staff, and of the blurring boundaries between these two historically divided professional roles within a 'third space' of academic practice. Further, it will also be worthwhile to consider how we can create additional opportunities to prioritise students' voices via student–staff partnership models of working. In recent years, partnership models have been shown to have the potential to disrupt institutional cultures (Matthews, Cook Sather, & Healey, 2018) and to enable a more dialogic relationship between staff and students (Bovill, 2017).

Conclusion

Literacy development is pivotal to students' success within higher education. However, the anxieties some students report about even the basic structures and processes of academic practice can lead them to seek out help in superficial ways that we struggle to move beyond. Moving forward, perhaps more collaborative and partnership work is needed between professional and academic colleagues, and between students and staff, to increase our understanding of students' experiences, enabling a deeper examination of the nuances of students' difficulties, as well as exploring further how to make learning happen in a generative, enriching, way.

References

Anthoney, J., Stead, R., & Turney, K. (2017). Making connections and building resilience: Developing workshops with undergraduates. *Knowledge Management and E-Learning, 9*(93), 404–418.

Ashworth, P., Banister, P., Thorne, P., & Students on the Qualitative Research Methods Course Unit. (2006). Guilty in whose eyes? University students' perceptions of cheating and plagiarism in academic work and assessment. *Studies in Higher Education, 22*(2), 187–203.

Barnett, L. (2018). Learning development. In I. M. Kinchin & N. E. Winstone (Eds.), *Exploring pedagogic frailty and resilience: Case studies of academic narrative* (pp. 187–204). Rotterdam: Sense.

Bent, M. (2013). Developing academic literacies. In J. Secker & E. Coonan (Eds.), *Rethinking information literacy: A practical framework for supporting learning* (pp. 27–40). London: Facet.

Bernstein, B. (1975). Class and pedagogies: Visible and invisible. *Educational Studies, 1*(1), 23–41.

Bewick, B., Koutsopoulou, G., Miles, J., Slaa, E., & Barkham, M. (2010). Changes in undergraduate students' psychological well-being as they progress through university. *Studies in Higher Education, 3*(6), 633–645.

Bourdieu, P. (1984). *Distinction: A social critique of the judgement of taste*. London: Routledge & Kegan Paul.

Bovill, C. (2017). Breaking down student-staff barriers: Moving towards pedagogic flexibility. In I. M. Kinchin & N. E. Winstone (Eds.), *Pedagogic frailty and resilience in the University* (pp. 151–162). Rotterdam: Sense.

Burke, P. J. (2012). *The right to higher education*. Oxon: Routledge.

Carless, D. (2006). Differing perceptions in the feedback process. *Studies in Higher Education, 31*(2), 219–233.

Chartered Institute of Library and Information Professionals Information Literacy Group. (2018). *Information literacy*. Retrieved from https://infolit.org.uk/new-il-definition.

Christie, H., Tett, L., Cree, V. E., Hounsell, J., & McCune, V. (2008). 'A real rollercoaster of confidence and emotions': Learning to be a university student. *Studies in Higher Education, 33*(5), 567–581.

Crozier, G., & Reay, D. (2011). Capital accumulation: Working-class students learning how to learn in HE. *Teaching in Higher Education, 16*(2), 145–155.

Ecclestone, K. (2011). Emotionally-vulnerable subjects and new inequalities: The educational implications of an 'epistemology of the emotions'. *International Studies in Sociology of Education, 21*(2), 91–113.

Fischer, T. (2017, August 10). My fellow lecturers won't say it in public, but students today are moaning, illiterate snowflakes. *The Telegraph*. Retrieved from https://www.telegraph.co.uk/news/2017/08/09/fellow-lecturers-wont-say-public-students-today-moaning-illiterate/.

Gale, T., & Parker, S. (2012). Navigating change: A typology of student transition in higher education. *Studies in Higher Education, 39*(5), 734–753.

Gilmore, S., & Anderson, V. (2016). The emotional turn in higher education: A psychoanalytic contribution. *Teaching in Higher Education, 21*(6), 686–699.

Gourlay, L. (2009). Threshold practices: Becoming a student through academic literacies. *London Review of Education, 7*(2), 181–192.

Gourlay, L., & Deane, J. (2012). Loss, responsibility, blame? Staff discourses of student plagiarism. *Innovations in Education and Teaching International, 49*(1), 19–29.

Gravett, K., & Kinchin, I. M. (2018). Referencing and empowerment: Exploring barriers to agency in the higher education student experience. *Teaching in Higher Education*, 1–14.

Gravett, K., & Winstone, N. E. (2018). "Feedback interpreters": The role of learning development professionals in facilitating university students' engagement with feedback. *Teaching in Higher Education*, 1–16.

Grayling, A. C. (2009, November 10). Universities are not there to spoon-feed. *The Guardian*. Retrieved from https://www.theguardian.com/commentisfree/2009/nov/10/university-contact-hours-mandelson.

Gulley, N. Y. (2016, August 5). The myth of the nontraditional student. *Inside Higher Ed*. Retrieved from https://www.insidehighered.com/views/2016/08/05/defining-students-nontraditional-inaccurate-and-damaging-essay.

Hockings, C., Thomas, L., Ottaway, J., & Jones, R. (2017). Independent learning—What we do when you're not there. *Teaching in Higher Education, 23*(2), 145–161.

Hutchings, C. (2013). Referencing and identity, voice and agency: Adult learners' transformations within literacy practices. *Higher Education Research and Development, 33*(2), 312–324.

Ibrahim, A. K., Kelly, S. J., Adams, C. E., & Glazebrook, C. (2013). A systematic review of studies of depression prevalence in university students. *Journal of Psychiatric Research, 47*(3), 391–400.

Joint Information Systems Committee (JISC). (2015). *Developing students' digital literacy.* Retrieved from https://www.jisc.ac.uk/guides/developing-students-digital-literacy.

Jönsson, A. (2013). Facilitating productive use of feedback in higher education. *Active Learning in Higher Education, 14*(1), 63–76.

Keane, E. (2011). Dependence-deconstruction: Widening participation and traditional-entry students transitioning from school to higher education in Ireland. *Teaching in Higher Education, 16*(6), 707–718.

Land, R. (2017). Enhancing quality to address frailty. In I. M. Kinchin & N. E. Winstone (Eds.), *Pedagogic frailty and resilience in the university* (pp. 179–194). Rotterdam: Sense.

Lea, M., & Street, B. (1998). Student writing in higher education: An academic literacies approach. *Studies in Higher Education, 23*(2), 157–172.

Lea, M., & Street, B. (2006). The "academic literacies" model: Theory and applications. *Theory Into Practice, 45*(4), 368–377.

Lillis, T. (2010). Student writing as 'academic literacies': Drawing on Bakhtin to move from critique to design. *Language and Education, 17*(3), 192–207.

Lillis, T., & Tuck, J. (2016). Academic literacies: A critical lens on writing and reading in the academy. In K. Hyland & P. Shaw (Eds.), *The Routledge handbook of English for academic purposes* (pp. 30–43). London: Routledge.

Macaskill, A. (2012). The mental health of university students in the United Kingdom. *British Journal of Guidance and Counselling, 41*(4), 426–441.

Mann, S. (2001). Alternative perspectives on the student experience: Alienation and engagement. *Studies in Higher Education, 26*(1), 7–19.

Mann, S. (2008). *Study, power and the university: The institution and its effects on learning.* Maidenhead, UK: McGraw Hill/Society for Research into Higher Education and Open University Press.

Matthews, K. E., Cook-Sather, A., & Healey, M. (2018). Connecting learning, teaching, and research through student-staff partnerships: Toward universities as egalitarian learning communities. In V. Tong, A. Standen, & M. Sotiriou (Eds.), *Shaping higher education with students: Ways to connect research and teaching* (pp. 23–29). London: UCL Press.

Mazer, J. P., McKenna-Buchanan, T. P., Quinlan, M. M., & Titsworth, S. (2014). The dark side of emotion in the classroom: Emotional processes as mediators of teacher communication behaviors and student negative emotions. *Communication Education, 63*(3), 149–168.

Murphy, M. (2011). Troubled by the past: History, identity and the university. *Journal of Higher Education Policy and Management, 33*(5), 509–517.

Price, M., Rust, C., O'Donovan, B., & Handley, K. (2012). *Assessment literacy: The foundation for improving student learning.* Oxford: Oxford Centre for Staff Learning Development.

Quinlan, K. (2016a). *How higher education feels: Commentaries on poems that illuminate emotions in learning and teaching.* Rotterdam: Sense.

Quinlan, K. (2016b). How emotion matters in four key relationships in teaching and learning in higher education. *College Teaching, 64*(3), 101–111.

Robinson, C., & Taylor, C. (2007). Theorizing student voice: Values and perspectives. *Improving Schools, 10*(1), 5–17.

Scanlon, L., Rowling, L., & Weber, Z. (2007). You don't have like an identity … You are just lost in a crowd: Forming a student identity in the first-year transition to University. *Journal of Youth Studies, 10*(2), 223–241.

Scott, D., Hughes, G., Burke, P., Evans, C., Watson, D., & Walter, C. (2014). *Learning transitions in higher education.* London: Palgrave.

Secker, J. (2015, December). *The trouble with terminology: Rehabilitating and rethinking 'digital literacy'.* Paper presented at the SRHE Research Conference, Celtic Manor, Newport, Wales, UK.

Secker, J. (2017). The trouble with terminology: Rehabilitating and rethinking 'digital literacy'. In K. Reedy & J. Parker (Eds.), *Digital literacy unpacked* (pp. 3–16). London: Facet.

Secker, J., & Coonan, E. (2013). *Rethinking Information Literacy: A practical framework for supporting learning.* London: Facet.

Smith, H. (2008). Spoon-feeding: Or how I learned to stop worrying and love the mess. *Teaching in Higher Education, 13*(6), 715–718.

Tapp, E. (2013). *Being and becoming a student: An investigation into how a pedagogic approach built on collaborative participation in academic literacy practices supports students' academic practice, knowledge and identity* (Unpublished PhD thesis). University of Nottingham.

Thomas, L., & Quinn, J. (2007). *First generation entry into higher education an international study.* Maidenhead, UK: Open University Press.

Thompsett, A., & Ahluwalia, J. (2015). Students turned off by Turnitin? Perception of plagiarism and collusion by undergraduate Bioscience students. *Bioscience Education, 16*(1), 1–15.

United Nations Educational, Scientific and Cultural Organization. (2005). *Communication and information.* Retrieved from http://www.unesco.org/new/en/communication-and-information/access-to-knowledge/information-literacy/.

Walker, J. (2010). Measuring plagiarism: Researching what students do, not what they say they do. *Studies in Higher Education, 35*(1), 41–59.

Whitchurch, C. (2013). *Reconstructing identities in higher education: The rise of third space professionals.* London: Routledge.

Winstone, N. E. (2017). The '3 Rs' of pedagogic frailty: Risk, reward and resilience. In I. M. Kinchin & N. E. Winstone (Eds.), *Pedagogic frailty and resilience in the university* (pp. 33–48). Rotterdam: Sense.

Winstone, N. E., Nash, R. A., Rowntree, J., & Parker, M. (2017). 'It'd be useful, but I wouldn't use it': Barriers to university students' feedback seeking and recipience. *Studies in Higher Education, 42*(11), 2026–2041.

12

Collaborating with Students to Support Student Mental Health and Well-being

Dawn Querstret

Mental health is a resource for daily living and a state of well-being that allows individuals to think, feel, cope with stress, work productively, interact with others and generally enjoy life (WHO, 2004). The promotion of mental health is important in the context of enabling individuals to flourish and contribute to society, and it results both from individual skills and community assets (Kobau et al., 2011; WHO, 2004). Universities represent a unique setting for the promotion of mental health due to the distinct, yet interrelated populations of students and staff (Fernandez et al., 2016). University students are considered a high-risk population due to their age, as most mental health issues have their onset before 24 years of age (Reavley & Jorm, 2010). In conjunction, students are exposed to personal and academic stressors that can negatively impact on their mental health. For example, university students usually need to establish greater autonomy from parents; form new relationships; adjust to a new social and in some cases cultural environment; master a new educational cur-

D. Querstret (✉)
University of Surrey, Guildford, UK
e-mail: dawn.querstret@surrey.ac.uk

© The Author(s) 2019
S. Lygo-Baker et al. (eds.), *Engaging Student Voices in Higher Education*,
https://doi.org/10.1007/978-3-030-20824-0_12

riculum; and develop career plans (Schulenberg, Sameroff, & Cicchetti, 2004; Towbes & Cohen, 1996).

Additionally, over the duration of their university experience, students need to become more autonomous individuals who can effectively manage priorities and pressures related to personal, academic, and social needs, demands and interests. As Alexander's case (Chapter 2) highlighted, one of the biggest challenges is that of developing a new sense of self, or personal identity. There is a lot of change to contend with over a relatively short period of time; therefore, it is not surprising that some students find their university experience challenging. However, the story is not one-sided. It is also important to note that exposure to change and stress does not necessarily have a negative impact and can be stimulating for students (see Chapter 10). Engaging in higher education can provide a purposeful environment with opportunities for academic and personal achievement, potentially leading to a fuller sense of personal identity and increased self-esteem. It also offers the opportunity for students to learn to manage multiple demands, build self-confidence and reduce isolation through the development of new and diverse friendships. Finally, opportunities are provided for exercise, creativity and community involvement and contribution (Universities UK, 2015), all protective factors when it comes to good mental health and well-being.

Student Mental Health Problems and Help-Seeking Behaviour

In the early 1990s, relationship problems were the most frequently reported at university counselling centres; however, since then reports of stress, anxiety, depression, eating disorders, self-harm and obsessive-compulsive disorder have become more common (Benton, Robertson, Tseng, Newton, & Benton, 2003; Conley, Durlak, & Kirsch, 2015; Davies, Morriss, & Glazebrook, 2014; Warwick, Maxwell, Statham, Aggleton, & Simon, 2008), with rates of suicidal students tripling (Benton et al., 2003). The level of emotional distress experienced by students is often very high (Rosenthal & Wilson, 2008), and this has many consequences including poor grades, academic probation leading to depression, decreased emotional and behavioural skills and a sense of social isolation (Megivern, Pellerito, & Mowbray, 2003). Furthermore, many students report cutting down on time spent on studies due to their emotional problems, and a proportion consider dropping out of university (Megivern et al., 2003). A conclusion that could be drawn from this is that the ability to deal successfully with emotional stresses in university life is an important factor in student retention (Pritchard & Wilson, 2003).

Two stages have been proposed in the research literature with regard to help-seeking: (1) perceiving the need for care and (2) acting on that perception by accessing services (Mechanic, 1966; Rosenstock, 1966). Many studies on higher education students' help-seeking and access to mental health services have documented substantial unmet needs and barriers to accessing services, including financial constraints, attitudes and knowledge (including stigma), concerns about privacy and lack of time (Furr, Westefeld, McConnell, & Jenkins, 2001; Mowbray et al., 2006; Tjia, Givens, & Shea, 2005). Two major factors appear to contribute to inadequate help-seeking: the stigma of having a mental illness and individual characteristics of the student.

Stigma associated with mental health problems is well documented and is a major cause for discrimination and exclusion (WHO, 2004). Symptoms of mental ill health (and the associated stigma) negatively affect people's self-esteem and disrupt relationships with a knock on effect on obtaining housing, jobs and an education (Storrie, Ahern, & Tuckett, 2010). University students are often unwilling to seek help because of perceived stigma (Blacklock, Benson, Johnson, & Bloomberg, 2003; Collins & Mowbray, 2005) and experience a sense of social isolation (Megivern et al., 2003). Help-seeking is often avoided because students perceive that mental health problems indicate weakness, which could have implications for successful career progression (Chew-Graham, Rogers, & Yassin, 2003). For example, medical students (especially ethnic minority and clinical students) perceive their professional lives to be at risk where psychiatric or emotional health problems are revealed (Roberts et al., 2001). Young people have identified perceived stigma, embarrassment, a preference for self-reliance and inability to recognise mental health symptoms (poor mental health literacy) as the most important barriers when it comes to seeking help. While research regarding facilitators is lacking, positive past experiences, social support and encouragement all appear to aid help-seeking behaviour (Gulliver, Griffiths, & Christensen, 2010). A common theme throughout this body of literature is that some students are unwilling to seek or receive help from university services because they are concerned that their emotional problems might not be understood and they will be stigmatized (Megivern et al., 2003; Stanley & Manthorpe, 2001; Warwick et al., 2008).

A related problem lies in the narrative around mental health in many universities. Even though mental health difficulties are experienced by a variety of different students, from different sociocultural and sociodemographic backgrounds, the expression of these difficulties is inconsistent. Students experience mental health difficulties in different ways, and universities tend to take a 'one-size-fits-all' approach to accessing support for mental health. There is generally an 'expert' community of mental health support (e.g. an on-campus well-being centre) supplemented by courses run by qualified mental health 'experts'. However, many students firstly seek support from a personal tutor or academic advisor and most academic staff either feel inadequately trained or do not feel it is part of their job to do so. As such, an unhelpful narrative of mental health difficulty being 'special' or 'not normal' is implicitly communicated; however, mental health difficulty is very common and often completely normal for anyone experiencing massive change over a short period of time. Therefore, universities need to create environments in which stigma associated with mental health is reduced and where staff and students alike feel comfortable discussing mental health with each other, while still respecting culturally diverse views.

However, stigma is not the only concern when considering students' access to mental health services both on and off campus. Factors individual to the student are also important. For example, students who are good at managing their emotions have generally had more positive experiences in the past with regard to help-seeking and therefore have better outcome expectations and are more willing to seek help (Ciarrochi & Deane, 2001). Conversely, students who find it more difficult to manage their emotions are less willing to seek help, resulting in those being most in need of help being least likely to seek it (Ciarrochi & Deane, 2001). Students who possess adaptive social and emotional skills hold positive self-perceptions and nurture supportive interpersonal relationships are much better placed to cope with the negative effects of emotional distress (Bouteyre, Maurel, & Bernaud, 2007; Burris, Brechting, Salsman, & Carlson, 2009; Pritchard, Wilson, & Yamnitz, 2007). Such skills in these intrapersonal and interpersonal domains are often associated with better adjustment (Conley, 2015). For example, evidence suggests that various aspects of self-perceptions (e.g. self-esteem), social and emotional skills (e.g. adaptive coping) and interpersonal relationships (e.g. social integration) predict academic success and retention (Eisenberg, Golberstein, & Hunt, 2009). However, research has also demonstrated that some university students sometimes struggle with regard to their self-perceptions (e.g. self-efficacy), social-emotional skills (e.g. adaptive thinking) and interpersonal relationships (e.g. poor relationship quality) (Conley, Kirsch, Dickson, & Bryant, 2014; Surtees, Wainwright, & Pharoah, 2002). Additionally, students experiencing high levels of psychological distress may not recognise that their psychological state is unusual and they may also lack any understanding that there are ways to cope with the distress or know how to obtain help (Rosenthal & Wilson, 2008). Therefore, it is reasonable to posit that enhancing personal and interpersonal competencies can play a role in preventing various types of emotional distress and adjustment problems, promoting students' mental health and well-being and academic performance (Conley et al., 2015). And, as mentioned above, creating an environment where students and staff feel comfortable discussing mental health with each other is a good first step.

Interventions to Support Student Mental Health and Well-being

Over the last few decades, many studies of preventive mental health programs in higher education have appeared. These investigations have generally adopted two different strategies: psychoeducational interventions and skills training interventions. Psychoeducational interventions work on the premise that receiving accurate information will motivate students to act effectively to prevent various negative outcomes, whereas skills training (systematically teaching students how to apply new skills) is based on the premise that behavioural skills are instrumental in preventing negative outcomes (e.g. anxiety, depression, stress) (Conley et al., 2015). For example, with regard to psychoeducational interventions, universities may inform new students about how to anticipate commonly encountered challenges and about techniques and coping strategies that may help students to cope more effectively (e.g. Moss, 2003; Walker & Frazier, 1993). The majority of research evidence suggests that psychoeducational interventions have not been successful in reducing stress, eating or weight problems, problematic drinking behaviour, or interpersonal violence (see Anderson & Whiston, 2005; Cronce & Larimer, 2011; Dennhardt & Murphy, 2013; Stice, Shaw, & Marti, 2007; Yager & O'Dea, 2008), although they can sometimes prove effective for increasing knowledge and improving attitudes. Van Deale, Hermans, Van Audenhove, and Van den Bergh (2012) reported that psychoeducational interventions were effective in the reduction of stress ($d = 0.27$); however, this review was not limited to higher education samples and included several studies which appeared to include skills training, and studies specifically targeting participants reporting clinical levels of psychological distress which may have contributed to the positive findings.

In contrast to the more passive psychoeducational programs, skills training interventions include such procedures as cognitive restructuring (helping students to think about situations and events in a different way), relaxation, mindfulness (being in the present moment), conflict resolution, various coping strategies and effective communication (e.g. Pool & Qualter, 2012). Skills training interventions often include emotional, cognitive and behavioural elements, helping the students to understand the link between these different factors in order to develop a more functional approach. As such, while skills training interventions have an informational element, they are just one component of a more intensive intervention which requires more effort on the part of the student. There is extensive evidence that skills training interventions are effective in helping students to adjust and maintain better mental health and well-being (Botvin & Griffin 2007; Stice et al., 2007). A recent meta-analysis investigated the effectiveness of mental health prevention programmes for higher education students (Conley et al., 2015). This review of 103 controlled published and unpublished interventions involving university undergraduate, graduate or professional students reported that skill-training programmes that included supervised practice were significantly more effective overall ($d = 0.45$) compared with skill training programmes without supervised practice ($d = 0.11$) and psychoeducational (information-only) interventions ($d = 0.13$) (Conley et al., 2015). Conley et al. showed that this pattern of results held for various outcomes by significantly reducing depression, anxiety, stress and general psychological distress, and by improving socio-emotional skills, self-perceptions, and academic behaviours and performance. Given the reluctance of some university students to seek help for mental health difficulties, it is important that universities offer access to self-help mental health materials and courses (e.g. via online platforms and apps); with meta-analytic research results suggesting that Cognitive Behaviour Therapy (CBT) delivered online improves anxiety (SMD $= -0.56$; 95% CI [-0.77, -0.35]), depression (SMD $= -0.43$; 95% CI [-0.63, -0.22]) and stress (SMD $= -0.73$; 95% CI [-1.27, -0.19]) in university students (Davies et al., 2014).

Several reviews have focused on the effectiveness of interventions for mental health and well-being that are aimed at students as individuals (e.g. Conley et al., 2015; Davies et al., 2014; Reavley & Jorm, 2010); however, much less is known about organisation level or 'setting-based' interventions. The setting-based model recognises that health is a function not only of individual factors, but also of the interaction of those factors with environmental, economic, social, organisational and cultural circumstances (Fernandez et al., 2016). The setting-based model can, therefore, be framed as a socio-ecological and salutogenic approach and interventions aim to improve 'the place' where the person lives, studies and/or works (Fernandez et al., 2016). These approaches focus on organisational and structural factors (that can potentially be changed) that have an impact on health, rather than on the individual risk factors alone (Dooris, 2009). Setting-based approaches aim to integrate health-related elements as part of the routine life of the higher education institution to create an environment that promotes health and productivity, connectedness and global well-being (Fernandez et al., 2016). Setting-based approaches generally include strategies that fall under two main categories: those that are policy-based and those that are academic-based.

Policy-based approaches represent institutional plans that define procedures and guide action (Fernandez et al., 2016). One of the most high-profile policy areas with regard to mental health and well-being relates to the prevention of suicide in students. Longitudinal research has shown that the implementation of a suicide policy, with clarity around the process to follow in the event of a student expressing suicidal ideation, reduced the rate of suicide by up to 50% over three years (see Joffe, 2008). These findings contrasted with an increasing rate of suicide at similar universities that did not have a suicide policy in place. Other policies related to mental health involve guidance for staff as to operating only within their level of expertise; signposting students to appropriate areas of support; highlighting on- and off-campus support related to mental health; outlining the institution's approach to helping students to manage their studies through mental health difficulties (as it relates to disability law); procedures for helping students in crisis; and requirements around confidentiality and data protection regarding mental health difficulties. One of the challenges for these policy-based approaches is that they are often developed 'by experts' or by engaging with research evidence, but without actually speaking to the staff or students themselves. This can lead to policies which, taken on face value, appear to satisfy the identified need; when in reality they are not quite nuanced enough to reflect the diversity of student experience or to be useful for busy academic staff.

Academic-based interventions focus on improving the mental health and well-being of students by including mandatory courses on topics related to mental well-being, by adopting different assessment strategies, and by altering curriculum design. Many of the mandatory courses focus on increasing knowledge about mental health (e.g. Becker et al., 2008), include mindfulness skills as part of the learning (e.g. Bergen-Cico, Possemato, & Cheon, 2013; Hassed, de Lisle, Sullivan, & Pier, 2009) and have shown significant improvements in outcomes related to mental health. However, these studies often do not have any follow-up measurement to assess change over time, so it is not clear whether these effects are maintained, and many of the studies do not employ a robust study design so the results need to be viewed with caution. Other institutions have trialled changing grade interval systems with results suggesting that grading schemes with more intervals were associated with improved mental health in students (Bloodgood, Short, Jackson, & Martindale, 2009; Reed et al., 2011; Rohe et al., 2006). Some universities have additionally trialled changes in the curriculum to assess the impact on the mental health and well-being of students (Jones & Johnston, 2006; Slavin, Schindler, & Chibnall, 2014). For example, one study employed a multi-tiered approach where they: changed the grading system (from 5-interval to 2-interval [pass/fail]); reduced the contact hours for students in the first two years; introduced more longitudinal electives; established learning communities composed of students and staff with common interests; and included a required course based on mindfulness and resilience in the curriculum (Slavin et al., 2014). Slavin et al. found that levels of depression, anxiety and stress were lower in students exposed to the changed curriculum verses previous student cohorts who had not been exposed. However, the results of studies like these suffer because there may well be a cohort effect at play which cannot be controlled for in the design, and the complexity of the intervention makes it difficult to assess which of its constituent components explains its effectiveness. Furthermore, because the results of these studies are based on aggregated group-level data, it is not possible to understand how these types of changes are experienced by individual students, some of whom may actually have experienced higher levels of emotional distress.

At an organisational level, often universities do not consider the interaction between a student's mental health and the way in which learning and teaching activities are organised. In Chapter 2, Alexander reported that he often couldn't identify the link between his lectures and laboratory activities; and also that he was disappointed that such an 'oral' discipline (engineering) was not taught this way. Due to some of Alexander's personal characteristics (i.e. being male, white, middle class), he was considered to be part of the majority (of engineering students) but there were many ways in which he experienced himself as a minority. It was difficult for him to identify with his subject (engineering) and himself within that discipline (as an engineer). In Alexander's case, completing the foundation year established him as part of a minority but he did not feel this was recognised. It is not clear whether or not Alexander's experiences impacted on his mental health but they did seem to impact on his ability to develop a personal identity. If academics do not have the time or motivation to prioritise foundation year training, designed to scaffold students into an adult-learning model, then students' ability to develop a new sense of identity may be compromised. Universities frequently focus on supporting 'recognised' minority group students (e.g. those from specific ethnic religious, or sexual orientation groups) and prioritise the voices of these students. When it comes to mental health, there is really no such thing as a minority group to be prioritised. All students may experience mental ill health under specific conditions (many of which are specific to the individual student). Therefore, when developing interventions or strategies for helping students, engaging as many student voices as possible in the development of these resources (rather than imposing a 'one-size-fits-all' 'off-the-shelf' solution) is really important.

Students as Collaborators in Mental Health Initiatives

Most universities have an on-campus counselling service for face-to-face support for students' mental health. However, press headlines suggest that in the UK, USA, Hong Kong and Australia demand for mental health services is rising and universities are struggling to meet demand (Liu, 2018; NUS, 2015; Orygen, 2017; Reilly, 2018). Therefore, finding other means to supplement the face-to-face offer is of great importance. An effective university well-being strategy should take a multi-tiered approach whereby students and staff can: (1) engage with psychoeducational content (e.g. online) to improve knowledge and reduce stigma associated with mental health; (2) access self-help courses (online) to build core skills (e.g. resilience, flexibility and patience); and (3) access to face-to-face therapeutic support where needed. There are many and varied suppliers of online mental health interventions with some specialist university suppliers or those that have been developed more broadly (e.g. www.bigwhitewall.com). Some universities are choosing to build their own online courses which are then free for use by all students, or to pay a fee for their students and staff to access an externally hosted solution.

   Growth in the number and range of initiatives that are either student-led or co-developed with students reflects the increasing emphasis students and student bodies place on mental health and well-being, as well as recognising the increased demand for mental health support (Universities UK, 2015). Many higher education institutions in the UK have established local peer support mental health programs for students and have active and passionate student unions promoting discussion campaigns to destigmatise mental health difficulties. The National Union of Students (NUS) has taken an active role working with HEIs in the development of policies and practices relating to the destigmatisation of mental health, and they have also worked closely with mental health charities like Mind and Rethink Mental Illness to reduce the stigma and discrimination that people with mental health difficulties experience. Furthermore, there are many national student-led initiatives offering free advice and support. For example, Student Minds is an organisation that trains students and staff in UK universities to deliver student-led peer support programs and workshops (www.studentminds.org.uk); Students Against Depression (www.studentsagainstdepression.org) is an online resource offering advice, information, guidance and resources to students; Nightline (www.nightline.ac.uk) offers peer support and information for students out of hours at many institutions across the UK; and the Alliance for Student-Led Well-being (www.alliancestudentwellbeing.weebly.com) is an umbrella group for student-led organisations that aims to raise awareness, reduce the stigma of mental ill health and provide practical help and emotional support. While many of the services referenced here are prevalent in the UK, the development of mental health strategies for higher education students is a core aim of most other countries' higher education institutions.

Conclusions

Many of the chapters in this book have referenced the importance of affording students an equal voice in aspects of their university experience, with specific chapters focused on ensuring students' involvement in developing university systems and processes (Chapters 16 and 17), and as co-researchers (Chapter 18). While it is important to ensure student voices are represented in the development of mental health and well-being interventions, at both individual and institutional levels, it is also important to ensure that any intervention is evidence-based, founded from the research literature which helps us to understand what does and does not prove effective. Where students' voices can be the loudest is in helping HEIs to develop and present mental health content in a way that is digestible and to develop interventions with which students will engage. By taking a participatory design approach (Chapter 18), students can be co-designers of both offline and online interventions for mental health and well-being. The challenge for universities is to ensure that the diverse voices of students from different backgrounds and with different life experiences can be adequately represented. In practice, in university populations of students and staff numbering in the tens of thousands, this is difficult to achieve. What is clear is that all voices (both student and staff) have something to contribute to the discussion around mental health and well-being.

References

Anderson, L. A., & Whiston, S. C. (2005). Sexual assault education programs: A meta-analytic examination of their effectiveness. *Psychology of Women Quarterly, 29*, 374–388.

Becker, C. M., Johnson, H., Vail-Smith, K., Maahs-Fladung, C., Tavasso, D., Elmore, B., & Blumell, C. (2008). Making health happen on campus: A review of a required general education health course. *Journal of General Education, 57*(2), 67–74.

Benton, S. A., Robertson, J. M., Tseng, W., Newton, F. B., & Benton, S. L. (2003). Changes in counseling center client problems across 13 years. *Professional Psychology: Research and Practice, 34*, 66–72.

Bergen-Cico, D., Possemato, K., & Cheon, S. (2013). Examining the efficacy of a brief mindfulness-based stress reduction (brief MBSR) program on psychological health. *Journal of American College Health, 61*(6), 348–360.

Blacklock, B., Benson, B., Johnson, D., & Bloomberg, L. (2003). *Needs assessment project: Exploring barriers and opportunities for college students with psychiatric disabilities.* Minneapolis: University of Minnesota Disability Services.

Bloodgood, R. A., Short, J. G., Jackson, J. M., & Martindale, J. R. (2009). A change to pass/fail grading in the first two years at one medical school results in improved psychological well-being. *Academy of Medicine, 84*(5), 655–662.

Botvin, G. J., & Griffin, K. W. (2007). School-based programmes to prevent alcohol, tobacco and other drug use. *International Review of Psychiatry, 19*, 607–615.

Bouteyre, E., Maurel, M., & Bernaud, J. (2007). Daily hassles and depressive symptoms among first year psychology students in France: The role of coping and social support. *Stress & Health: Journal of the International Society for the Investigation of Stress, 23*, 93–99.

Burris, J. L., Brechting, E. H., Salsman, J., & Carlson, C. R. (2009). Factors associated with the psychological well-being and distress of university students. *Journal of American College Health, 57*, 536–543.

Chew-Graham, C., Rogers, A., & Yassin, N. (2003). 'I wouldn't want it on my CV or their records': Medical students' experiences of help-seeking for mental health problems. *Medical Education, 37*, 873–880.

Ciarrochi, J., & Deane, F. (2001). Emotional competence and willingness to seek help from professional and non-professional sources. *British Journal of Guidance and Counselling, 30*, 173–188.

Collins, M., & Mowbray, C. (2005). Higher education and psychiatric disabilities: National survey of campus disability services. *American Journal of Psychiatry, 75*, 304–315.

Conley, C. S. (2015). SEL in higher education. In J. A. Durlak, C. E. Domitrovich, R. P. Weissberg, & T. P. Gullotta (Eds.), *Handbook of social and emotional learning: Research and practice* (pp. 197–212). New York: Guilford.

Conley, C. S., Kirsch, A. C., Dickson, D. A., & Bryant, F. B. (2014). Negotiating the transition to college: Developmental trajectories and gender differences in psychological functioning, cognitive-affective strategies, and social well-being. *Emerging Adulthood, 2*(3), 195–210.

Conley, S., Durlak, J. A., & Kirsch, A. C. (2015). A meta-analysis of universal mental health prevention programs for higher education students. *Preventative Science, 16*, 487–507.

Cronce, J. M., & Larimer, M. E. (2011). Individual-focused approaches to the prevention of college student drinking. *Alcohol Research & Health, 34*, 210–221.

Davies, E. B., Morriss, R., & Glazebrook, C. (2014). Computer-delivered and web-based interventions to improve depression, anxiety, and psychological well-being of university students: A systematic review and meta-analysis. *Journal of Medical Internet Research, 16*(5), e130.

Dennhardt, A. A., & Murphy, J. G. (2013). Prevention and treatment of college student drug use: A review of the literature. *Addictive Behaviors, 26*, 2607–2618.

Dooris, M. (2009). Holistic and sustainable health improvement: The contribution of the settings-based approach to health promotion. *Perspective in Public Health, 129*(1), 29–36.

Eisenberg, D., Golberstein, E., & Hunt, J. B. (2009). Mental health and academic success in college. *The BE Journal of Economic Analysis and Policy, 9*(1). https://doi.org/10.2202/1935-1682.2191.

Fernandez, A., Howse, E., Rubio-Valera, M., Thorncraft, K., Noone, J., Luu, X., … Salvador-Carulla, L. (2016). Setting-based interventions to promote mental health at the university: A systematic review. *International Journal of Public Health, 61*, 797–807.

Furr, S. R., Westefeld, J. S., McConnell, G. N., & Jenkins, J. (2001). Suicide and depression among college students: A decade later. *Professional Psychology Research and Practice, 23*, 97–100.

Gulliver, A., Griffiths, K. M., & Christensen, H. (2010). Perceived barriers and facilitators to mental health help-seeking in young people: A systematic review. *BMC psychiatry, 10*(1), 113.

Hassed, C., de Lisle, S., Sullivan, G., & Pier, C. (2009). Enhancing the health of medical students: Outcomes of an integrated mindfulness and lifestyle program. *Advances in Health Science Education: Theory and Practice, 14*(3), 387–398.

Joffe, P. (2008). An empirically supported program to prevent suicide in a college student population. *Suicide & Life Threatening Behavior, 38*(1), 87–103.

Jones, M. C., & Johnston, D. W. (2006). Is the introduction of a student-centred, problem-based curriculum associated with improvements in student nurse well-being and performance? An observational study of effect. *International Journal of Nursing Studies, 43*(8), 941–952.

Kobau, R., Seligman, M. E., Peterson, C., Diener, E., Zack, M. M., Chapman, D., & Thompson, W. (2011). Mental health promotion in public health: Perspectives and strategies from positive psychology. *American Journal of Public Health, 101*(8), e1–e9.

Liu, M. (2018). *The secret burden of mental illness in Hong Kong.* CNN. Retrieved from https://edition.cnn.com/2018/04/29/health/mental-health-suicide-hong-kong-asia/index.html.

Mechanic, D. (1966). Response factors in illness: The study of illness behavior. *Social Psychiatry, 1*(1), 1–20.

Megivern, D., Pellerito, C., & Mowbray, C. (2003). Barriers to higher education for individuals with psychiatric disabilities. *Psychiatric Rehabilitation Journal, 26*, 217–232.

Moss, S. B. (2003). *The effects of cognitive behavior therapy, meditation, and yoga on self-ratings of stress and psychological functioning in college students* (Unpublished doctoral dissertation). Retrieved from ProQuest Dissertations and Theses (3103673).

Mowbray, C. T., Megivern, D., Mandiberg, J. M., Strauss, S., Stein, C. H., Collins, K., ... Lett, R. (2006). Campus mental health services: Recommendations for change. *American Journal of Orthopsychiatry, 76* (2), 226–237.

NUS. (2015). *Digital support for student mental health*. National Union of Students. Retrieved from https://www.nus.org.uk/en/advice/health-and-wellbeing/digital-support-for-student-mental-health/?load=5&top=1836.

Orygen. (2017). *Mental health of Australian university students flying under the radar*. Orygen: The National Centre of Excellence in Mental Health. Retrieved from https://www.orygen.org.au/About/News-And-Events/Mental-health-of-Australian-university-students-fl.

Pool, L. D., & Qualter, P. (2012). Improving emotional intelligence and emotional self-efficacy through a teaching intervention for university students. *Learning and Individual Differences, 22*, 306–312.

Pritchard, M. E., & Wilson, G. S. (2003). Using emotional and social factors to predict student success. *Journal of College Student Development, 44*, 18–28.

Pritchard, M. E., Wilson, G. S., & Yamnitz, B. (2007). What predicts adjustment among college students? A longitudinal panel study. *Journal of American College Health, 56*, 15–21.

Reavley, N., & Jorm, A. F. (2010). Prevention and early intervention to improve mental health in higher education students: A review. *Early Interventions in Psychiatry, 4*(2), 132–142.

Reed, D. A., Shanafelt, T. D., Satele, D. W., Power, D. V., Eacker, A., Harper, W., ... Dyrbye, L. N. (2011). Relationship of pass/fail grading and curriculum structure with well-being among preclinical medical students: A multi-institutional study. *Academy of Medicine, 86* (11), 1367–1373.

Reilly, K. (2018). *Record numbers of college students are seeking treatment for depression and anxiety—But schools can't keep up*. Retrieved from http://time.com/5190291/anxiety-depression-college-university-students/. Accessed on 28 November 2018.

Roberts, L. W., Warner, T. D., Lyketsos, C., Frank, E., Ganzini, L., & Carter, D. (2001). Perceptions of academic vulnerability associated with personal illness: A study of 1027 students at nine medical schools. *Comprehensive Psychiatry, 42*, 1–15.

Rohe, D. E., Barrier, P. A., Clark, M. M., Cook, D. A., Vickers, K. S., & Decker, P. A. (2006). The benefits of pass-fail grading on stress, mood, and group cohesion in medical students. *Mayo Clinic Proceedings, 81*(11), 1443–1448.

Rosenstock, I. M. (1966). Why people use health services. *The Milbank Quarterly, 44,* 94–106.

Rosenthal, B., & Wilson, C. (2008). Mental health services: Use and disparity among diverse college students. *Journal of American College Health, 57,* 61–67.

Schulenberg, J. E., Sameroff, A. J., & Cicchetti, D. (2004). The transition to adulthood as a critical juncture in the course of psychopathology and mental health. *Developmental Psychopathology, 16,* 799–806.

Slavin, S. J., Schindler, D. L., & Chibnall, J. T. (2014). Medical student mental health 3.0: Improving student wellness through curricular changes. *Academy of Medicine, 89*(4), 573–577.

Stanley, N., & Manthorpe, J. (2001). Responding to students' mental health needs: Impermeable systems and diverse users. *Journal of Mental Health, 10,* 41–52.

Stice, E., Shaw, H., & Marti, C. N. (2007). A meta-analytic review of eating disorder prevention programs: Encouraging findings. *Annual Review of Clinical Psychology, 3,* 207–231.

Storrie, K., Ahern, K., & Tuckett, A. (2010). A systematic review: Students with mental health problems—A growing problem. *International Journal of Nursing Practice, 16,* 1–6.

Surtees, P. G., Wainwright, N. W. J., & Pharoah, P. D. P. (2002). Psychosocial factors and sex differences in high academic attainment at Cambridge University. *Oxford Review of Education, 28,* 21–38.

Tjia, J., Givens, J. L., & Shea, J. A. (2005). Factors associated with undertreatment of medical student depression. *Journal of American College Health, 53,* 219–224.

Towbes, L. C., & Cohen, L. H. (1996). Chronic stress in the lives of college students: Scale development and prospective prediction of distress. *Journal of Youth Adolescence, 25,* 199–217.

Universities UK. (2015). *Student mental wellbeing in higher education: Good practice guide.* London: Universities UK.

Van Daele, T., Hermans, D., Van Audenhove, C., & Van den Bergh, O. (2012). Stress reduction through psychoeducation: A meta-analytic review. *Health Education & Behavior, 39,* 474–485.

Walker, R., & Frazier, A. (1993). The effect of a stress management educational program on the knowledge, attitude, behavior, and stress level of college students. *Wellness Perspectives, 10*(1), 52–60.

Warwick, I., Maxwell, C., Statham, J., Aggleton, P., & Simon, A. (2008). Supporting mental health and emotional well-being among younger students in further education. *Journal of Further and Higher Education, 32*, 1–13.

WHO. (2004). *Promoting mental Health: Concepts, emerging evidence, practice* (Summary report: A report of the World health Organization Department of Mental health and Substance Abuse in Collaboration with the Victorian Health Promotion Foundation and the University of Melbourne). Geneva: World Health organization.

Yager, Z., & O'Dea, J. A. (2008). Prevention programs for body image and eating disorders on university campuses: A review of large, controlled interventions. *Health Promotion International, 23*, 173–189.

13

Reconciling Diverse Student and Employer Voices on Employability Skills and Work-Based Learning

Katarina Zajacova, Erica Hepper and Alexandra Grandison

Arguably, one of the core roles of higher education (HE) is to help make graduates employable and 'job ready'. Despite debates on the responsibilities of HEIs, gaining employment is one of the primary motivations for applying to university (Higher Education Academy, 2015; Molesworth, Nixon, & Scullion, 2009; Tymon, 2013) and many universities are focusing considerable resources on developing 'employability skills' (Yorke, 2006). Although there are numerous definitions of employability, it can be broadly understood as a complex set of skills, attributes, and achievements that make an individual more likely to gain and retain employment (Tymon, 2013; Yorke, 2006). However, the current landscape of graduate employability faces fundamental challenges. Research in a number of world regions has suggested that many graduates still lack the employability skills that are required by employers (Rasul, Rauf, Mansor, & Puvanasvaran, 2012). Specifically, it has been recognised that graduates frequently fail to meet employers' expectations in terms of key transferable skills

K. Zajacova (✉) · E. Hepper · A. Grandison
University of Surrey, Guildford, England, UK
e-mail: k.zajacova@surrey.ac.uk

© The Author(s) 2019
S. Lygo-Baker et al. (eds.), *Engaging Student Voices in Higher Education*,
https://doi.org/10.1007/978-3-030-20824-0_13

such as communication, teamwork, and self-management (Branine, 2008; Jackson, 2012). This 'skills gap' leaves vacancies unfilled (UK Commission for Employment and Skills, 2016) and may feed into lower productivity, dissatisfaction for employers and employees, and higher turnover. With changes to both compulsory education and the HE sector coming thick and fast, attention is needed to ensure that universities and their graduates keep up with the shifting landscape of employability.

One much-lauded approach to reducing the skills gap is the integration of work-based learning (WBL) into HE programmes (Lemanski, Mewis, & Overton, 2010; Little, & ESECT (Enhancing Student Employability Co-ordination Team), 2006; Morley, 2018). Comprising professional placements, internships, and other types of work experience in organisations, WBL provides opportunities for training, skills development, and personal development, which may increase students' job readiness upon graduation and their success in the graduate employment market (Harvey, 2005; Lemanski et al., 2010). Nevertheless, the road to effective WBL is not necessarily smooth. Notwithstanding the array of positive contributions, WBL brings a number of new considerations and challenges, resulting in a need for HEIs to update their understanding and practices to encompass the diversity of students. A key reason for this is a lack of coherence among the voices of different stakeholders: How do varying students, employers, and HE providers view employability and the role of WBL?

This chapter discusses two key challenges that HEIs face when embedding WBL into their curricula, and the roles that disparate voices play in each. First, we consider diversity among students in terms of their needs for WBL and the role this might play in their employability. In the light of such diversity, we focus on international students as one key example of a heterogeneous group characterised by a multitude of voices. It is crucial that the voices within this group can be heard and acted upon in combination with the many other voices that represent other under-represented, marginalised or persecuted groups, whilst not forgetting or ignoring the many voices within the 'privileged majority'. Second, we discuss tensions that potentially arise between the voices of students and employers in terms of what employability is. Much focus is laid on the actions involved in employment itself (e.g. statistics for graduates applying and employers offering jobs; see Chapter 8). We argue that greater insight into the voices that underpin these actions is needed to move towards a shared understanding of employability. In turn, this will enable HEIs to maximise the value of their programmes (e.g. by embedding employability and WBL in the most effective ways), and students and employers to maximise their benefit from HE.

Diversity Between Students' Needs for Employability and Work-Based Learning

One of the government's most ambitious targets for HE in recent years has been to widen access and participation in order to diversify its student population (Department for Business Innovation & Skills, 2016). Although not constant across the sector, some success with widening participation has been achieved, with the diversity of students increasing. This greater diversity in age, gender, disability, ethnicity, nationality, and socio-economic status is undoubtedly a positive step towards the equality of opportunities for individual students (Brighouse, Howe, & Tooley, 2010) but also for the academic and the wider community. Specifically for HE, engagement by a wider range of nationalities has enriched the learning environment and broadened teaching practices (Jones & Brown, 2007), bringing new insights and new challenges.

The increased diversity within student bodies, partly achieved by widening participation initiatives, has been recognised by a number of leading institutions that have adapted their curricula effectively. This includes the London School of Economics (LSE; McKenna, 2017), University of Surrey, and University of Sussex. Often one of the first steps towards making adjustments to existing practices is the examination of the content, ethos, and objectives of curricula in terms of their diversity and inclusivity. Compared to some of the more immediately visible challenges, the concept of employability has been a relatively recent consideration when making revisions to curricula in the light of student diversity. However, to ensure that students from diverse backgrounds are offered and benefit from wide-ranging employability opportunities, universities must work in collaboration with employers. This need for collaboration highlights the role of different yet connected voices within this landscape. Any increase in diversity within the student population leads to a broadening of different types of graduates, which arguably must be mirrored by an increase in the range and types of employability opportunities available. Employers are therefore key to expanding traditional graduate jobs to accommodate this diversity and so their changing voices must also be heard.

Different groups of students bring diverse needs and considerations, and the increase in the representation in higher education highlights the diversity of student voices both across and within groups such as LGBTQ+ (lesbian, gay, bisexual, transgender, queer/questioning) community (e.g. Hawley, 2015), individuals from lower socio-economic backgrounds (e.g. Reay, 2016) or those entering higher education over the age of 21, often referred to as 'mature students' (e.g. Swain & Hammond, 2011), to name but a few examples. It is also important to remember that enormous diversity exists within the voices of the 'privileged majority' for whom representation is also crucial (see Chapter 2). A full review of the many different groups within the student community is beyond the scope of this chapter and so to illustrate some of the issues relating to employability we focus our discussion on the example of internationalisation. We argue that not only is it important to make sense of the full range of students' voices regarding expectations of and engagement with employability, but also to extract the range of voices representing the views of international students. Furthermore, it is equally crucial to consider the voices of educators and employers to provide context for their actions around these voices. Some of the issues below apply to a number of groups, whereas others are particular to the heterogeneous collective that is international students (see also Chapter 5). One effect of 'internationalisation' within the HE sector is to create greater competition within local job markets whilst opening up overseas opportunities, changing the face of the global employment market, and broadening and constantly shifting the concept of employability. Another, more proximal effect is the varying needs and views about employability and WBL that students from different nationalities bring. Here, we focus on two aspects of education that are shaped by these pressures: inclusion of employability-related skills into the curriculum and engagement with WBL.

In a WBL context, the acknowledgement of the variety of students' needs becomes especially crucial, given that a student is typically expected to leave the relatively protected university environment and enter the world of a professional workplace. The value of WBL lies in the ongoing dialogue between HE and industry by equipping students with relevant transferable skills that are equally valued in academia as well as in the workplace. This dialogue requires an awareness of the variability of what exactly is valued by employers across the globe. It cannot be assumed that WBL holds equal value to students of different nationalities, given that expectations regarding the role of HE are likely to be very different in their countries of origin, as are the varying landscapes of future graduate employment (Education for Engineering, 2011). For example, Little and Harvey (2006) highlight that international students are more likely to aim to complete a degree in three years, reducing their likelihood of taking a sandwich course. Moreover, the prospect of entering a professional environment when one has never been exposed to or worked professionally in that country or language before may be daunting, and heightened costs for an international student are even more significant than they are for a home student (Wilson, 2012). Somewhat alarmingly, a study by Crawford and Wang (2016) suggests that even after overcoming the potential barriers to engaging with WBL, international undergraduates actually gain less from work placements than their UK counterparts. This is despite evidence of no significant difference in performance between UK and international students across the first two years of a degree. Together, these factors highlight the need for the sector to do more to support students to value WBL, to feel ready to enter the workplace, and/or to maximise the benefits whilst engaging with WBL. To do this, it is essential that curricula are regularly reviewed and that such reviews acknowledge the full range of voices that reflect diverse student experiences.

Within higher education curricula, students' expectations and engagement must now relate to both academic and transferable skills in order to foster employability. This dual outlook is essential for added value to students, universities, and industry, and employability is now a priority agenda in curriculum design (e.g. Higher Education Academy, 2015). However, as previously implied, awareness of the concept of employability and the connection between work readiness and academic study at the point of entry vary greatly between different groups of students (Daniels & Brooker, 2014), with nationality being only one of many intersections of a student's identity. As outlined by Aamodt, Hovdhaugen, and Bielfeldt (2010), different job markets across the world have different needs and requirements and so the competencies and skills that are essential to maintain employability also differ. This naturally leads to a variety of conceptualisations of employability for students from different countries with the aim for teaching staff to address this variability. In addition, even if we were to find an international agreement on the value of a particular skill that students ought to acquire during their university studies, the definition of the most valuable aspect or application of that skill is again likely to vary significantly, depending on the location of their graduate destination. To take an example of writing skills, even though both undergraduate and postgraduate students have typically acquired advanced skills in formal essay writing, graduates nowadays need to be more flexible in terms of their writing competencies, something that could be achieved by diversifying assessment patterns. By including formats such as blog writing, report writing, presentation/poster preparation, persuasive and creative writing styles, universities are more likely to produce an agile and adaptable individual who is comfortable working with a variety of communication formats. However, more traditional views of academic skills acquisition that are still held in many countries, such as in parts of Eastern Europe (Wile & Ulqini, 2003), may dissociate some of these more diverse writing formats from HE-related skills and place less value on them when selecting future employees. Thus, not only does any new approach need to recognise the necessity to broaden the use and application of certain skills (such as written skills, for example), but it also needs to be aware that different variations on any given competency will be expected of graduates and valued differentially by employers across the globe.

In both WBL and within-curriculum contexts, when developing the most effective employability curriculum that aims to engage all groups and subsections of students, it is important to be aware that a one-size-fits-all format is unlikely to be effective. Additionally, the diverse range of voices that make up the broad category of international students (and other non-traditional groups) are often lost in mainstream data collected through the NSS or internal teaching evaluation questionnaires. As outlined in Chapter 5, the diversity within international student voices is often grossly oversimplified by the comparison between UK students, European Union (EU) students, and non-EU students. However, the voices represented within this group are wide-ranging and complex. We have focused on the example of internationalisation to stimulate the debate on tailored approaches to employability and WBL more broadly, and to highlight the challenges such diversity brings for effectively listening to and acting on student voices from all groups. Similarly, we call for more explicit consideration of the employability needs of postgraduate students and doctoral researchers (see also Chapter 9), who are often forgotten in mainstream literatures and within-institution discussions.

Employer and Student Perspectives on Employability

Initiatives to prepare students for the changing job market must be informed by employer perspectives and consider how well students and educators currently understand and share these perspectives. Although there appears to be little clarity on what the voices of students say about their expectations for and experiences of WBL and other forms of employability support, there is some relatively objective information about the needs of (some groups of) employers, even if those needs are diverse. As the number of graduates increases, so too does competition for jobs that require higher skill levels, and so skill development alone becomes insufficient (Baciu & Lazar, 2011). Moradi (2011) illustrates the need for developing transferable skills such as communication, critical thinking, decision-making, and problem-solving, in addition to the technical and academic knowledge that employers demand. Such skills are also cited by employers as key aspects of person specifications and recruitment criteria. Further, employers are beginning to emphasise not only skills but also personal attributes such as attitudes, resilience, and self-awareness. Such characteristics equip graduates to be 'life-long learners' who can adapt to fast-changing technologies and markets. As today's workplace changes constantly, employees must too be able to adapt, and indeed, the concept, meaning, and components of employability itself keep shifting (Williams, Dodd, Steele, & Randall, 2015). Nevertheless, graduate recruiters have reported that they expect some skills to be learned during HE (e.g. problem-solving) or in WBL before employment (e.g. commercial and organisational awareness; Association of Graduate Recruiters, 2016). Thus, HE providers must seek to support students as best they can in developing a range of skills and attributes as well as keeping abreast of the continually changing landscape. As a further complexity, as mentioned earlier, emphases may vary across cultures for students seeking to enter the global job market. Although most employers around the world place high value on (e.g.) communication skills, there can be some variation in how the key attributes are understood and valued in different cultural contexts. The reality of being able to consider each individual nationality and their interpretation of employability is impossible; however, valuable knowledge can be gained from dialogue with international placement providers. Nevertheless, in the light of all of this, it is no wonder that student voices on employability become lost as they inevitably flounder in the wake of the transient and ever-changing global job market.

Although employer perspectives are key for helping to guide students in their preparation for employment, HE providers are naturally guided by the academic literature and communities when turning to curriculum or WBL design. Due in part to the constant changes highlighted above, and the natural lag in academic publication processes, the concept of employability has numerous definitions within the literature. For example, Hillage and Pollard as far back as 1998 suggested that employability is having the capability to obtain and maintain work that is fulfilling by using knowledge, skills, and attitudes to realise one's potential. However, this and similar definitions have been criticised for their simplicity, and the concept continues to be contested and redefined (Williams et al., 2015). Tymon's (2013) review highlights that of six dominant frameworks for employability in the academic literature, there is considerable divergence in terms of component parts, with only *teamwork* and *communication* appearing in all six. This suggests that these frameworks are not necessarily conceptualised as integrated networks of skills, rather as collections of isolated attributes that are not clearly interlinked. This approach arguably fails to capture the holistic application of employability skills in the real world. Unsurprisingly, then, there is uncertainty in HE institutions about the most valuable skills or attributes to focus on and how to use scarce resources to build these into curricula and WBL.

Some of these employment-related skills have been incorporated into HE curricula in the UK by diversifying the learning outcomes and broadening the assessment patterns of undergraduate and postgraduate modules (Medland, 2016). Although from certain perspectives the diversification of curricula primarily aims to enhance inclusivity and ensure that as wide a range of voices as possible is represented in courses and programmes, for the purpose of this chapter, it is also believed that it greatly enhances student employability and improves graduate employment statistics (see Chapter 8). Diversifying assessment is believed to promote learning in a way that is more suited to real-world practice. Not only does this help to accommodate the wide-ranging needs and aptitudes of the diverse student community, but it also serves to make that student community more employable to a range of global employers upon graduation (McLean, 2018).

Whilst broadly accepted as a positive development, the implementation of WBL into academic curricula has not been without its challenges, one of which is listening to and accommodating the myriad of student voices. As previously implied, the definition of employability is challenging as it is transient and context-specific. However, when the aims and objectives of a curriculum are being created, this is inevitably being done with the UK employment (or 'western' international) context in mind, despite the internationally diverse student body. From the international perspective, employability in different countries often relates to distinct skills and competencies that are influenced by national contexts, cultural values, and social hierarchies (Gribble, 2014). This perspective is something that international students bring with them and it is reflected in their many different voices throughout their studies, especially if they are planning to return to their countries of origin post-graduation. Overall, the concept of employability is complex and is impacted by factors that may be outside an individual's control, such as market conditions and pressures within the social and political landscape. When engaging with the concept of employability as a theoretical exercise, as traditional academic approaches might dictate, it is therefore difficult to gain certainty about the magic formula required. Rather, active engagement with WBL enables students to immerse themselves in real-world problems. Such experiences can help to develop tangible, transferrable skills that are adaptable, as well as enabling students to gain experience and network with employers to better understand their perspectives and needs at any given time.

So, what do students' voices tell us about employability? Currently, given the many potentially conflicting voices from employers and the academic literature on the very nature of employability, it is perhaps unsurprising that students express uncertainty about how to become employable. Moreover, there is little understanding of how students understand employability and what they think is important in promoting it. Students recognise that they need to demonstrate skills to add value to their degree (Tomlinson, 2008). However, Qureshi, Wall, Humphries, and Balani (2016) found that students report poor understanding of employability, and Tymon (2013) demonstrates disparity between students' and employers' views. Although students acknowledged the importance of skills, they appear to be thinking less long-term than employers and only final-year students recognised the value of experience. Lemanski et al. (2010) similarly highlight a range of concerns and barriers that might arise from students' perspectives on WBL (e.g. workload, support, personal relevance). Other students, such as Alexander in Chapter 2, may not identify with the employment goals of the majority on their course and disengage as a result. As per earlier discussions on widening participation initiatives and the diversification of the curriculum, it is possible that with the gradual inclusion of employability-related skills into all degree levels, students' recognition of their value will increase from the start of their degrees or even before they enter HE. However, educators may need to take a proactive role in ensuring that this value is clearly communicated and understood by the diverse student body. Currently, even after graduation, graduates prioritise different aspects of employability compared to employers (Wickramasinghe & Perera, 2010) and this clash of voices poses challenges. It is important to help students develop a strong voice around employability so that they can articulate their skills and attributes clearly and persuasively when applying for roles—learning to speak the language of employers will pay dividends in the recruitment process.

Students' actions are another means to understand the commitment and value they place on employability. This includes engagement with employability development opportunities (which in universities are often optional sessions), as well as engaging with WBL. Whilst some students are highly focused on their personal development, others report lower engagement with employability opportunities (Qureshi et al., 2016; Tymon, 2013). When students do undertake WBL (such as sandwich courses), this is shown to increase graduate employment success (Harvey, 2005). It can be speculated that this may be a result of the sandwich year providing an opportunity and time frame for the expectations of both students and employers to align with each other. Yet, it is recognised within HE that many students fail to engage with WBL or other activities that are billed as employability-oriented (Little & Harvey, 2006). Thus, lack of engagement may be holding students back, perhaps for some of the reasons highlighted by Lemanski et al. (2010) above. Given the issues around diversity discussed throughout this chapter, such lack of engagement might be especially prevalent and risky in some groups, creating inequalities that HE institutions should be mindful of mitigating. One route to facilitating employability-promoting actions is to capitalise on the voices of student peers. For example, the voice of a student returning from a placement year can provide valuable knowledge and lay the foundations for alumni connections. This should be considered when developing curricula and university-led extra-curricular activities. One tried and tested practice in our institution to collate such valuable input from students—including those undertaking their work placements abroad——is via discussions between academic placement tutors, students, and employers during (physical or virtual) placement visits and during placement debrief sessions. Equally, encouragement and embedding of peer-networking activities that enable dialogue between returning placement students and their more junior cohorts promote awareness and help to align the expectations of future student cohorts and future employers. The role of HE is therefore likely to be multifaceted, as its aim is not only to deliver employability-related education, but even more importantly to act as the facilitator and enabler of such dialogues.

More research is needed in this area but it is clearly essential to educate students about what employers are actually looking for and the value of engaging with employability and WBL opportunities. We argue that this can partly be achieved by: (a) better understanding the range of student voices on employability, which will help to inform the way that approaches to employability are embedded and promoted in HE curricula; (b) better understanding employers' voices, taking into account different sectors and geographical regions; and (c) recognising that HE institutions need to communicate and mediate between employers and students more effectively to help students fulfil their responsibility to engage with employment opportunities and help employers provide relevant opportunities that maximise the potential of our ever-changing graduate communities.

Moving Forward: The Role of Higher Education

Overall, the HE and graduate recruitment sectors are facing a fast-changing landscape and an increasing need to consider and build employability into HE courses. To achieve this goal, it will be essential to inform and align the voices and perspectives of the various stakeholders to work towards the best outcomes for students, institutions, and employers. Clearly, institutions need to invest prudently in designing employability-focused curricula, activities, and WBL opportunities that provide real value, whilst encouraging and supporting as wide a range of students as possible to engage with these opportunities. Such efforts need to begin with a clearer understanding of the different needs and voices that exist in the diverse student body. Such voices include the broad and diverse group of international students providing a focus within this chapter, but also students of different ages, genders, socio-economic backgrounds, sexual identities, those with financial or caring responsibilities for example, as well as students within the 'privileged majority', all of whom contribute to the student community in all its diversity. At the same time, a clearer understanding and communication are needed of the voices of employers and the needs of their graduate roles. So, one might ask, who is responsible for seeking out, listening to, and disseminating these voices? An understandable tension exists in HE between the importance of employability and the perception and pressures faced by academics (e.g. concerns that it is outside of their role or beyond the scope of their workload to offer specific WBL activities; Jackson,

2012; Qureshi et al., 2016). Nevertheless, we return to our opening claim that HE carries the role of readying graduates for the world of work—and ultimately, it is HE institutions who have access to both groups of student and employer voices with the power to connect the two.

We make four recommendations to the sector that we hope will help to achieve this aim. First, further systematic research is needed into the meanings of employability and the skills and attributes that different stakeholders use to define this nebulous term (specifically exploring the diversity of different groups of students and employers, including undergraduate and postgraduate, as well as those from international backgrounds and markets). Second, more open communication and connections between students and employers would help to create shared understandings of these issues, for example via employer engagement and networking events, field visits, and online platforms. Third, research is also needed to explore the reasons why some students do not engage with employability and WBL opportunities, including investigation of the wider incentives around pursuing higher education. Fourth, programmes should aim to embed such opportunities into core curricula so that students are able to increase their employability even if they lack motivation or have work or caring commitments. Here, we can learn from and engage with employers or perhaps alternative HE providers who, arguably, could be better placed than universities in some cases to equip graduates with skills such as commercial awareness. We hope that raising and discussing these issues will help to stimulate further movement in the positive directions that many HE institutions are already pursuing, and ultimately better equip graduates at all levels to enter their chosen job market and workplace not only job-ready but career-ready. We need to tackle these challenges as a community of voices to enable collective actions that empower and benefit students, educators, and employers alike.

References

Aamodt, P., Hovdhaugen, E., & Bielfeldt, U. (2010). Serving the society? Historical and modern interpretations of employability. *Higher Education Policy, 23,* 271–284.

Baciu, E., & Lazar, T. (2011). Skills supply and skills demand among youth: Object of concern or object of hope? *Revista De AsistentaSociala, 4,* 85–101.

Branine, M. (2008). Graduate recruitment and selection in the UK: A study of recent changes in methods and expectations. *Career Development International, 13*(6), 497–513.

Brighouse, H., Howe, K. R., & Tooley, J. (2010). *Educational equality.* London: Bloomsbury.

Crawford, I., & Wang, Z. (2016). The impact of placements on the academic performance of UK and international students in higher education. *Studies in Higher Education, 41*(4), 712–733.

Daniels, J., & Brooker, J. (2014). Student identity development in higher education: Implications for graduate attributes and work-readiness. *Educational Research, 56*(1), 65–76.

Department for Business Innovation & Skills. (2016). *Success as a knowledge economy: Teaching excellence, social mobility and student choice.* London: Higher Education Reform Directorate.

Education for Engineering (E4E). (2011). *Sandwich courses in higher education: A report on current provision and analysis of barriers to increasing participation.* Retrieved from https://educationforengineering.org.uk/reports/.

Gribble, C. (2014). *Exploring 'employability' in different cultural contexts.* London: Society for Research into Higher Education. Retrieved from https://www.srhe.ac.uk/downloads/gribble-cate.pdf.

Harvey, L. (2005). Embedding and integrating employability. *New Directions for Institutional Research, 128,* 13–28.

Hawley, J. C. (Ed.). (2015). *Expanding the circle: Creating an inclusive environment in higher education for LGBTQ students and studies.* New York: SUNY Press.

Higher Education Academy. (2015). *Framework for embedding employability in higher education.* New York: Higher Education Academy. Retrieved from https://www.heacademy.ac.uk/knowledge-hub/framework-embedding-employability-higher-education.

Hillage, J., & Pollard, E. (1998). *Employability: Developing a framework for policy analysis.* London: Department for Education and Employment.

Jackson, D. (2012). Testing a model of undergraduate competence in employability skills and its implications for stakeholders. *Journal of Education and Work, 27*(2), 220–242.

Jones, E., & Brown, S. (Eds.). (2007). *Internationalising higher education.* London: Routledge.

Lemanski, T., Mewis, R., & Overton, T. (2010). An introduction to the recent literature on approaches to work-based learning. *New Directions in the Teaching of Physical Sciences, 6,* 3–9.

Little, B., & ESECT (Enhancing Student Employability Co-ordination Team). (2006). *Employability and work-based learning.* Retrieved from www.heacademy.ac.uk.

Little, B., & Harvey, L. (2006). *Learning through work placements and beyond: A report for HECSU and the higher education academy's work placements organisation forum.* Retrieved from https://hecsu.ac.uk/assets/assets/documents/Learning_through_work_placements_and_beyond.pdf.

McKenna, C. (2017). *Diversifying the curriculum—Recent developments and projects at LSE.* Retrieved from http://blogs.lse.ac.uk/education/2017/06/13/4581/.

McLean, H. (2018). This is the way to teach: Insights from academics and students about assessment that supports learning. *Assessment and Evaluation in Higher Education, 43*(8), 1228–1240.

Medland, E. (2016). Assessment in higher education: Drivers, barriers and directions for change in the UK. *Assessment and Evaluation in Higher Education, 41*(1), 81–96.

Molesworth, M., Nixon, E., & Scullion, R. (2009). Having, being and higher education: The marketisation of the university and the transformation of the student into consumer. *Teaching in Higher Education, 14*(3), 277–287.

Moradi, M. A. (2011). *A case study of how students enrolled in CTE programs and faculty understand and assess the implications of globalization on career preparation.* Unpublished PhD Thesis, Western Michigan University.

Morley, D. (Ed.). (2018). *Employability in higher education through work-based learning.* London: Palgrave Macmillan.

Qureshi, A., Wall, H., Humphries, J., & Balani, A. B. (2016). Can personality traits modulate student engagement with learning and their attitude to employability? *Learning and Individual Differences, 51,* 349–358.

Rasul, M. S., Rauf, R. A. A., Mansor, A. N., & Puvanasvaran, A. P. (2012). Employability skills assessment tool development. *International Education Studies, 5,* 43–56.

Reay, D. (2016). Social class in higher education: Still an elephant in the room. In J. E. Côté & A. Furlong (Eds.), *Routledge handbook of the sociology of higher education* (pp. 131–141). London: Routledge.

Swain, J., & Hammond, C. (2011). The motivations and outcomes of studying for part-time mature students in higher education. *International Journal of Lifelong Education, 30*(5), 591–612.

Tomlinson, M. (2008). 'The degree is not enough': Students' perceptions of the role of higher education credentials for graduate work and employability. *British Journal of Sociology of Education, 29*(1), 49–61.

Tymon, A. (2013). The student perspective on employability. *Studies in Higher Education, 38*(6), 841–856.

UK Commission for Employment and Skills. (2016, May). *Employer skills survey 2015: UK results.* Retrieved from https://www.gov.uk/government/uploads/system/uploads/attachment_data/file/525444/UKCESS_2015_Report_for_web__May_.pdf.

Wickramasinghe, V., & Perera, L. (2010). Graduates', university lecturers' and employers' perceptions towards employability skills. *Education and Training, 52*(3), 226–244.

Wile, J. M., & Ulqini, L. (2003, March 24–25). *Developing critical thinking skills in Eastern Europe.* Paper presented at the World Bank's International workshop, curricula, textbooks, and pedagogical practices and the promotion of peace and respect for diversity.

Williams, S., Dodd, L. J., Steele, C., & Randall, R. (2015). A systematic review of current understandings of employability. *Journal of Education and Work, 29*(8), 877–901.

Wilson, T. (2012). *A review of business—University collaboration.* Bristol: Higher Education Funding Council for England.

Yorke, M. (2006). *Employability in higher education: What it is-what it is not (learning & employability series 1).* New York: Higher Education Academy.

14

Students' Perceptions of Graduate Attributes: A Signalling Theory Analysis

Anna Jones and Judy Pate

In recent years, discussions concerning the linkages between higher education (HE) and the economy have been rekindled and have spurred stakeholders to revisit the age-old debate on the role of education. At a governmental level, policy communicates the economic imperative of enhancing human capital in the labour market. Unsurprisingly, employers reinforce this economic focus in the backdrop of fierce global competition and require students to be 'work-ready' on graduation (see Chapter 8). One response from universities has been to articulate graduate attributes to provide more concrete and tangible outcomes of HE.

In considering graduate attributes, the voices of students have been largely ignored, despite the agenda being closely associated with both stu-

A. Jones (✉)
King's College London, London, UK
e-mail: anna.jones@kcl.ac.uk

J. Pate
Alliance Hotels Consultants, Glencoe House, Glencoe, Near Fort William, West Highlands, Scotland, UK
e-mail: jpate@glencoe-house.com

© The Author(s) 2019
S. Lygo-Baker et al. (eds.), *Engaging Student Voices in Higher Education*,
https://doi.org/10.1007/978-3-030-20824-0_14

dents' learning and their future employability. There has been some consideration of the student perspective (Cavanagh, Burston, Southcombe, & Bartram, 2015; Daniels & Brooker, 2014; Fraser & Thomas, 2013; Hill, Walkington, & France, 2016; Mager & Spronken-Smith, 2014; Oliver, 2013; Su, 2014) yet no systematic examination of students' views. In forming their perspectives, students are subject to a variety of messages from numerous and varied sources both within the confines of the university and further afield through public policy, media, and industry; such signals are inextricably linked to the assumptions and vested interests of particular stakeholders and to the individual perspectives of each student. So, our central question is this: how do students conceptualise graduate attributes and to what extent are their interpretations influenced by other stakeholders? In this chapter, we (a) seek to understand student perspectives on graduate attributes and (b) to explore the signals that influence their understanding. We argue that while students are uncertain about the term 'graduate attributes', nevertheless they have a clear view of the capabilities they will leave university with, how these are acquired, and why they are valuable for their future. We also argue that there is no single 'student voice' but rather a range of viewpoints and perspectives.

Conceptualising Graduate Attributes

The economic narrative appears to have overwhelmed recent discussions around the interface between HE and the labour market where 'education should logically coordinate with the requirements of work because that is how societies function' (Saunders, 2006, p. 3). This dominant paradigm appears to have pervaded the thinking of policy makers, employers, and to a growing degree, the student body, to an extent that it appears to have become normalised as the accepted wisdom (Collini, 2017). Employment destinations are a crucial indicator of employability (Bridgestock, 2009; Mason, Williams, & Cranmer, 2009; Yorke, 2006; see Chapter 8), regardless of inherent social inequalities in an imbalanced labour market (Moreau & Leathwood, 2006).

The terminology surrounding HE and the labour market is crowded but not necessarily transparent. Within HE, graduate attributes are frequently defined as 'the qualities, skills and understandings a university community agrees its students would desirably develop during their time at the institution and, consequently, shape the contribution they are able to make to their profession and as a citizen' (Bowden, Hart, King, Trigwell, & Watt, 2000, para. 2). Significantly, Tomlinson (2012) commented that 'while notions of graduate skills, competencies, and attributes are used interchangeably, they often convey different things to different people and definitions are not always likely to be shared among employers, university teachers and graduates themselves' (p. 412). Moreover, it has been argued that concepts of skills are too narrow and fail to encapsulate all social practices, such as critical reflection, expected by universities and employers (Yorke & Knight, 2007). The situation becomes yet more complicated when particular skills can be seen as socially constructed and recognised as holding different meanings for HE and employers (Holmes, 2001). The concept of graduate attributes has attempted to move the debate towards a more holistic approach which includes scholarship, global citizenship, and lifelong learning (de la Harpe & David, 2012; Fraser & Thomas, 2013), although there is a far from shared understanding even within the academic community (Barrie, 2006, 2012; Jones, 2009).

Signalling theory provides the theoretical framework to examine how intended and unintended messages from key stakeholders are read and interpreted by students and how they are affected by the content of the message (Spence, 1973; Connelly, Certo, Ireland, & Reutzel, 2011). In the context of this chapter, the key parties all act as *signallers* of their expectations and perceptions concerning graduate attributes. The student body acts as active *receivers* and interpreters of cues and signals from the other parties. Thus, key stakeholders are producers of communication signals although it is likely that the content and nature of these messages will differ in strength, intensity, clarity, and reliability. Moreover, some signals may be deliberate and intended, others may be inadvertent or unintended. Signals may be distorted on the journey from signaller to intended receiver. Therefore, the relative consistency of signals is significant. By drawing on signalling theory, the plurality of student interpretations will be elucidated to uncover divergent understandings and a multiplicity of voices. The strength of signalling theory is that it focuses on the message and its interpretation and the gaps or miscommunication.

The Study

This study explored perceptions of undergraduate students in four disciplines (medicine, law, history, and management) at one research-intensive university in Scotland. It is a qualitative study based on 18 in-depth interviews. Each interview was audio-recorded and transcribed in full. Analysis was emergent, and coding was developed through re-reading and validation through cross-checking across all transcripts. From this coding, patterns were identified and refined. Hypothetical relationships identified in the coding were confirmed, modified, or rejected on the basis of this process. Themes and patterns were then analysed using the framework of signalling theory, and findings were verified by both researchers.

By drawing on signalling theory as an analytical lens, students identified several sources of signals that informed their perceptions of graduate attributes, albeit to varying degrees. These signallers were as follows: lecturers in the classroom and messages from those within the academic discipline; signals from university policy and communications including from the careers office; messages gained through work experience in both paid employment and voluntary work; and finally, perceived signals from future potential employers.

The university's graduate attribute policy was developed seven years ago through extensive consultation with staff and students in conjunction with input from external policy bodies. The formal policy encompassed a range of graduate attributes including: critical thinking; independent learning; effective communication; adaptability; confidence; ethics; and social awareness, together with subject-specific values, knowledge, and techniques. The policy was available on the university's website, and the careers office took the lead in communicating issues associated with graduate attributes.

Findings

The findings of this study are discussed by discipline in order to explore possible differences in the signals received.

Medicine

Signals from Teaching

Medical students saw aspects of communication as central, both for their work as clinicians and for gaining employment. They described this as problem-solving and teamwork, both integral to their training:

> Medicine has dedicated time to improving communication skills. We do role plays, actors come in and we get to practice role plays through third year with complex scenarios.

Students saw communication as part of the course; it was made clear to them by formal teaching (clinical and campus) and assessed through the objective structured clinical examination (OSCE) and talking to patients.

Signals from the Profession

Students suggested that they received clear signals concerning the attributes required of medical practitioners. This was from overt teaching and from more tacit understandings of what medicine entails. As one student said:

> You need to be able to communicate with people, speak to them – it's not just about knowing the things, you need to know but being able to talk to people... Communication, certainly and other things are just part of what we do.

Communication was therefore perceived as integral to the role whether managing a team, interacting with other professions, or communicating with patients.

Medical students were aware of the need to enhance their employability and 'build a CV'. They were conscious that they needed to pass their finals but also concentrate on securing junior jobs. As one participant suggested, 'some jobs will have about 130 applicants for a post so you need to be able to stand out as different and more able'. Those we spoke to were clear that it was 'not just all about grades' but also about 'being able to market yourself', and many were involved in extra-curricular activities such as orchestras, sport and understood that these facilitated the development of teamwork, leadership, and 'life skills'.

In addition, comments were deeply embedded in a professional context. Graduate attributes such as communication, problem-solving, and teamwork were not seen as generic in a non-disciplinary sense, although they *may* be considered as transferrable between specialties and contexts.

Law

Signals from Teaching

Students identified graduate attributes associated directly with coursework, including teamwork, communication, managing information, constructing a case, and research. Students suggested these skills were developed as part of the formal curriculum to varying degrees. Through the dissertation, they learned research skills, an ability to focus, negotiate large amounts of information, and develop fluent writing skills. They learned communication skills through shorter writing exercises and presentations. Problem-based courses facilitated development of skills such as teamwork, time management, communication, managing information, giving and receiving feedback, dealing with stressful situations, and taking on a case that modelled the 'real world'. They viewed development of these skills as an integral part of their coursework although they took them more seriously if they were assessed. Students expressed greater clarity about the messages received from the classroom rather than the professional context and ideas about 'being a lawyer' seemed to be mediated through the classroom. This is perhaps because law students, unlike medical students, have less active contact with the profession before graduation.

Signals from Outside the Classroom

Alongside developing skills and attributes in the classroom, law students gained confidence from activities outside the classroom such as committees and clubs. They argued that these activities developed the ability to organise and to try new things:

> If I was given something new by an employer and I hadn't a clue how to do it... it wouldn't phase me. If you are doing that kind of thing around your peers and friends you don't want to look a fool in front of, it can give you that extra bit of confidence you maybe wouldn't get in class.

History

Signals from the University

With regard to signals from the university from tangible sources, students were not entirely clear as to what graduate attributes were, suggesting 'I assume you mean the skills you leave university with'. One student said it was the first time she had heard of them, others thought they were learning outcomes or the 'things you can put on a CV'. Another suggested that there was a disjuncture between the (vague) idea of graduate attributes that they had received from university communications and the messages they were receiving in class:

> I don't know if [graduate attributes] always correlates with what we actually do in class. I think they sometimes write things down and obviously it doesn't quite correlate in class really. It depends on how much they get you to do group work and that kind of thing.

Signals from the Classroom

Students were ambivalent about signals received from class about graduate attributes:

> I don't know if many historians or history students would be that interested. We got a lecture at the beginning of the year basically telling us that history students need to think about their careers after university...I don't know, maybe we are too stuck in the past and we don't want to think about that kind of thing.

This student also suggested that graduate attributes could be made more overt in class; for example, tutors could explain what attributes were being taught and then students may be better able to transfer these skills outside of the classroom. However, another suggested that it *was* present in their formal teaching although she was a bit dismissive:

> It is sometimes in course documents. What they are trying to aim for and sometimes they bandy around the term.

Signals from the Discipline

When talking about history as a discipline, participants were clear that they could identify the attributes of a historian and speak about this with enthusiasm and a certain confidence and assurance:

> You have to pick from [secondary sources] and give a presentation. So you are trying to communicate something quickly and concisely. So the skill is which bit to use.

Other attributes that history students identified as essential for historians included research skills, confidence, time management, self-motivation, communication (written and spoken), analytic skills, weighing up evidence, and understanding ambiguity. A sophisticated understanding of the ways in which historians think was evident: 'everything is in the detail and silences, actually what they don't say. You really have to read between the lines'. Students spoke eagerly of the 'passion' of being an historian.

Signals from Potential Employers

Paradoxically, although history students suggested they were not interested in graduate attributes for employability and did not think a great deal about post-university employment, they were able to articulate the ways in which the attributes gained at university could be valuable for employment. For example, clear links between research skills learned in history and their applicability in employment were drawn:

History is all about research, you have to learn to love the research...I just did a presentation which I had to show my staff how dealing with customer service is financially beneficial to them in terms of the tips and statistics... This is the skill set given to me at university.

As history students often did not gain employment in history, many took cues regarding graduate attributes from elsewhere. For example, one student referred to someone who had studied at the same university: 'she has taken on a lot of skills that she learnt at university but she also said that she didn't really need her degree'.

Skills learnt in a work context contributed to their understanding of graduate attributes. For one student, her work in the archives and museum promoted the importance of communicating with different audiences and research skills. For another, her career outside history in combination with her studies gave her confidence and awareness of attributes required for employment. At 21, she had been a student and a manager and so understood the importance of attention to detail: 'this is something that history does particularly well and the fact that you can do things very methodically. I think they are interchangeable, definitely'. Another said teamwork and communication were valued in her summer work at an accounting firm.

Students suggest they are under pressure to get good grades and enhance their competitiveness through developing 'unique' qualities in addition to their studies. Indeed, some students suggest that a good degree will not be the most important thing in an interview because it doesn't 'speak':

So while you are working hard and you want to get a good degree, I think it doesn't really speak in an interview. There is a lot more you should be doing and I am thinking about what people look for and what is unique.

Like students in medicine, these students were receiving clear signals that they needed to 'sell themselves' and that it was not enough to get good grades and have a range of skills, they must also be able to articulate these in a way that is attractive to employers.

Business and Management

Signals from the University

These students linked the idea of graduate attributes directly with post-university employability. One suggested that the messages were not sufficiently clear:

> I think people should pick it up but I suppose not everybody is forward thinking so maybe it should be pointed out from first and second year.

Moreover, students suggested that their peers assumed things about future employment opportunities that were not necessarily true and if messages were clearer this would be helpful:

> I think when a lot of people graduate they say there are no jobs out there but there are hundreds of jobs. They don't realize it from uni. For instance I have been up for trainee accountancy roles. People on my course say but you haven't studied accountancy and I say well, you don't have to have studied accountancy. You need to have skills and a 2:1.

Signals from the Classroom

The key graduate attributes students identified from formal teaching included critical thinking, analysis, teamwork, communication skills and giving presentations but this was not always overt:

> Essay writing improves your transferrable skills and if you do presentations it improves your confidence. It's not directly taught but they come through the classes.

However, for some, the signals were clear and they understood, for example, about presentation skills, teamwork, and time management, and these were a fundamental part of some projects and assessed accordingly:

Right from second year management we had a group project that involved working in a group. So we were picking up teamwork skills, problem solving skills, organizational skills.

Students suggested that there was a distinction between skills and dispositions, suggesting:

I don't know if you need to have skills, rather than showing you have initiative and drive.

The key graduate attributes students developed from coursework were critical thinking and time management, particularly as part of the dissertation. However, the signals were not explicit:

I would maybe make it more integral to the courses and not just what they are trying to teach in the subject area but maybe integrate so that attributes are more prominent. Not just trying to teach you about this x y or z or this subject area but attributes are a priority as well. For the students it would make a lot of the courses seem more relevant.

Some of the students interviewed argued that it would be helpful to be clearer about what attributes they have learnt. They argued that while many graduate attributes were acquired as an integral part of coursework, they often seemed buried within it. As a consequence, students focused on the task and content knowledge without necessarily reflecting on other attributes such as critical thinking that were potentially more beneficial for their future.

Signals from the Discipline

Management students did not express a coherent understanding of the ways in which graduate attributes were central to their discipline. This may be because management, as an eclectic field, does not have a clear disciplinary identity, drawing on a number of academic and professional areas including marketing, finance, psychology, and sociology. Students identified particular class activities rather than a holistic disciplinary view.

Signals from Potential Employers

Students discussed links between their studies and employment and the need to identify and develop attributes that employers required. Some saw their degree as a small part of job-finding success:

> Obviously your overall degree grade counts but that is like just minimal percentage of what they actually look for. So what they look for is time management skills, leadership skills, if you have all these things and you can demonstrate that you have done them, that is what they care about.

Skills, such as time management, were developed through employment rather than from coursework alone. Working for a bank while studying gave one student a sense of responsibility:

> Your course work is just for yourself. When you are working for a bank and you make a mistake you are going to lose money, you pick up this higher level of responsibility. You know how to be more precise because there is more weight on it that what you get at university.

Students received messages from potential employers through job applications and interviews and understood that employers were looking for more than a degree alone:

> I don't think getting a degree is enough. They want you, I guess, to have pushed yourself. Put yourself into situations where you aren't that comfortable.

Discussion and Conclusions

This chapter seeks to contribute to our understanding of graduate attributes by examining how students conceptualise graduate attributes and to what extent their interpretations are influenced by other stakeholders; an area that has been largely overlooked in the literature, drawing on signalling theory as a theoretical lens to unpack the ways in which students socially construct and frame the notion of graduate attributes. We argue that students actively make sense of a myriad of signals from a variety of sources and are far from passive agents. Their view of the attributes with which they will leave university is varied, and as the analysis of the interviews has demonstrated, there is no unified voice.

Our findings revealed that the term 'graduate attributes' was not central to student thinking. In essence, the concept effectively holds meaning for those within the academy but has failed to filter through to those who are the principal focus of the concept and associated policies. Although there was a central university commitment to graduate attributes, this had not effectively been communicated to students.

However, students were clear that there were a number of important capabilities that they would take with them on graduation, some of which would facilitate future employment. More specifically, students saw a clear connection between attributes and employability, albeit not uniformly. Importantly, students' ideas about what they would take with them varied—between disciplines particularly but also within disciplines. Many students perceived the notion as a list of skills and abilities that graduates should possess in order to be 'work ready'. Unsurprisingly, the detail differed across academic disciplines; for example, medical students focused on communication and history students on research. However, while employability was clearly on the radar, this was disciplinary in focus (with the possible exception of the management students) even if they did not anticipate employment in their field of study. Students argued that concentration on the 'content' areas of their chosen fields developed a range of capabilities that would be essential in employment, augmented by extra-curricular activities.

A minority of students considered graduate attributes in holistic terms placing greater weight on tacit experiences garnered at university. For example, one student (management) commented:

I don't think you're formally learning about it and nobody stands there and tells you, this is what you will need to know but I think in general a university experience, you're subconsciously learning or becoming aware, it's not printed out and given to you on a bit of paper.

The notion of global citizenship and the broader social agenda of universities was conspicuous by its absence. No student, regardless of the discipline, alluded to graduates as socially informed global citizens. The meaning attached to economic messages appears to have crowded out social and democratic imperatives to the extent that they did not figure in students' conversations.

Signals from the central university were not received clearly by the students. This may not be because the university neglected to transmit messages but rather that students identified more strongly with their department and course. Possibly students did not pick up these signals, because they were buried in infrequently visited websites, or because they were deemed 'generic' hence too vague to be applicable. In addition, signals from the central university may have been drowned out by more immediate signals from those in closer proximity—their teachers and employers.

In making sense of the array of signals associated with graduate attributes, students interpret and draw meaning from the term in a multi-layered way that is deeply embedded within their discipline; such interpretations are in sharp relief from espoused university strategies which appeared to be muffled at best. This may in part stem from how students prioritise the myriad messages from the university. Given their identity is often firmly rooted in their discipline or future profession, students interpreted communication from departments and individual teachers as more meaningful and as such gave these messages precedence. As such, although the university's approach to graduate attributes was monolithic, students' responses varied—primarily by discipline but also within each discipline.

A strong theme was the importance attributed to the prevailing disciplinary paradigm in framing graduate attributes. Medical students unequivocally viewed graduate attributes as central to their training. Such attributes were not construed as generic but as essential to be good *doctors* and integral to the application of medical knowledge. These students privileged signals from teaching staff, both clinical and university, articulated as curriculum and allied with employability and 'marketability'.

For law students, the most powerful signals were from the classroom and most valued if assessed and centred around those skills perceived to be useful for law such as analysing large amounts of information and fluent communication.

History students were categorically disinterested in 'generic' skills yet able to provide a textured analysis of the attributes of the discipline and the very essence of what it meant to be a historian. The identity of a historian encompassed critical elements of graduate attributes such as criticality, writerliness, attention to detail, and the ability to find evidence. While they expressed interest in a clearer articulation of ways in which these skills could be transferred to other contexts, such as employment settings, they were emphatic about how their skills and capabilities could be applied. Moreover, they did not voice any doubts that they would gain employment. Nonetheless, such thoughts of the future were perceived to be a distraction from their existing academic endeavours as their main interest, source of pride, and identity stemmed from being historians and the skills that this engenders.

Business and management students, in contrast, linked graduate attributes firmly with employability and suggested that messages came both from the classroom and their reading of potential employers' requirements. They felt, however, that graduate attributes were not overt or consistently evident in their courses but rather that a focus on academic content meant that they were 'buried'.

Graduate attributes are not 'de-disciplined' skills that can be taught independently of subject matter (Jones, 2009). Students expressed very little interest in central university signals, which were seen as separate from their immediate interests. Instead, they were concerned with the ways in which presentation skills, the ability to write well, the ability to research and organise material, work under pressure, communicate clearly, or analyse complex material were honed *as part of their learning*. While an earlier study considered the views of academic staff (Jones, 2009), the present student-centred study supports this. What is apparent is that if graduate attributes are to be taken seriously and to have a useful function in articulating what students leave university with, it is essential that they be expressed through, identified with, and taught within the context of the formal, discipline-based curriculum as well as encouraged through opportunities in the informal curriculum.

One apparent silence in the signals regarding graduate attributes in this particular context was counter signals from students. From our research, it appeared to be a unidirectional conversation and while students had strong and coherent opinions about graduate attributes expressed in the interviews, there seemed no clear channel for expression and no interest in the range of their views. At the moment, most of the focus on feedback to and from students is about coursework. Students receive feedback in the form of assessment, class contact, and so on, and teaching staff received feedback in the form of course evaluations and the NSS survey. However, there is less focus on dialogue between the university and its students regarding graduate attributes. This perhaps serves to weaken the signals. While students are not engaged in a conversation and not required to think critically about graduate attributes, then the university cannot know how students are engaging with these. The 'standard' student voice heard by the institution does not represent the myriad of perspectives presented here. By ignoring the range of views, the institution has no way of understanding how its messages are heard and interpreted.

One way of addressing this issue is for institutions to take a more nuanced approach to feedback and to value multiple ways of communicating with students (see also Chapter 7). In this way, there is greater opportunity for institutions to hear the range of student voices.

In conclusion, this chapter contributes to theorising graduate attributes by focusing on students' voices, thus giving expression to unheard perspectives. As this study shows, students are not passive. While existing studies focus on the definition and application of graduate attributes, by using signalling theory, this chapter makes some progress towards considering the process of facilitating the development of graduate attributes and where this appears to be faltering. In addition, this chapter also makes a clear contribution to academic practice. By considering how students prioritise messages, signalling theory begins to unpack the ways in which communication (and miscommunication) happens in universities. While there is still a lot more work to be done in this area, it raises questions about communication pathways and effectiveness.

References

Barrie, S. C. (2006). Understanding what we mean by generic attributes of graduates. *Higher Education, 51*(2), 215–241.

Barrie, S. C. (2012). A research-based approach to generic graduate attributes policy. *Higher Education Research and Development, 31*(1), 79–92.

Bowden, J., Hart, G., King, B., Trigwell, K., & Watt, O. (2000). *Generic capabilities of ATN University graduates.* Retrieved from http://www.clt.uts.edu.au/ATN.grad.cap.project.index.html.

Bridgestock, R. (2009). The graduate attributes we've overlooked: Enhancing graduate employability through career management skills. *Higher Education Research and Development, 28*(1), 31–44.

Cavanagh, J., Burston, M., Southcombe, A., & Bartram, T. (2015). Contributing to a graduate-centred understanding of work readiness: An exploratory study of Australian undergraduate students' perceptions of their employability. *The International Journal of Management Education, 13,* 278–288.

Collini, S. (2017). *Speaking of universities.* London: Verso.

Connelly, B. L., Certo, S. T., Ireland, D., & Reutzel, C. R. (2011). Signaling theory: A review and assessment. *Journal of Management, 37*(1), 39–67.

Daniels, J., & Brooker, J. (2014). Student identity development in higher education: Implications for graduate attributes and work-readiness. *Educational Research, 56,* 65–76.

de la Harpe, B., & David, C. (2012). Major influences on teaching and assessment of graduate attributes. *Higher Education Research and Development, 31*(4), 493–510.

Fraser, K., & Thomas, T. (2013). Challenges of assuring the development of graduate attributes in a Bachelor of Arts. *Higher Education Research and Development, 32*(4), 545–560.

Hill, J., Walkington, H., & France, D. (2016). Graduate attributes: Implications for higher education practice and policy. *Journal of Geography in Higher Education, 40*(2), 155–163.

Holmes, L. (2001). Reconsidering graduate employability: The graduate identity approach. *Quality in Higher Education, 7*(2), 111–119.

Jones, A. (2009). Re-disciplining generic attributes: The disciplinary context in focus. *Studies in Higher Education, 34*(1), 85–100.

Mager, S., & Spronken-Smith, R. (2014). Graduate attribute attainment in a multi-level undergraduate geography course. *Journal of Geography in Higher Education, 38,* 238–250.

Mason, G., Williams, G., & Cranmer, S. (2009). Employability skills initiatives in higher education: What effects do they have on graduate labour market outcomes? *Education Economics, 17*(1), 1–30.

Moreau, M.-P., & Leathwood, C. (2006). Graduates' employment and the discourse of employability: A critical analysis. *Journal of Education and Work, 19*(4), 305–324.

Oliver, B. (2013). Graduate attributes as a focus of for institution-wide curriculum renewal: Innovations and challenges. *Higher Education Research and Development, 32*(3), 450–463.

Saunders, M. (2006). From organisms to boundaries: The uneven development of theory narratives in education, learning and work connections. *Journal of Education and Work, 19*(1), 1–27.

Spence, M. (1973). Job market signalling. *Quarterly Journal of Economics, 87,* 355–374.

Su, Y. (2014). Self-directed genuine graduate attributes: The person-based approach. *Higher Education Research and Development, 33*(6), 1208–1220.

Tomlinson, M. (2012). Graduate employability: A review of conceptual and empirical themes. *Higher Education Policy, 25,* 407–431.

Yorke, M. (2006). *Employability in higher education: What it is—What it is not.* New York: Higher Education Academy.

Yorke, M., & Knight, P. (2007). Evidence-informed pedagogy and the enhancement of student employability. *Teaching in Higher Education, 12*(2), 157–170.

Part IV

The Influence of Student Voices
on Academic Work

15

Valuing Uncertainty

Simon Lygo-Baker

Chapters within this book provide a series of articulations that suggest how the higher education sector has begun to recognise that hearing and then responding to the student voice and then working with it are important. However, as they also note, the notion that it is one single voice that can be engaged with is problematic and may alienate many such as Alexander (Chapter 2). The reasons higher education has recognised a student voice and how it has been engaged with are however complex and potentially multifaceted. They appear to range from positive engagement based on a pedagogical value placed on the co-creation of learning opportunities (Bovill, 2013), to a more negative element surrounding the additional authority given to the student body (Kandiko & Mawer, 2013). This latter development has been encouraged through the development of a transactional relationship prompted in the UK by the introduction of a tuition fee regime from 1998 and significant increases to this starting from 2006 (see Chapter 4). This has increased the influence of the student voice

S. Lygo-Baker (✉)
Department of Higher Education, University of Surrey, Guildford, UK
e-mail: s.lygo-baker@surrey.ac.uk

© The Author(s) 2019
S. Lygo-Baker et al. (eds.), *Engaging Student Voices in Higher Education*,
https://doi.org/10.1007/978-3-030-20824-0_15

but it is not the only shift that universities have had to contend with. The higher education sector has witnessed significant shifts in the past fifty years since Nisbet (1972) warned that universities were beginning to betray themselves in the ways that they responded. An end result of what Nisbet outlined, with significant power of prediction, was that the university would no longer be the real centre of learning.

This accusation has seen other writers follow this argument and present their own evidence. Readings (1996) and Barnett (2000), for example, both echo Nisbet, suggesting that the university has lost the identity it once possessed and is no longer the centre of knowledge creation, nor is it the place where ideas tend to surface. Instead, pressured by new discourses, universities have become preoccupied with the provision of greater efficiency (Deem, 1998) and with staff being required to achieve more with less (Cuthbert, 1996). As Clegg (2010) argued, the university has become increasingly focussed on producing graduates who are 'employment ready' and recent developments in the Teaching Excellence Framework (BIS, 2016) have reinforced this, furthering metrics that will reward universities whose students gain well-paid roles following graduation (see Chapter 8).

Is all lost therefore? This chapter argues not. It suggests that if we make use of the evidence base we have available to us and act upon this collaboratively with students then we can make use of the diverse voices that exist to reinvigorate approaches within our higher education institutions. This requires us to embrace uncertainty rather than try to reduce it because it is an important basis for learning (Jarvis, 2010). In so doing, the sector also has the opportunity to maintain our integrity (Palmer, 1998). Rather than seeing diverse student voices as threatening, such an approach I argue can help us to repurpose our teaching. For some time, it has been people beyond university who have questioned the role of those within higher education and suggested that the student voice should be more closely listened to. Through a range of 'market driven' responses, Tomlinson (2017) argues that student expectations about their university experience have been raised. It is time that the academy responded and took back the professional autonomy that has been eroded. How? By doing what academic practice provides the opportunity to undertake: the ability to articulate and then explore particular questions relating to the complex interrelationship between learning and teaching. A key initial question is to ask what the different voices are and to find ways to engage them in meaningful discourse. This may provide evidence upon which future actions can be established. To not do this risks further eroding our autonomy as educators (Biesta, 2015), removing the professionalism that previously defined the role (Piper, 1992).

This is not to encourage arrogance or an aloof approach to others by those from within the academy. Such behaviour is only likely to be met with negative responses that may be used to justify further limits being placed upon the profession that erode the opportunities of academic staff to act independently. This can undermine professionalism, which Friedson (1994) argued was defined by individuals through an ability to deal with complex knowledge structures and to be able to regulate how this was utilised and therefore ultimately how the role was performed. However, there is evidence to suggest that trust in the professions to undertake such self-regulation has been eroded. In higher education, the repercussions have been greater state involvement and manipulation of the context within which learning occurs. This has seen a corresponding rise of managerialism as senior university staff have attempted to respond to the complex challenges they face through an increase in bureaucracy (Davis, Jansen van Rensburg, & Venter, 2016). It has been suggested that in part this has manifested itself through greater coercion being applied towards academic staff, who have responded by increasingly surrendering aspects of their autonomy as a way of retaining some element of control (Alvesson & Spicer, 2016). Against a backdrop of increased central recognition of a student voice, greater pressure has been placed on academics to respond with less authority to the wishes of their learners, leading to accusations by some academics of pressure to spoon-feed students (Dehler & Welsh, 2014). Ultimately, this serves neither the learner nor the teacher well.

The changes in behaviour by university management are perhaps not unexpected and may not be entirely without foundation. In a situation where society faces an increasingly challenging future (Beck, 1992), in a fluid (Bauman, 2000) and unpredictable world (Giddens, 2003), attempting to bring a sense of control, a sense of order to the uncertainty being faced, is perhaps understandable human trait. After all, much of our university research is based upon a human desire to bring understanding and to be able to predict that following action A the likely outcome is B. As such it follows that in response to greater uncertainty, university management seek to limit risk through prediction in order to create greater stability. This appears to be done by engaging with the sources (voices) that appear to be speaking the loudest and have the greatest potential influence.

Prediction

According to psychologists, attempts to predict what will happen are deeply embedded within humans as a survival mechanism. The philosopher Kant (1979) argued that we look to the past in order for us to 'foresee' what is ahead: in other words, to predict the future. However, the desire for the certain, the knowable, is a feature that Beck (1992) argues is ultimately no longer possible. The risks faced have become 'omnipresent' and, to make it even more difficult, somewhat invisible (Hollway & Jefferson, 1997).

However, it would appear we remain determined wherever possible to try to bring some order to the uncertainty that prevails. The development of learning analytics and the creation of 'big data', for example, suggest opportunities to establish a variety of algorithms that purport to enhance our predictive capabilities, despite the potential for such to come at a cost of removing the outliers who may actually offer alternatives (Rosenblat, Kneese, & Boyd, 2014). However, as humans we typically ask questions, seeking to find an answer that can be seen to reduce our uncertainty. According to Hollway and Jefferson (1997), this has been encouraged by the science of probability and the suggestion that, on this basis, more rational decisions can be made. As such, risk becomes visible and subsequently we appear to be able to remove the discomfort of uncertainty. Such an approach appears to work on the premise that the more we understand the less is unknown.

Rebalancing the Value of Uncertainty

So far we have seen that the notion of uncertainty appears to be aligned to an unwelcome experience that leads to forms of instability and wherever possible should be reduced. Uncertainty causes concern because it suggests that we are not able to control our destiny or the outcomes of our actions. This, rather than being acknowledged as inevitable given the complexity that exists, has rather been posited as a failing, a flaw in our character that suggests an inability to respond to the challenges faced. However, I would argue that uncertainty can be viewed differently. It need not be seen as a purely negative experience. Rather it can be used as a way to draw people in, as a way of engaging them with their curiosity which can bring forth an increase in our interest of the area under examination. Subsequently, we pay more attention and potentially it can cause us to think more about our actions.

There is a tendency to suggest that learners wish to have uncertainty removed. Much of the conversation I hear suggests that our learners enter higher education with a desire to be 'spoon-fed' following schooling that has removed alternative perspectives and provided a clarity that appears to be comforting (Wingate, 2007). This is not the fault of school teachers; they are encouraged by targets and policy directives to ensure that pupil uncertainty is reduced. These actions have been encouraged by the increased strength of parental voices based on a notion of their right to intervene and require particular responses from teachers and schools. The arrival at university of students, where parents have less influence, may offer an opportunity to rebalance this approach, a role the university has fulfilled perhaps more adeptly within previous decades. More recently however I have recognised the pressure felt by academic staff to teach content and 'the known' rather than embrace uncertainty through questions to which we have yet to establish plausible responses. Universities appear to be increasingly enticed by student evaluations, management requirements for consistency and quality assurance to behave in ways that alleviate the uncertain: seduced by an apparent removal of risk.

However, uncertainty is an unavoidable and necessary element to the learning process. Whilst there remain significant debates, particularly within psychology, as to how to define learning (De Houwer, Barnes-Holmes, & Moors, 2013), the notion of change is somewhat constant within the different narratives. If learning is therefore related to elements of a change from a particular state of not recognising, knowing, or doing to a point where we do recognise, know, or can do, then it suggests that uncertainty is an essential aspect of the learning process. To become aware of something, or to learn it, is to recognise that prior to that point you were unaware or unable to make use of it. Whilst we may only know this following the point at which it becomes clear, much of the time, particularly in formal education, we begin from the perspective that the role of the teachers is to take the learner from this point of not being aware or able to one where they are cognisant. The difficulty arises when the new understanding is viewed as an end: learning therefore appears finite. When the learner believes that they have reached a point where there is nothing else to know, or perhaps more importantly nothing new to question (Firestein, 2012), then uncertainty is removed and no longer appears problematic, which can appear seductive. Increasingly, I hear academic staff concerned that learners are ultimately concerned with knowing which point they need to reach before they can stop, an aspect that may lie behind the criticisms of learning outcomes (Hussey & Smith, 2002); the point at which uncertainty is removed and they can be comfortable that this knowledge will suffice, as if reaching a particular threshold. It will answer the question that will be framed within a summative test. Whilst this is clearly not generalisable, there is a concern that this experience is a growing trend, encouraged increasingly from an early age where students are taught to a particular point and the opportunity to explore outside known frames is something that is not encouraged. Rather than celebrating uncertainty as an area to explore, the removal of it becomes the ultimate aim.

However, if learning comes from change this suggests that uncertainty is always present in some form, and that it is a necessary part of the evolution as learners. We may wish to remove it; indeed, it is uncertainty that acts as the spur but ultimately complete removal is impossible. Peter Jarvis (2009) argued that whilst being in harmony with our surroundings is a comfortable state to experience, we are mostly in a state of disjuncture. Here we find ourselves presented with challenges for which our current understanding is not sufficient and cannot provide an adequate answer. According to Jarvis, our options are to reject the issue or to change by employing a different idea or approach.

Teaching

The premise of teaching may appear troubled by these definitions. Surely a teacher is there to provide clarity and reduce uncertainty by providing the correct answer, or at least showing the way, making the troubled waters calm and navigable? If uncertainty must remain, then we may need to reconceive of our understanding of the role of the teacher. This is particularly the case within higher education, where there are qualitatively different ways of experiencing and explaining teaching that come forward when this question is posed (Dall'Alba, 1994).

For those who have been teaching in university in the UK and not directly influenced by the development of the universal framework established initially by the Institute of Learning and Teaching in Higher Education (subsequently the Higher Education Academy and now Advance HE), there has been significant freedom in developing an independent teaching approach celebrating difference and uncertainty. Even for those working towards fellowship, and therefore working within the UKPSF framework, there remains a wide variety of practice and definitions of how to describe and articulate the role of the teacher and much of what exists remains contested. However, some have questioned whether the focus of such a framework has potentially a more Machiavellian purpose (Furedi, 2004) or at least outcome. These people see that applied in the absence of personal values the end result is the depersonalisation of approaches to teaching. There is a reduction of alternatives, and this may appear to be encouraged through a combination of external groups helping to provide greater authority to the student body through a particular definition of a student voice. This voice, channelled through such a framework, can make demands that aim to reduce uncertainty through a particular approach to teaching that may appear rational, although ultimately flawed.

The argument can be made as follows. Following the Dearing Report (1997) and the recommendation to focus more upon the quality of teaching, scrutiny has increased. However, over time the language that has surrounded the debates has shifted away from a direct focus on teaching itself, to a broader remit considering student learning and the student experience and now even encompasses student employability (see Chapter 8). As these discourses have developed, there has been an increase both in the questioning of the autonomy of professionals to manage themselves, and the financial commitment of those attending as learners (Bunce, Baird, & Jones, 2017; see Chapter 4). It would perhaps be expected that when these arguments are put together there is a swell of support that appears to legitimise a dominant discourse that questions the authority of an academic to design and develop learning without recourse to involving the voice of the learner.

Whilst the majority of teachers I have had the privilege to work with in higher education would undoubtedly support the notion of engaging productively with learners, in reality it is more difficult than policy-makers may have people believe. Does a class all speak with one unified voice? That may depend in part on the question asked or the experience they have been through. As researchers, we tend to know that you get data that you screen for. Therefore, it depends a great deal on the question we ask our learners. If, for example, we ask learners following a series of lectures whether they would like access to recorded lecture material, the answer is likely to be almost universally affirmative. However, if we were to ask, 'how would you like to engage with the learning material?' the answers may be more variable. The former question is leading and therefore likely to gain a more unified response. This then raises further questions. First, if we ask the latter, more pedagogically sound, question, How do we get to hear the different responses? If we are not careful, we are likely to merely hear the loudest or most regular voice in the group. For example, there are a range of voices in any one classroom: Which of these do you connect with as a teacher? Second, is it, as Bentham asked, a question of the greatest happiness for the greatest number? But what if the greatest happiness is actually only for the few, often the loudest or more assertive? Is that what we mean by engaging with the student voice? And how do we respond to enable the greatest happiness? Take away the uncertainty to make things appear comfortable? Is this what brings forth effective learning?

So do we need to respond to all the different voices? Can we? To try would be to take an extreme interpretation of differentiation and is likely to prove counterproductive. Nobody can adapt to each individual voice that they teach. A more measured understanding of differentiation suggests the need for teachers to offer alternatives, to provide a diverse approach that is likely to offer opportunities for learners that may not otherwise be activated, responding to different voices but not all at once; in other words, teaching through uncertainty.

Teaching Through Uncertainty

With the increased focus on the quality of teaching in higher education towards the end of the last century, there was an increased number of publications and research that suggested how this could be enhanced (e.g. Fry, Ketteridge, & Marshall, 1999; Ramsden, 1992). Unfortunately, this may have proved problematic as people were seeking certainty from an emerging discipline that lacked a substantial evidence base (Helsing, 2007). Staff in university, asked to reconsider the role of teaching, looked to others for support and ideas that could enhance their practice. Many of the ideas purported to offer a panacea, or even if they did not were initially appropriated as if they did. Some however remained deeply sceptical of such suggestions. The challenge was often that the idea being offered needed adaptation to a particular disciplinary context. Often this was missing, or at least the lack of imagination or willingness to adapt was apparent. As a consequence, whilst approaches were put forward that may have provided greater opportunities for successful learning, ultimately a search for a generalisable approach that could be adopted 'off the shelf' proved illusory and academic development as a field was often distrusted.

That is not to suggest that progress has not been made. Without a doubt, the quality of teaching that students receive at university has generally improved. But this is worth further reflecting upon. There always were outstanding teachers in universities and there still are. In addition, the increased scrutiny has undoubtedly raised the general quality of the student learning experience. The learning environment is often unrecognisable from that which existed twenty years ago. The consequence is that the student results have certainly improved, although the notion of 'grade-inflation' (Bachan, 2017) may have masked the improvement that has taken place, or at least reduced the visible impact. In addition, the massification (Giannakis & Bullivant, 2016) that has occurred in the UK whilst offering opportunities for more of the population to attend university also causes additional challenges. Whilst there are positive aspects to the increase, it asks more questions of the curriculum, with more voices involved. Additionally, the context against which the changes have occurred should be critically evaluated.

Few of those in the university would resist opportunities to enhance the quality of student learning. However, it is not necessarily as simple as that may appear. The pressure upon staff to constantly improve the opportunities available, to be responsive to the learners, to ensure that standards are always on the increase, is inevitably ultimately flawed. Without doubt, a significant benefit has been a growing willingness, or perhaps in some instances pressure, to engage more closely with the recipients of our teaching. This has established a dialogue between university staff representing different roles and our learners (e.g. senior management with the student union, and teaching staff with student course representatives). These different dialogues offer opportunities to explore how teaching and learning relate to one another, to explore the opportunities that can be exist if we work to embrace uncertainty and not attempt to reduce it.

The link between the role of the teacher and how learning occurs is interconnected but remains complex which brings us back to uncertainty and the student voice. We have teachers, newly invested either intrinsically or extrinsically, with enhancing their teaching approach in order to improve opportunities for learning with an emergent and strengthening student voice. The problem is that both the link and the voice can prove to be illusions or at best, variable. As a teacher, for example, which voice do you listen to? It may appear a cacophony at times—with so many voices available, causing confusion and the temptation is to listen to the loudest voice or that which appears to have the greatest authority and label this the student voice. For the individual academic, this may be a voice that has been translated through senior management and into a particular policy and is reframed through a number of different interpretations within a department even before being heard by the individual teacher. However, it may sometimes be hard to hear this voice against the background of the voices of the different students present in your own classroom, and the voice you have that speaks to you from your own values (Breakwell, 1986).

The danger is that in trying to respond to different expectations, we try to remove things that cause discomfort and yet this may be counterproductive. Think back to the teacher that extended your own thinking: the teacher who got you to see alternatives, to become the learner you have become. Did they do so by providing you with all the knowledge and understanding you have today, or did they allow you to apply your thoughts, to see alternatives, to be creative with an enthusiasm that inspired you? The different voices that exist do not necessarily need to be seen as threatening; rather, they can be viewed as providing an opportunity to explore new directions. They provide new contexts, new ideas and new ways of establishing dialogue that allows teaching to occur not through a series of answers that are prescribed but are exciting by being uncertain themselves. Rather than seeking to hear and engage with the dominant voice, we can instead enjoy listening and engaging with diverse voices, enjoying the added uncertainty that this brings to our class. In doing so, we may not miss the voices of students such as Alexander (see Chapter 2) whose experience is ultimately one of feeling that nobody was listening.

Teaching with uncertainty is not to be viewed as the same as teaching without care or thought. It allows the celebration of the fact that what we have control over is somewhat limited and that we can share the responsibility for the exploration of the unknown with others—learners, colleagues and collaborators. To celebrate the uncertainty, enjoying the experience of exploring with others interested in a similar journey, without knowing where that may take us to by the end. As a teacher, we retain responsibility for setting some of the parameters within which that journey can occur. As the physicist Eric Mazur (1996) suggests however, teaching the known may be less valuable than exploring the uncertainty that moves each discipline forward. There is so much we do not understand in each discipline (Firestein, 2012) and the opportunity to celebrate this with those who have chosen to study our discipline and who may ask new and as yet unformed questions, reverting to more childlike enjoyment of asking 'why', offers significant possibilities but only if we embrace these opportunities and celebrate the uncertainty.

Approaching teaching with uncertainty may be challenging if we look to the frames within which we develop our teaching as limiting, moving towards a consensus that ultimately suggests that the best teacher is not armed with free will but rather follows a set and predetermined format. Such an interpretation of the role of the teacher requires us merely to provide a consistent approach at all times, to ensure all the learners achieve a particular level based on a set of learning outcomes that outline the minimum to be achieved. At the extreme, this appears to mirror a somewhat Orwellian outcome based on a positivist view of learning that may preclude what it is to be human: that is the ability to act differently, to have a different voice. Rather it suggests that teachers should speak with one voice, objectively developing teaching opportunities for learners who whilst increasingly vocal, are ultimately all asking the same thing: What is the answer?

However, I suggest that to maintain our integrity as teachers (Palmer, 1998) we should embrace uncertainty and use this as the basis for our teaching. This offers the additional benefit of drawing together two often disparate aspects of academic work. As Boyer (1990) argued, rather than fragmenting our role into teaching and research, we can use an understanding of scholarship as potentially uniting. The opportunity to engage in inquiry offers this, as it enables us to pose questions and challenges to our learners, to encourage adventures into uncertainty and then to embrace and listen to the different voices of those present. As our classes grow in diversity, we have the opportunity to have more divergent conversations that bring in more that we may not have previously considered. This is not to encourage chaos in the curriculum but rather to see the known not as an end point but as the start. As such, we take the suggestion of Mazur forward, that the skill of the teacher is not to merely to replicate the text but to see how we can use this with the learners to establish new combinations and establish new ideas. That is and has to be teaching with uncertainty. It may seem brave, it may seem counter-intuitive, but only because we currently only engage with a voice that has encouraged us to view learning and teaching in a limited manner. If we open our ears to the other voices, then we have the opportunity to be the inspirational teachers who we remember and who infused our learning with questions, inculcating within us a sense of opportunity to create and to contribute to future questions that can excite future generations.

References

Alvesson, M., & Spicer, A. (2016). (Un)Conditional surrender? Why do professionals willingly comply with managerialism? *Journal of Organisational Change Management, 29*(1), 29–45.

Bachan, R. (2017). Grade inflation in UK higher education. *Studies in Higher Education, 42*(8), 1580–1600.

Barnett, R. (2000). University knowledge in an age of supercomplexity. *Higher Education, 40*(4), 409–422.

Bauman, Z. (2000). *Liquid modernity.* Cambridge: Polity.

Beck, U. (1992). *Risk society: Towards a new modernity.* London: Sage.

Biesta, G. (2015). What is education for? On good education, teacher judgement and educational professionalism. *International Journal of Education, 50*(1), 75–87.

Bovill, C. (2013). Students and staff co-creating curricula: An example of good practice in higher education? In E. Dunne & D. Owen (Eds.), *The student engagement handbook: Practice in higher education* (pp. 461–476). Bingley, UK: Emerald Publishing.

Boyer, E. L. (1990). *Scholarship reconsidered: Priorities of the professoriate.* New York: Wiley.

Breakwell, G. (1986). *Coping with threatened identities.* London: Methuen.

Bunce, L., Baird, A., & Jones, S. E. (2017). The student-as-consumer approach in higher education and its effects on academic performance. *Studies in Higher Education, 42*(11), 1958–1978.

Clegg, S. (2010). Time future—The dominant discourse of higher education. *Time and Society, 19*(3), 345–364.

Cuthbert, R. (1996). *Working in higher education.* Buckingham: Open University Press.

Dall'Alba, G. (1994). The role of teaching in higher education: Enabling students to enter a field of study and practice. *Learning and Instruction, 3,* 299–313.

Davis, A., Jansen van Rensburg, M., & Venter, P. (2016). The impact of managerialism on the strategy work of university middle managers. *Studies in Higher Education, 41*(8), 1480–1494.

Dearing, R. (1997). *The Dearing report, higher education in the learning society.* London: The National Committee of Inquiry into Higher Education. Retrieved from http://www.educationengland.org.uk/documents/dearing1997/dearing1997.html.

Deem, R. (1998). 'New managerialism' and higher education: The management of performances and cultures in universities in the United Kingdom. *International Studies in Sociology of Education, 8*(1), 47–70.

Dehler, G. E., & Welsh, M. A. (2014). Against spoon-feeding: For learning. reflections on students' claims to knowledge. *Journal of Management Education, 38*(6), 875–893.

De Houwer, J., Barnes-Holmes, D., & Moors, A. (2013). What is learning? On the nature and merits of a functional definition of learning. *Psychonomic Bulletin & Review, 20*(4), 631–642.

Department for Business, Innovation, and Skills. (2016). *Success as a knowledge economy: Teaching excellence, social mobility and student choice.* London: BIS.

Firestein, S. (2012). *Ignorance: How it drives science.* Oxford: Oxford University Press.

Friedson, E. (1994). *Professionalism reborn.* Chicago: Chicago University Press.

Fry, H., Ketteridge, S., & Marshall, S. (Eds.). (1999). *A handbook for teaching and learning in higher education.* London: Kogan Page.

Furedi, F. (2004, January 30). Don't underestimate managers' ability to treat you as an idiot. *The Times Higher Educational Supplement.*

Giannakis, M., & Bullivant, N. (2016). The massification of higher education in the UK: Aspects of service quality. *Journal of Further and Higher Education, 40*(5), 630–648.

Giddens, A. (2003). *Runaway world.* New York: Routledge.

Helsing, D. (2007). Regarding uncertainty in teachers and teaching. *Teaching and Teacher Education, 23,* 1317–1333.

Hollway, W., & Jefferson, T. (1997). The risk society in an age of anxiety: Situating fear of crime. *British Journal of Sociology, 48*(2), 255–266.

Hussey, T., & Smith, P. (2002). The trouble with learning outcomes. *Active Learning in Higher Education, 3*(3), 220–233.

Jarvis, P. (Ed.). (2009). *The Routledge international handbook of lifelong learning.* Abingdon, UK: Routledge.

Jarvis, P. (2010). *Adult education and lifelong learning: Theory and practice* (4th ed.). Abingdon, UK: Routledge.

Kandiko, C. B., & Mawer, M. (2013). *Student expectations and perceptions of higher education.* London: King's Learning Institute.

Kant, I. (1979). *The conflict of the faculties.* New York: Arabis.

Mazur, E. (1996). *Peer instruction: a user's manual.* Mahwah, NJ: Prentice Hall.

Nisbet, R. A. (1972). The degradation of the academic dogma. *British Journal of Educational Studies, 20*(3), 335–336.

Palmer, P. (1998). *The courage to teach.* San Francisco: Jossey Bass.

Piper, D. W. (1992). Are professors professional? *Higher Education Quarterly, 46*(2), 145–156.

Ramsden, P. (1992). *Learning to teach in higher education.* London: Routledge.

Readings, W. (1996). *The university in ruins.* Cambridge, MA: Harvard University Press.

Rosenblat, A., Kneese, T., & Boyd, D. (2014, March). Predicting human behaviour. *The Social, Cultural & Ethical Dimensions of "Big Data".*

Tomlinson, M. (2017). Student perceptions of themselves as 'consumers' of higher education. *British Journal of Sociology of Education, 38*(4), 450–467.

Wingate, U. (2007). A framework for transition: Supporting 'learning to learn' in higher education. *Higher Education Quarterly, 61*(3), 391–405.

16

Pluralising 'Student Voices': Evaluating Teaching Practice

Adun Okupe and Emma Medland

Student Voice: Rising Power and Ensuing Tensions

The student voice has become increasingly powerful. This power is evident internationally: from the National Student Survey in the UK, to the Course Experience Questionnaire in Australia, and the National Survey of Student Engagement in the USA. In the UK, the perceived marketisation of the higher education sector due, in part, to the introduction of tuition fees (see Chapter 4), has resulted in rising student expectations and increasing competitiveness in the global education marketplace (Harvey, 2003). This has fuelled a rise in demand for the student voice to document the students' experience (Wong & Chiu, 2019), which, in turn, contributes to its power.

A. Okupe
The Sahara Centre, Lagos, Nigeria

E. Medland (✉)
Department of Higher Education, University of Surrey, Guildford, UK
e-mail: e.medland@surrey.ac.uk

© The Author(s) 2019
S. Lygo-Baker et al. (eds.), *Engaging Student Voices in Higher Education*,
https://doi.org/10.1007/978-3-030-20824-0_16

Within the UK, part of the power of the student voice lies in its influence over the position of higher education institutions in national league tables (Rienties, Li, & Marsh, 2015). Teachers are increasingly required to refer to student evaluations as evidence of their teaching effectiveness, although this rise in power has not been balanced by a commensurate focus on student responsibility in the learning and teaching process (Wong & Chiu, 2019). Indeed, the pressure to be popular and interesting can conflict with the role of the teacher as educator. This can result in teaching practice becoming a service with the teacher as provider, working on teaching efficiency so that students do not provide negative feedback (Wong & Chiu, 2019). As a result, students' comments can be viewed by teachers through a sceptical lens because they are often imposed on teachers by the institution, and students' responses 'cannot be challenged even if they are clearly contrary to the lecturer's own experience' (Leckey & Neill, 2001, p. 26).

Students' comments are important because this allows them to provide their views and experiences of teaching. Furthermore, in requesting student evaluation, the institution signals that it respects their views and takes them into account in decision-making. However, students' experience of university is gathered using national and institutional feedback instruments—typically questionnaires—to provide information on how the student population perceives the higher education institution (Leckey & Neill, 2001; Shah, Cheng, & Fitzgerald, 2017; Wong & Chiu, 2019). We argue that this use of questionnaires attempts to present a monolithic, coherent and homogenous student voice, resulting in a misguided conceptualisation of the students' experience. This conceptualisation fails to represent the diversity of the student population that typically includes part-time, distance, mature, international students, as well as those with disabilities and additional learning needs (Li, Marsh, & Rienties, 2016; Temple, Callender, Grove, & Kersh, 2016), to name but a few. In addition, as each student comes to university with a unique background that will colour his/her student life and expectations of teaching practice, the extent to which such students' experience can be understood and represented in a questionnaire requires critique.

Whilst questionnaires provide some insight into the students' experience, the multiple ways in which they are used—for quality assurance, teacher development, teacher assessment, teacher promotion (Johnson, 2000) and research on teaching (Richardson, 2010; Wiggins, 2010)—present complexity in the extent to which one instrument can meet the requirements of diverse stakeholders (i.e. government, institutions, employers, teachers, future students, and funding bodies; Shah et al., 2017). Given the multiple uses of students' evaluative comments, the power of the student voice becomes evident, as does the inherent complexity, requiring a pluralisation of its conceptualisation. We attempt to explore this premise by focusing on the relationship between students' evaluative comments and teaching practice.

In our attempt to understand the influence of students' evaluative comments on teaching practice, we considered the student evaluation process and the extent to which students' evaluative comments derived from different sources (i.e. individually and institutionally framed surveys) have different influences on teaching practice. The research underpinning this chapter indicates that even when asking the same group of students to evaluate their experiences of the same module, institutionally framed surveys can result in qualitatively different types of evaluative comments when compared to individually framed instruments developed by teaching staff. As such, our chapter highlights the heterogeneity of student voices and presents evidence of the influence of the tools designed to elicit these voices on the development of teaching practice.

Institutionally Framed Evaluation: A Flawed Instrument?

There is an increasing expectation for staff to adopt reflective and adaptive practices, informed by the students' experience. Reflection involves an element of observing challenges and focused attempts to solve problems by questioning the status quo (Larrivee, 2000). Student evaluation provide teachers with insights to the effectiveness of their teaching (Richardson, 2005), and can contribute to the process of reflection (Huxham et al., 2008) while also working to eliminate teacher danger of being 'trapped in unexamined judgements, interpretations, assumptions and expectations' (Larrivee, 2000, p. 294). Key to evaluation of teaching practice is how it is used to inform decision-making and/or teaching practice on a basis of continuous improvement.

Students' evaluative comments provide the opportunity to record students' experience and bring to the fore issues that may be unidentified and unresolved. The process of collecting feedback also provides a means to learn from the student population about how students perceive teachers. The instruments to collect student feedback range from informal discussions, group discussions and forums, to casual comments made by students in and outside the classroom or during student-staff faculty meetings, focus groups, and/or student diaries (Huxham et al., 2008). Rapid feedback instruments may also be used, where students provide individual and anonymous answers to short questions (e.g. What do you like about this module? What changes would you suggest making?; Huxham et al., 2008). This method obtains quick feedback, and the open-ended nature allows students to provide deeper information on fewer issues, providing more time to reflect. It also provides a form of focused guidance to teachers, enabling them to improve their teaching, and is quick to analyse (ibid.).

The student questionnaire is the most widely used form of teaching evaluation in the UK. However, it is not without criticism. The extent to which it is able to inform teaching enhancement has been debated due to its lack of flexibility, and its basis on traditional forms of teaching. Huxham et al. (2008, p. 676) have argued that the questionnaire 'often fails to improve teaching'. More recent articles highlight how these questionnaires are increasingly being used to examine and enhance the learning and teaching experience (e.g. Rienties, 2014). However, they are strongly resisted by staff (Crews & Curtis, 2011) as they '…don't ask quite the right questions in quite the right way for their practices, and are seen as a management instrument' (Bamber & Anderson, 2012, p. 13). In other words, module evaluation questionnaires (MEQs) can be used by institutional management to assess teaching effectiveness when considering promotion and tenure (Baldwin & Blattner, 2003). They can also condense student voices into a singular voice that does not reveal the multiplicity of student perspectives, and even where the student body is divided into categories (e.g. mature, international, part-time, etc.) in an attempt to provide a more diverse overview of students' experiences, this can still result in a dialogue with a particular group, or section of a university, often preventing or negating the voice of others being heard.

A further source of conflict perhaps lies in failing to acknowledge the different forms of questionnaires that exist, which serve different purposes. For instance, Harvey (2003, p. 6) notes that student questionnaires generally take one of five forms based on a hierarchy of levels: (1) Institution level; (2) Faculty level; (3) Programme level; (4) Module level; and (5) Teacher appraisal of student learning. More recently, an additional form has been established, that of national level, which has seemingly reduced the focus on institution- and faculty-level questionnaires as individual accountability increases (i.e. module- and individual-level). In essence, the appeal of engaging with a seemingly cohesive student voice appears to be irresistible, as both nationally and institutionally framed surveys proliferate and gain increasing credence. However, if one of the intentions of evaluating teaching practice is to enhance it, we question whether a standardised questionnaire, issued at the end of the semester, is the best tool for achieving this intention? (see also Chapter 7).

When designed appropriately, the teaching evaluation process can be used not only to benefit pedagogic practice, but also to provide students with the opportunity to reflect on their learning experiences and question their assumptions and expectations of their teachers. However, where evaluation is end-loaded and institutionally framed (e.g. the MEQ), the focus is overwhelmingly on teaching practice—what the teacher does and does not do—thereby handing the responsibility for learning, and for teaching, to teachers. Given that academic experience refers to learning *and* teaching (Harvey, 2003), to what extent are students engaged in *their* learning, within and outside of the classroom? Institutionally framed MEQs can neglect this in preference to aligning their instruments with the nationally framed student satisfaction surveys, once again handing responsibility back to the teachers for the entire learning experience of their students. In addition, the anonymous nature of comments provided by students may contribute to a focus on negative and poor performance, rather than providing qualitative information on how teaching practice may be enhanced. This is perhaps informed by the role of student evaluations in quality assurance decisions, which arguably do not focus on what students think is important, but rather on what teachers and managers think is important to the students (Harvey, 1999). The question then becomes, to what extent are MEQs the best tool for informing teaching development and where does responsibility lie for the evaluation and development of pedagogic practice?

Among other key criticisms of institutionally framed instruments is that MEQs are issued at the end of semester meaning that students are often not informed and do not benefit from the impact of their evaluation on the development of pedagogic practices. In other words, the feedback loop is not closed, as noted in Chapter 7. Other influential variables to take into consideration are response rates and the ability of students to evaluate teaching, as well as the nature, content, and purpose of students' evaluative comments. This is because the intent behind the evaluative comments will influence the instrument used and has the capacity to yield different results. Response rates are important as inferences are made about the population. Little consideration in relation to institutionally framed MEQs is given to developing students' ability to evaluate teaching, particularly in relation to their learning and teaching expectations. Yet, this is a fundamental point as students' comments are generally not challenged (Leckey & Neill, 2001), and this can serve to limit the extent to which they may be constructive (Cleary, Happell, Lau, & Mackey, 2013). Further, students' comments tend to focus on performance, such that teachers then become more strategic and focus on teaching efficiency to meet assessment requirements, without the same focus on teaching effectiveness (Richardson, 2010).

Different groups of students have different expectations of a teacher which requires a reflexive approach to teaching. Therefore, students' evaluative comments gathered earlier on in the semester may provide opportunities for the teacher to understand and clarify student expectations. In such cases, individually framed rapid response instruments can provide an avenue for students to reflect on the difference between their expectations of learning and teaching and also enable the teacher to provide an earlier response. As the instrument can be tailored to a particular purpose, it provides opportunities for teachers (and students, if handled appropriately) to acknowledge and appreciate the plurality of student voices. Such an appreciation can, in turn, illuminate the various angles from which teaching practice may be evaluated, depending on the characteristics of the student population. As such, rapid response instruments can provide opportunities for teacher development whilst also enhancing teaching effectiveness.

It is not the intention of the authors to encourage a move away from the use of institutionally framed instruments, but rather a call to acknowledge the different purposes and impact that each can result in, and the weaknesses associated with basing the evaluation of teaching practice on one instrument. For example, the qualitative comments tending to emerge from individually framed rapid response surveys provide a snapshot of each student's most pertinent experience of teaching at that point in time, which can provide greater insight into the reasons behind students' responses and the variety of students' experiences within a class. The quantitative comments from institutionally framed MEQs, on the other hand, provide a clear overview of the overall cohort experience that can allow for benchmarking teaching practice over time (Williams, Kane, Sagu, & Smith, 2008), but provide less information regarding the learning experience at an individual level (Richardson, 2010). Furthermore, when the feedback is analysed centrally or by an external agency, it becomes further removed from the teaching process and therefore can limit ownership and engagement, which can impact on response rates (Richardson, 2010). In other words, whilst MEQs focus on quality assurance through identifying consensus and generalising the students' experience through the identification of a singular student 'voice', rapid response instruments focus on quality enhancement through allowing multiple voices to come to the fore with a focus on the diversity of the students' experience.

Whilst institutions are required to 'demonstrate the value of their work' (Bamber & Anderson, 2012, p. 15), staff are perhaps more concerned with the evaluation and enhancement of teaching and learning. This has led Bamber and Anderson (2012, p. 15) to call for:

> ...separating out evaluation for assurance and evaluation for enhancement. The two will have some common ground, but the latter is much more likely to engage academics in action.

As a result, alternatives to the often reductionist and performative focus of institutionally framed surveys are beginning to emerge that encompass a range of student roles as a means of attempting to embrace the notion of pluralistic student voices. The student as evaluator is one of the five main roles that have been assumed for students (Seale, 2009) within the zeitgeist of the student voice movement. However, even if the pluralistic notion of student voices is accepted, it could be argued that this assumes that such voices are fixed and complete, which the personal experience outlined below would seem to contradict.

Personal Reflection of a Novice Teacher's Evaluative Journey

Receiving students' evaluative comments can be deeply emotional for novice teachers understandably nervous about the process of being evaluated (Flodén, 2016). The rationale for this chapter arose from the reflection on teaching practice by one of the authors (A. Okupe) when she was undertaking a Graduate Certificate in Learning and Teaching (GCLT), and her tutor (E. Medland). It was during one of the reflections that the realisation of the influence of students' evaluative comments on teaching practice, particularly for novice teachers, came about. In this section, we present a reflection on receiving students' comments as an evaluation of teaching practice by a novice teacher from two sources [(1) Institutionally framed MEQ; (2) Individually framed rapid response instrument], and how these evaluations influenced teaching practice.

As a novice teacher, I was not prepared for the experience of receiving students' evaluative comments and, as such, the experience of receiving the first set of comments on my teaching practice was emotional. As a student, I had given feedback on several occasions even though, upon reflection, I had little understanding of how to provide constructive comments or how these comments were going to be utilised by the university. Now as a novice teacher on the receiving end of students' evaluative comments, I reflect upon the impact of this highly emotive experience.

I taught a class of 25 undergraduate students over the course of two semesters. My Programme Director asked me to use a rapid response instrument to ask my students to respond anonymously to three questions: (i) What did you particularly like about the class?; (ii) What did you not like about the class?; and (iii) How could the class be improved?

Interestingly, he had asked me to conduct this before the university issued its MEQ at the end of the semester. Perhaps this was due to his teaching experience and fore-knowledge on the impact of the MEQ on a novice teacher. This collection of students' evaluative comments using two instruments from the same class provided an avenue to compare the results from the instruments and the impact of the comments on my teaching practice. The process yielded several findings.

Firstly, the time taken to conduct the rapid response was short; I only had to ask students to answer the three questions written on the whiteboard. Secondly, the response rate was high (90%) as it was easy for students in attendance at the class to complete it. Thirdly, and most relevant, was the content of the feedback which was all qualitative and constructive, where students had taken the time to share what they liked about the class, providing positive comments and suggestions for improvement. The students' comments from the institutionally framed MEQ were markedly different. The results took far longer to receive and were not collected until the end of semester; the response rate was significantly lower (56.85%); and I perceived the MEQ comments to be largely negative and unconstructive.

My response to the two instruments was significantly different and led to a range of emotions from surprise, to dejection, anger and eventually to rejection of the results (Titus, 2008). The MEQ comments made me feel like I was being examined by my students: a role reversal where the assessor becomes the assessed and the student becomes the evaluator (Seale, 2009). I reported my surprise to the Programme Director and his response was interesting—'*don't take comments too personally, but they will give us something to discuss*'. This in itself was revealing; evidence of the importance of experience on the impact of students' evaluative comments.

The rapid response comments, on the other hand, appeared more sympathetic. I acknowledge that my awareness of the fact that I was issuing the rapid response instrument may have influenced my teaching. However, it is also possible that student evaluation is influenced by the time it is requested, and the MEQ conducted at the end of the module could have been influenced by the imminent exams and potentially less positive emotions associated with this.

Following discussion with the Programme Director and upon reviewing the contents of the data from the two instruments, the shock gave way to a moment of reflection. This reflection was supported by my enrolment onto the GCLT programme, which contributed to the more reflexive nature of the process and moving from rejection, to trying to understand how the students' comments could be used to enhance teaching practice.

The reflection yielded a few discoveries. Firstly, having evidence of the evaluation of teaching practice from two instruments, provided an avenue to diffuse the shock from the MEQ. I was able to reflect on my expectations of students and evaluate pre-conceived notions of my students. It opened my mind to the presence of teacher bias as to the nature of the 'implied student' (Ulriksen, 2009). This led to a marked change in my perception of teaching as a novice teacher, as I was able to get to grips with what I had assumed to be the students' expectations (which had been formed by my experience as a student in the UK and my own expectations of my teachers). I was also able to come to terms with their *actual* expectations of me as detailed in the comments received. I had to move from a passive expectation of students and teaching practice, towards more active engagement in teaching practice, in which I shared responsibility in the enhancement of my teaching practice with my students.

On further reflection, I realised that many of the students in my class were not from the UK and were, therefore, unfamiliar with participative forms of learning. There was a need to reconsider the module timetable, the role of each lecture within this timetable, and the importance of introducing the module and detailing the expectations of students in different ways to be able to resonate with the diverse student population. This active reflection helped me to come to terms with my own biases as a teacher, informed by dialogue with the students and a need for regular reflection to develop my teaching practice.

Taken together, the two instruments were useful. As a novice teacher, what was important was the juxtaposition between how individual students perceived my teaching and its development, and how the generalised student voice emerging from the MEQ presented my teaching at an institutional level. The singular student voice elicited from the MEQ was far more judgemental and critical in tone and meant that my first reaction was to ensure that my teaching practice fulfilled certain measurement parameters. The focus was very much on knowing what the school wanted and ensuring that I tried to address this as a 'box-ticking' exercise (e.g. making sure I mentioned the word feedback several times in class). With the multiple student voices elicited through the rapid response feedback, this provided more information on what elements of my teaching each student liked and felt could be developed, and I used this to inform my immediate development and shared these with the students in subsequent sessions. I also used the critically constructive comments as ammunition to encourage the development of the broader programme by discussing the comments with other staff involved in delivering the module. As a result, not only were the students' comments more developmental in nature, but so too was my response to their multiple voices and experiences. Exposure to multiple student voices and acknowledgement of their heterogeneous transiency has, therefore, had much more of a positive developmental impact on my teaching practice than the more judgemental, singular student voice emerging from the MEQ.

My experience confirms Flodén's (2016) observations that evaluative comments are more likely to affect the teaching practice of those new to teaching. The opportunity to receive comments from two instruments also improved my willingness to enhance my teaching practice, where the rapid response comments provided were constructive and the MEQ helped me to understand how my teaching practice was compared with other teachers on the same programme. I also learnt, in line with Larrivee's (2000) conclusion, that reflective teaching is challenging. It requires the teacher to have an attitude of 'integrity, openness and commitment' and not 'compromise, defensiveness or fear' (Larrivee, 2000, p. 295). It requires the teacher to be open to active inquiry, and to search for explanations for action. It requires teachers to take time out to engage in critical inquiry, through a deep examination of teaching practices and consideration of the effect of these practices on students. And, it requires self-reflection, a process of reviewing and challenging existing assumptions, values and beliefs about student learning (Richardson, 2005).

Recommendations

For evaluation to enhance teaching practice, teachers need to be adaptable and flexible, aware of the diverse student population, and the different forms of learning. The evaluation process needs to be an iterative and responsive collaboration between students, their teachers, and the institutions. Teachers need to take time to reflect and re-engage with developing and enhancing their teaching practice through continuing professional development. Whilst the added pressure of multiple responsibilities means that such time may not be readily available, reflection can vastly improve teaching practice (Larrivee, 2000). Even with more teaching experience, it is useful to return to self-reflection and critical review of teaching practice to reduce biases and assumptions that are prone to develop with time. The process of collecting evaluative comments can be managed in a way to maintain teacher morale and motivate teachers such that evaluation is able to enhance teaching practice. Where teachers are open to learning and adapting their behaviour according to the environment, the teacher can create strategies that improve teaching. By using student evaluation as a tool for learning, the teacher and students are located within an interactive environment—a dynamic relationship where both parties are co-creators of knowledge that impacts on teaching.

Some of the key criticisms of the institutionally framed MEQ have led to challenges associated with disengagement, cohort specificity, and lack of impact. This had led to questions as to whether comments are improvement-oriented, and issues with low response rates (Shah et al., 2017). This positions students' evaluative comments as a static and transmissive experience. However, as highlighted above, a shift is required to view student evaluation as a dynamic process associated with responsive teaching practices (Li et al., 2016), in which students and teachers share responsibility for the continuing development of pedagogic practice. Therefore, effective teaching requires the teacher to be able to work with students to integrate multiple voices to develop his/her pedagogic practice, whilst acknowledging its time- and context-bound nature (Wiggins, 2010). This requires that teachers and students co-construct an evaluative process that begins early in the semester to enable the development of teaching and learning processes whilst it is taking place, rather than retrospectively (see Chapter 7). That is, it requires teachers and students to be self-aware, reflective and adaptive, underpinned by an explicit rationale central to teaching practice (Hatziapostolou & Paraskakis, 2010; Huxham et al., 2008).

Novice teachers, in particular, require support and guidance in implementing partnership approaches to the evaluation of teaching and learning practices that allow for the plurality of student voices to be surfaced. Students also require support and guidance in engaging in partnership with their teachers and developing their feedback literacy (Carless & Boud, 2018). It is also important that both staff and students are aware of the impact that the evaluative process has on teaching and learning behaviour, informed by dialogue and based on a number of evaluative instruments to provide greater insight into the diversity of experiences within the same class. For example, rapid response instruments, student-led teaching observations (Huxham et al., 2017), and students as educational 'consultants' as part of a pedagogical team to support staff to step out of their 'pedagogical solitude' (Hayward, Ventura, Schuldt, & Donlan, 2018), are just some of the approaches that might be adopted. In so doing, the evaluative process is viewed as a joint responsibility that is dynamic, iterative and ongoing, rather than static, transmissive, and end-loaded. Commitment to a partnership approach to evaluation will provide space and time to allow individual student voices to be surfaced on multiple occasions, which will serve to harness the benefits of heterogeneous transiency of student voices, rather than framing them as a barrier in pursuit of the singular student voice.

Conclusion

Through reflection upon the experiences of a novice teacher using different evaluative instruments, this chapter aimed to critique the concept of the singular, consensual student voice. Further, it sought to acknowledge the heterogeneous transiency of students' evaluative comments. Such comments can shift depending on the perceived purpose of the process, timing of the evaluation, level of anonymity of the responses, and the students' level of engagement in the evaluative process. Teachers' reactions to these comments are also likely to be diverse, coloured by the level of ownership over the evaluation process, perceptions of the purpose of evaluation, and affective responses to the evaluative comments received. Further, the challenges associated with reliance on a single, institutionally framed evaluation instrument that focuses on identifying commonality within a single student voice have been identified. This has been compared with an individually framed rapid response instrument focusing on gaining insight into the diversity of student voices.

Student voice has become increasingly important given the neoliberal nature of higher education, which has been accompanied by the ubiquitous use of institutional measures for evaluating the students' experience. However, in isolation, this approach to evaluation is transmissive, reductive and limits the impact. Furthermore, it places responsibility for teaching development primarily with the teacher, thus positioning the student as consumer or recipient of learning (see Chapter 4). Within this chapter, we have argued that the process of evaluation can be greatly enhanced through the acknowledgement and harnessing of the benefits of the heterogeneous transiency of individually framed evaluation instruments. Key to this enhancement is a shift in perspective to students as partners in evaluation. This requires more regular (perhaps continuous) evaluation-focused events that surface individual students' experiences, providing a balanced overview not just of teaching practice, but also of the overall module/programme experience. Engagement in a continuing, iterative dialogue will serve to familiarise students and teachers with the evaluative process, so that students see the impact of their comments on the development of teaching practices, thereby emphasising their responsibility within the pedagogic development process in higher education. To conclude, we argue for increasing student involvement as co-constructors or educational consultants in the evaluation process, and for teachers to engage in dialogue with students on a regular basis throughout the semester to ensure that teaching is a dynamic process. Student voices can inform reflexive teaching and we encourage colleagues to explore and continue to reflect on how they can work in partnership with their students in order to engage the multiple voices present.

References

Baldwin, T., & Blattner, N. (2003). Guarding against potential bias in student evaluations: What every faculty member needs to know. *College Teaching, 51*(1), 27–32.

Bamber, V., & Anderson, S. (2012). Evaluating learning and teaching: Institutional needs and individual practices. *International Journal for Academic Development, 17*(1), 5–18.

Carless, D., & Boud, D. (2018). The development of feedback literacy: Enabling uptake of feedback. *Assessment and Evaluation in Higher Education, 43*(8), 1315–1325.

Cleary, M., Happell, B., Lau, S., & Mackey, S. (2013). Student feedback on teaching: Some issues for consideration for nurse educators. *International Journal of Nursing Practice, 19,* 62–66.

Crews, T., & Curtis, D. (2011). Online course evaluations: Faculty perspective and strategies for improved response rates. *Assessment and Evaluation in Higher Education, 36*(7), 865–878.

Flodén, J. (2016). The impact of student feedback on teaching in higher education. *Assessment and Evaluation in Higher Education, 42*(7), 1054–1068.

Harvey, L. (1999). The sense in satisfaction. *Times Higher Education.* Retrieved from http://www.timeshighereducation.co.uk/news/the-sense-in-satisfaction/144626.article.

Harvey, L. (2003). Student feedback [1]. *Quality in Higher Education, 9*(1), 3–20.

Hatziapostolou, T., & Paraskakis, I. (2010). Enhancing the impact of formative feedback on student learning through an online feedback system. *Electronic Journal of E-Learning, 8*(2), 111–122.

Hayward, L., Ventura, S., Schuldt, H., & Donlan, P. (2018). Student pedagogical teams: Students as course consultants engaged in process of teaching and learning. *College Teaching, 66*(1), 37–47.

Huxham, M., Laybourn, P., Cairncross, S., Gray, M., Brown, N., Goldfinch, J., & Earl, S. (2008). Collecting student feedback: A comparison of questionnaire and other methods. *Assessment and Evaluation in Higher Education, 33*(6), 675–686.

Huxham, M., Scoles, J., Green, U., Purves, A., Welsh, Z., & Gray, A. (2017). 'Observation has set in': Comparing students and peers as reviewers of teaching. *Assessment and Evaluation in Higher Education, 42*(6), 887–899.

Johnson, R. (2000). The authority of the student evaluation questionnaire. *Teaching in Higher Education, 5*(4), 419–434.

Larrivee, B. (2000). Transforming teaching practice: Becoming the critically reflective teacher. *Reflective Practice, 1*(3), 293–307.

Leckey, J., & Neill, N. (2001). Quantifying quality: The importance of student feedback. *Quality in Higher Education, 7*(1), 19–32.

Li, N., Marsh, V., & Rienties, B. (2016). Modelling and managing learner satisfaction: Use of learner feedback to enhance blended and online learning experience. *Decision Sciences Journal of Innovative Education, 14*(2), 216–242.

Richardson, J. T. E. (2005). Instruments for obtaining student feedback: A review of the literature. *Assessment and Evaluation in Higher Education, 30*(4), 387–415.

Richardson, J. T. E. (2010). Perceived academic quality and approaches to studying in higher education: Evidence from Danish students of occupational therapy. *Scandinavian Journal of Educational Research, 54*(2), 189–203.

Rienties, B. (2014). Understanding academics' resistance towards (online) student evaluation. *Assessment and Evaluation in Higher Education, 39*(8), 987–1001.

Rienties, B., Li, N., & Marsh, V. (2015). *Modelling and managing student satisfaction: Use of student feedback to enhance learning experience.* Gloucester, UK: Quality Assurance Agency.

Seale, J. (2009). Doing student voice work in higher education: An exploration of the value of participatory methods. *British Educational Research Journal, 36*(6), 995–1015.

Shah, M., Cheng, M., & Fitzgerald, R. (2017). Closing the loop on student feedback: The case of Australian and Scottish Universities. *Higher Education, 74*(1), 115–129.

Temple, P., Callender, C., Grove, L., & Kersh, N. (2016). Managing the student experience in English higher education: Differing responses to market pressures. *London Review of Education, 14*(1), 33–46.

Titus, J. (2008). Student ratings in a consumerist academy: Leveraging pedagogical control and authority. *Sociological Perspectives, 51*(2), 397–422.

Ulriksen, L. (2009). The implied student. *Studies in Higher Education, 34*(5), 517–532.

Wiggins, A. (2010). *The courage to seek authentic feedback* [Ebook] (30th ed., pp. 19–21). Retrieved from http://www.edweek.org.

Williams, J., Kane, D., Sagu, S., & Smith, E. (2008). *Exploring the National Student Survey Assessment and feedback issues.* York, UK: Higher Education Academy.

Wong, B., & Chiu, Y. (2019). Let me entertain you: The ambivalent role of university lecturers as educators and performers. *Educational Review, 71*(2), 218–233.

17

Student Voice(s) on the Enactment of the Research-Teaching Nexus

Ian M. Kinchin and Camille B. Kandiko Howson

The discussion of research-teaching links has received considerable attention in the higher education literature (e.g. Brew, 2006; Jenkins, Breen, & Lindsay, 2003), and it is not the purpose of this chapter to review that literature. Instead, we seek to offer views from students of the nature of the relationship between research and teaching. This is a relationship of which many undergraduates are functionally unaware or have a negative view, perceiving research to come at the expense of teaching (Kandiko & Mawer, 2013).

Research-intensive institutions often claim that they can offer students a distinctively excellent student experience because of the proximity of research (Zamorski, 2002). Often research is positioned as the desired pinnacle of undergraduate education in research-intensive settings (Garde-

I. M. Kinchin (✉)
Department of Higher Education, University of Surrey, Guildford, UK
e-mail: i.kinchin@surrey.ac.uk

C. B. Kandiko Howson
Centre for Higher Education Research & Scholarship, Imperial College, London, UK

© The Author(s) 2019
S. Lygo-Baker et al. (eds.), *Engaging Student Voices in Higher Education*,
https://doi.org/10.1007/978-3-030-20824-0_17

Hansen & Calvert, 2007; Kaartinen-Koutaniemi & Lindblom-Ylänne, 2008; Tight, 2012), but there is less concern on how it is done (Malcolm, 2014), or what it would look like to students. However, many studies of links between research and teaching show that there is little or no necessary relationship between high-quality research and excellent teaching (Creighton, 2009; Hattie & Marsh, 1996).

A Unified View of Academic Work

It has been argued that there would be no need to link teaching and research if they were not divided in the first place (Locke, 2004). Traditionally, 'teaching' has been considered in isolation from other aspects of academic practice (e.g. Åkerlind, 2011) with the result that much of the literature on research-teaching links starts with the presumption that the activities are in tension with each other (e.g. Healey, 2005; Kinchin & Hay, 2007; Verburgh, Elen, & Lindblom-Ylänne, 2007). It is also evident, that when 'teaching' is considered as a separate entity, it can initiate a different set of unconscious assumptions about learning in comparison with 'research' (Kinchin, Hatzipanagos, & Turner, 2009). Starting with a focus on 'disciplinary learning' may avoid setting up a destructive binary that needs to be overcome before connections between research and teaching activities can be made.

It is relatively easy to outline research-led teaching initiatives when research skills are a feature of the learning outcomes, especially with more advanced students (e.g. King, Bowe, Sprake, & Kinchin, 2011), but how it can be done is less obvious within the main body of the undergraduate curriculum. In this chapter, the focus is on students' investigations of their disciplinary curriculum as a step to investigate the potential of 'undergraduate research as the pedagogy for the twenty-first century' (Dotterer, 2002, p. 81); a pedagogy in which the engagement of students must, by default, be at a level where they contribute to the flow of instruction (e.g. Reeve, 2013).

Many scholars have explored the possible benefits of linking research and teaching, and the ways in which it can be done (Brew & Boud, 1995; Healey, 2005). Kaartinen-Koutaniemi and Lindblom-Ylänne (2008) stress the central importance of this issue, claiming: 'The development of academic thinking and research skills in students should be considered as a main goal of academic studies in research-intensive universities' (p. 189). Garde-Hansen and Calvert (2007) advocate placing research at the heart of the curriculum and of students' processes of learning: '[research] needs to be promoted as the "flagship" activity of each discipline, not simply as a set of transferable skills. Students need to be made visible as research-active individuals and teams. They need to see that their research efforts are valued' (p. 115). Discussion of the research-teaching nexus is often diffuse, partly because a range of different assumptions are in play about the nature of the relationship (Tight, 2016). In their review, Robertson and Bond (2001) identified five qualitatively different relationships between research and teaching:

a. Research and teaching are mutually incompatible activities
b. Little or no connection exists between research and teaching at undergraduate level
c. Teaching is a means of transmitting new research knowledge
d. Teachers model and encourage a research/critical inquiry approach to learning
e. Teaching and research share a symbiotic relationship in a learning community.

Whilst it may seem removed from the nuts and bolts of course delivery, the role of research and its relationship with teaching activity is a fundamental aspect of a department, and the development of a curriculum that makes the best use of a research-rich environment requires a clear and shared view. Central to this chapter is the view of teaching, so well expressed by DiCarlo (2009, p. 260) when he stated: 'rather than telling students what we know, we should show students how we learn'. This comment is one of many that call for universities to adopt more research-like ways of teaching their students (exemplified by Fung, 2017) and embodies the view that teaching and research should not be viewed as polar opposites, but rather as complementary facets of academic practice. Research can have a positive impact on teaching if the conditions were right for it to do so, and if it were made explicit to students (Blackmore & Kandiko, 2012). Outcomes from a Higher Education Funding Council for England (HEFCE)-supported project (King's Learning Institute, 2010) suggested that a binary tension could be avoided if teaching and research were thought of as two aspects of a more central concept, learning, which is at the core of university work. The project proposed that an evidence base for research-informed and student-centred curriculum enhancement should be developed at the level of disciplines and that students should be encouraged to become research partners in curriculum change, which allows the curriculum to act as a vehicle for student feedback on their learning experience.

Methodology and Approach

Based in a research-intensive university, a group of students investigated the ways in which research and teaching were perceived by academics to be connected in each of the component nine academic areas. Students conducted interviews in their own disciplinary area, constructing reports which represented their data collection and analysis (Kandiko & Kinchin, 2013), and to this end they are a valuable resource, providing a student perspective of staff approaches to a research-led curriculum. This offered the opportunity for multiple student voices to be part of the research, contextualised within their own disciplinary context.

This approach offers a number of distinctive features: its employment of students as researchers; its rejection of a research-teaching binary division; and its wish to go beyond the mere development of research 'skills'. The project was different to the majority of undergraduate research projects reviewed by Zimbardi and Myatt (2014) in that it was not directly embedded into any of the students' disciplinary curricula, and the students were all working beyond the boundaries of their 'home' disciplines in their research approach and as such were working with their supervisors outside the comfort of the 'commonly known' (Willison & O'Regan, 2007).

Student researchers were recruited for this study within nine academic schools, covering the breadth of fields of study and disciplines available within the institution. Students were then invited to apply for the post in a competitive process undertaken within each school. Successful applicants were paired with an academic mentor from within their own school (who

Table 17.1 Disciplines and authors represented in the special issue

Discipline	Author[a]
Arts and Humanities	Kwok (2013)
Biomedical Sciences	Cleary (2013)
Dentistry	Worton (2013)
Psychiatry	Lynch (2013)
Law	Walker (2013)
Medicine	Wickenden (2013)
Natural and Mathematical Sciences	Varambhia (2013)
Nursing and Midwifery	Hall (2013)
Social Sciences	Abrahamsson (2013)

[a]For papers, see Kandiko and Kinchin (2013)

helped to identify and approach suitable candidates to be interviewed) and with a mentor from the academic development team, who helped prepare the students for the process of interviewing and writing up a final report.

The students were part of a co-constructive development process, learning interview techniques from tutors within the academic development team through a series of seminars in which the students were engaged in discussions to identify key questions and ways to phrase them that would use language suitable for their own disciplinary settings. Outputs included student presentations (Abrahamsson et al., 2012) and final student reports were then collated through a special issue journal volume (Kandiko & Kinchin, 2013; see Table 17.1). The reports detail the findings of the students' research, and here we provide a synthesis of student voices in relation to the research-teaching nexus.

Students each conducted nine interviews within their own school: with three leading researchers, three graduate teaching assistants (GTAs) and three academic staff who have a leading teaching role (e.g. module or programme leads). The description of potential interviewees using these category headings was simply a way of highlighting the diversity of academic staff when discussing the research process with the student researchers. In discussion, it was clear that these categories are not mutually exclusive (i.e. some leading researchers are also programme leaders), and the use of these categories was more or less appropriate in the different academic departments. However, they provided a basis for discussion of the need to talk to academics that might hold varying perspectives of activities within their departments. This was something that a few of the student researchers had not previously been aware of or considered.

Discussions with the student researchers considered the variety of staff who may be involved in teaching and/or research and factors such as age, seniority, gender and ethnicity were noted as variables to consider when inviting staff for interview. Whilst an interview sample of nine cannot fully represent a whole academic school, the students aimed to invite interviewees who were as representative as possible, within the limitations of the project. The students used anonymous quotes from their interviews to illustrate their reports on learning within their discipline and the relationship between learning in a research mode and the taught undergraduate curriculum. Not surprisingly, academic staff and students varied in their experience of such a research approach and the extent to which they felt at ease with it. Such a study cannot generate detailed quantitative data to describe a population of academic staff, but it does represent the co-construction of voices of 81 staff and the nine student researchers across an institution whose voices might not otherwise be heard. The study does not intend to extrapolate and generalise from the data, but simply represents the opinions of those who were interviewed, filtered through the students' voices. Some students also drew on wider resources, such as disciplinary literature, experiences in other institutions and wider perspectives from other students.

Students as Researchers

This work builds on published research on the development of student consultants as change agents—which have shown positive results (e.g. Bovill, Cook-Sather, & Felten, 2011; Butcher & Maunder, 2014; Cook-Sather & Alter, 2011; Dunne & Zandstra, 2011; Feldman, Divoll, & Rogan-Klyve, 2013). The recruitment of students as researchers is intended to provide a valuable insider perspective which has been previously overlooked by many studies (Partridge & Sandover, 2010).

The intention of this project was to include the students in the research process as much as possible as agentic learners (Reeve, 2013) rather than simply using students as 'data points' in a study on student voice. The established model provided by Brew (2013) offers a useful structure to guide a review of the development of the process undertaken with the student researchers (modified and redrawn in Fig. 17.1). The topic for this research was chosen by staff, and the task structure and the research outputs were also dictated by staff rather than students. Beyond that the inquiry was open-ended in that there was no clear answer to be achieved, and the questions used in the interviews were co-constructed between staff and students, allowing an opportunity for students to voice questions not normally raised. The sectors of Fig. 17.1 which lean most towards the outer rings of the model are those concerned with originality and knowledge. There was the potential to develop understanding that was new, not just to the students, but also to the wider discipline (i.e. the 'unknown'; described by Willison & O'Regan, 2007). There was no formal assessment tied to this activity in terms of credits or scores, but a 'successful outcome' would be achieved by gaining a published report. We feel that this profile is quite typical of an academic research activity.

Students at the Centre

This work also provides an opportunity to evaluate Brew's model in practice and to offer some constructive amendments based on our experiences working with the students. We offer two suggestions: changing the central focus and adding the notion of liminality. Firstly, Brew (2013) places students at the centre of the model. Whilst we would not disagree that students are at the centre of learning, we are not convinced that placing students at the centre of this model enhances its utility in terms of decision-making, particularly if students are party to decision-making processes. The implication of placing students at the centre of the model is that it suggests a student-centred teaching approach. Recently, researchers have called for a more nuanced discussion of teaching in higher education that overcomes the deficiencies of the broad categories (student-centred and teacher-centred) that are considered to be inadequate in capturing the essence of teaching practices. Neumann (2013, p. 161) offers the view that student-centred learning is a 'complicated and messy idea that has encompassed a wide range of meanings'. Unlike student-centred contexts

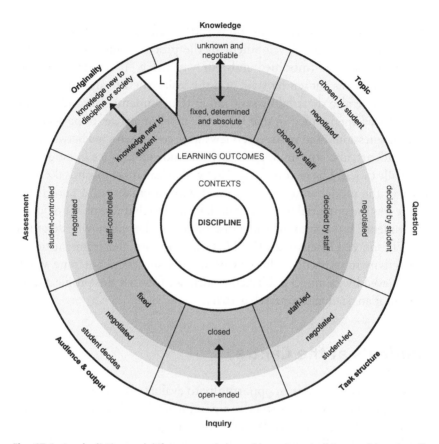

Fig. 17.1 A wholistic model for research-based learning decision-making (modified and redrawn from Brew, 2013)

that centre *on* students, or centre *in* students, those that centre *with* students are seen by Neumann to emphasise partnership between teachers and students in a reciprocal learning relationship and allow for multiple student voices. If we centre *with* students, then staff and students share a focus and that has to be the discipline. Guzmán-Valenzuela (2013) develops this to consider that the intellectual practice and field provides the ground on which complex pedagogical interactions are enacted.

Arguments in favour of discipline-centred approaches have been supported by commentators from a variety of sources. Palmer (1998, p. 116) stated that 'the classroom should be neither teacher-centred nor student-centred, but subject-centred'. Hobson and Morrison-Saunders (2013, p. 781) conclude that 'taking a subject-centred approach is a gentle and effective way to manage power differences', whilst Winch (2013, p. 138) states that to guide students to gain subject expertise student-initiated procedures are insufficient, and that it 'needs teachers with a clear conceptual map related to appropriate ways of learning the relevant subject matter'.

If we are considering 'research as pedagogy' (Dotterer, 2002; Kinchin, Kingsbury, & Buhmann, 2018), then we have to consider the authentic research experience in which the discipline would occupy centre stage in the decision-making process, with students and teachers contributing to the contexts in which the subsequent decisions have to be made. For these reasons, we have opted to place 'The Discipline' at the centre of the decision-making model and would locate students within the 'context' ring. In addition, placing the discipline at the centre of the model overcomes the visual literacy issue generated by the original figure. Putting 'students' in the centre of the three inner rings contradicts the pattern in the outer three rings in which moving from the centre towards the edge indicating greater student focus.

Secondly, adopting a 'students-as-researchers' stance changes the traditional dynamics of the relationship between the student as passive receiver of information and the teacher as active transmitter. The student starts to occupy the space of 'student as producer', and this 'catalyses a revision of students' relationships to their teachers and their responsibilities within their learning' (Cook-Sather & Alter, 2011, p. 37). Where research leads students into a space where they have to let go of some prior conceptions, they may enter a state of liminality where progress feels difficult and they may feel temporarily stuck between the familiarity of rote learning and the goal of expert understanding (e.g. Meyer & Land, 2006). This liminal space is acknowledged in our redrawing of Brew's model (Fig. 17.1) and is represented by the triangle labelled 'L'. The triangular shape indicates that the further one moves into the outer ring of the model, the larger the liminal space. Where research is generating knowledge that is new to discipline or society, the students will share the liminal space with their academic supervisors. Part of the supervisors' role may be seen to support students with the uncertainties that come with this situation (see also Chapter 15).

Discussion

Working with students as researchers into issues of curriculum and pedagogy raised issues about power relations and the roles of academics and students. Although comfortable being interviewed by students, some academics expressed negative views about students being able to understand research or to have sufficient capability to participate in research within their disciplines. In terms of research, most academics positioned themselves as experts and students as novices or even future novices. However, in terms of teaching, there was more openness to the place of research in the curriculum.

Ownership and Empowerment

The issue of 'ownership' appeared in a number of the case studies. This was given centre stage within the title of the report given by Wickenden (2013) who describes the tensions between the 'rigid' learning experiences of the lecture theatre and the experiences that are available within the 'gold standard' of bedside clinical teaching. He asks, 'Could this experience be used as an educational model to strengthen research-teaching links and promote student ownership?' (p. 73). Hall (2013, p. 84) considers the same issue from the nursing perspective, in which an interviewee expresses the need for students to be more empowered so that they do not justify their actions by saying that 'the doctor told me to do it'. This disempowerment is explored by Wheelahan (2010) in terms of students being denied access to powerful knowledge.

Ability

The teachers' perceptions of student ability and knowledge are seen to be critical determinants in granting students access to a research-rich teaching experience, with academics split between the ideas that students must either have the knowledge first before engaging in research or might gain the knowledge through a process of research. Wickenden (2013, p. 71) highlighted the comment that 'undergraduates don't tend to be in a position of knowledge to be able to influence what you're doing', whilst Abrahamsson (2013, p. 94) was told by one academic that 'first year undergrads are not theoretical enough'. However, it is clear that this 'knowledge first' perspective is not universal, and to highlight this, Abrahamsson (2013, p. 94) was also told by another academic from the same department, that: 'the lower the level of the students the better the questions, because they make me think what I am doing', whilst Walker (2013, p. 55) referred to an academic who 'stated that they gave students a draft of "scholarly material" in order to hear their comments'.

The 'knowledge-first' versus the 'knowledge through research' perspective may represent a reflection of the academics' conceptions of teaching, with the more positivist colleagues requiring the students to be given the facts in advance and the more constructivist teachers allowing for the understanding to emerge. Alternatively, it may reflect the academics' primary interests: either promoting their own research at an individual level (Fig. 17.1) with the students seen as only useful if they help to uncover that which is totally unknown, against a view in which the 'collective good' is seen as more important through the development of a research-embedded curriculum that has a much longer-term aim.

Purpose of Research

Maton (2013, p. 8) describes a widespread assumption that the goal of university education is to equip students with understanding that transcends the immediate context of the teaching when he states that 'Almost everyone in education shares a desire for cumulative knowledge-building. Researchers typically aim to generate ideas that have utility or appeal beyond the specificities of their originating contexts'. This view is complemented by policymakers proclaiming that education must prepare students for living and working in fast-changing societies by providing knowledge and skills that can build throughout 'lifelong learning'. However, for academics to be able to take a wider perspective of their own focussed research is quite difficult for many—particularly where they may feel that their research field is so cutting-edge that it may not yet have clear application.

While there was an emerging feeling throughout many of the interviews that teaching is for the good of someone else, research was seen by some as a vehicle for their own professional development. Cleary (2013, p. 21) quotes an academic who stated, 'To do research well I think you have got to be incredibly selfish … the motivational drive for any researcher has to be themselves … ultimately it's their own progression up the research hierarchy (that motivates them) … that doesn't necessarily come across in teaching, where the rewards don't come from their progression, but from the progression of others'.

Conclusion

Engaging students as researchers brings unique insights into how both students and academics consider research in relation to the curriculum. There was a noted dichotomy of teaching as a collective endeavour, both amongst academics and for a group of students, contrasted with the individualism of research, for the academic toiling away and for a student to understand. Students-as-researchers offer a way for students to be empowered in the research process, but are largely divorced from disciplinary research. Reconceptualising research-teaching links as 'research as pedagogy' may offer a bridge to bring academics and students together in the context of disciplinary learning. This view also brings together the individualistic side of research with the collectivist view of teaching. Repositioning the curriculum as a place for staff and students to co-construct 'disciplinary learning' and place it at the centre of the academic endeavour can be the foundation for an ethos of research-led student engagement.

From the reports constructed by the students, it is clear that they are not only reporting on the research-teaching nexus as described by the academics in their institution, but they are also developing their own voice(s). The freedom afforded by the research activity allowed them to reflect upon their data and interpret it from their own contextual starting point and showcases the heterogeneity of multiple student voices. As this group of students had a more formalised and coherent view of the range of opinions and perceptions about the research-teaching nexus across their disciplinary areas, their voices were supported by evidence and so gained authority. This then challenges notions of power and of powerful knowledge and confers an element of expertise to, and value of student voices (Kinchin, 2016).

Acknowledgements This project was supported in part through the King's-Warwick Project funded by the Higher Education Funding Council for England.

References

Abrahamsson, B.-E. (2013). Acquiring and sharing knowledge: Exploring the links between research and teaching in social science and public policy. *Higher Education Research Network Journal, 6,* 92–101.

Abrahamsson, B.-E., Cleary, S., Hall, R., Kwok, A. Y. H., Lynch, S., Varambhia, A., ... Kinchin, I. M. (2012, June 19). *Students as co-researchers of the curriculum.* Paper presented at the 6th Excellence in Teaching Conference, King's College London, UK.

Åkerlind, G. S. (2011). Separating the 'teaching' from the 'academic': Possible unintended consequences. *Teaching in Higher Education, 16*(2), 183–195.

Blackmore, P., & Kandiko, C. B. (2012). *Strategic curriculum change: Global trends in universities.* London: Routledge and SRHE.

Bovill, C., Cook-Sather, A., & Felten, P. (2011). Students as co-creators of teaching approaches, course design, and curricula: Implications for academic developers. *International Journal for Academic Development, 16*(2), 133–145.

Brew, A. (2006). *Research and teaching: Beyond the divide.* Basingstoke, UK: Palgrave Macmillan.

Brew, A. (2013). Understanding the scope of undergraduate research: A framework for curricular and pedagogical decision-making. *Higher Education, 66*(5), 603–618.

Brew, A., & Boud, D. (1995). Teaching and research: Establishing the vital link with learning. *Higher Education, 29,* 261–273.

Butcher, J., & Maunder, R. (2014). Going URB@N: exploring the impact of undergraduate students as pedagogic researchers. *Innovations in Education and Teaching International, 51*(2), 142–152.

Cleary, S. (2013). Perceptions of collaboration in research and teaching in a School of Biomedical Sciences. *Higher Education Research Network Journal, 6,* 19–28.

Cook-Sather, A., & Alter, Z. (2011). What is and what can be: How a liminal position can change learning and teaching in higher education. *Anthropology and Education, Quarterly, 42*(1), 37–53.

Creighton, J. (2009). *Learning in research-intensive environments: Do students benefit?* LTEA Conference, University of Reading.

DiCarlo, S. E. (2009). The Claude Bernard distinguished lecture: Too much content, not enough thinking, and too little FUN! *Advances in Physiology Education, 33,* 257–264.

Dotterer, R. L. (2002). Student-faculty collaborations, undergraduate research, and collaboration as an administrative model. *New Directions for Teaching and Learning, 90,* 81–89.

Dunne, L., & Zandstra, R. (2011). *Students as change agents: New ways of engaging with learning and teaching in higher education.* York, UK: Higher Education Academy. Retrieved from http://escalate.ac.uk/8242.

Feldman, A., Divoll, K. A., & Rogan-Klyve, A. (2013). Becoming researchers: The participation of undergraduate and graduate students in scientific research groups. *Science Education, 97*(2), 218–243.

Fung, D. (2017). *A connected curriculum for higher education.* London: UCL Press. Retrieved from http://www.oapen.org/search?identifier=630699.

Garde-Hansen, J., & Calvert, B. (2007). Developing a research culture in the undergraduate curriculum. *Active Learning in Higher Education, 8*(2), 105–116.

Guzmán-Valenzuela, C. (2013). Challenging frameworks for understanding teaching practices in higher education: The end or the beginning? *Qualitative Research in Education, 2*(1), 65–91.

Hall, R. (2013). Florence Nightingale School of Nursing and Midwifery: From university intention to student perception. *Higher Education Research Network Journal, 6,* 83–91.

Hattie, J., & Marsh, H. W. (1996). The relationship between research and teaching: A meta-analysis. *Review of Educational Research, 66,* 507–542.

Healey, M. (2005). Linking research and teaching to benefit student learning. *Journal of Geography in Higher Education, 29*(2), 183–201.

Hobson, J., & Morrison-Saunders, A. (2013). Reframing teaching relationships: From student-centred to subject-centred learning. *Teaching in Higher Education, 18*(7), 773–783.

Jenkins, A., Breen, R., & Lindsay, R. (2003). *Reshaping teaching in higher education: Linking teaching with research.* London: Kogan Page.

Kaartinen-Koutaniemi, M., & Lindblom-Ylänne, S. (2008). Personal epistemology of psychology, theology and pharmacy students: A comparative study. *Studies in Higher Education, 33*(2), 179–191.

Kandiko, C. B., & Kinchin, I. M. (Eds.). (2013). Student perspectives on research-rich teaching. *Higher Education Research Network Journal, 6* (Special Issue), 1–98. Retrieved from https://www.researchgate.net/publication/244483439_student_perspectives_on_research-rich_teaching.

Kandiko, C. B., & Mawer, M. (2013). *Student expectations and perceptions of higher education.* Report for the Quality Assurance Agency (QAA). London: King's College London.

Kinchin, I. M. (2016). *Visualising powerful knowledge to develop the expert student: A knowledge structures perspective on teaching and learning at university.* Rotterdam: Sense.

Kinchin, I. M., Hatzipanagos, S., & Turner, N. (2009). Epistemological separation of research and teaching among graduate teaching assistants. *Journal of Further and Higher Education, 33*(1), 45–55.

Kinchin, I. M., & Hay, D. B. (2007). The myth of the research-led teacher. *Teachers and teaching: Theory and practice, 13*(1), 43–61.

Kinchin, I. M., Kingsbury, M., & Buhmann, S. Y. (2018). Research as pedagogy in academic development. In E. Medland, R. Watermeyer, A. Hosein, I. M. Kinchin, & S. Lygo-Baker (Eds.), *Pedagogical peculiarities: Conversations at the edge of university teaching and learning* (pp. 49–67). Rotterdam: Brill and Sense.

King, A. J., Bowe, J., Sprake, J. A., & Kinchin, I. M. (2011). In vivo laboratory practicals in research-led teaching: An example using glucose tolerance tests in lean and obese mice. *Journal of Pharmacological and Toxicological Methods, 64*(2), 166–172.

Kwok, A. Y. H. (2013). Research-teaching links in the School of Arts and Humanities: An enquiry-based learning approach. *Higher Education Research Network Journal, 6*, 9–18.

Locke, W. (2004). Integrating research and teaching strategies: Implications for institutional management and leadership in the United Kingdom. *Higher Education Management and Policy, 16*(1), 101–120.

294   I. M. Kinchin and C. B. Kandiko Howson

Lynch, S. (2013). Research-teaching links at the Institute of Psychiatry. *Higher Education Research Network Journal, 6*, 43–49.

Malcolm, M. (2014). A critical evaluation of recent progress in understanding the role of the research-teaching link in higher education. *Higher Education, 67*(3), 289–301.

Maton, K. (2013). Making semantic waves: A key to cumulative knowledge-building. *Linguistics and Education, 24*, 8–22.

Meyer, J. H. F., & Land, R. (2006). Threshold concepts and troublesome knowledge: Issues of liminality. In J. H. F. Meyer & R. Land (Eds.), *Overcoming barriers to student understanding: Threshold concepts and troublesome knowledge* (pp. 19–32). London: Routledge.

Neumann, J. W. (2013). Developing a new framework for conceptualizing "student-centered learning". *The Educational Forum, 77*(2), 161–175.

Palmer, P. (1998). *The courage to teach.* San Francisco: Jossey-Bass.

Partridge, L., & Sandover, S. (2010). Beyond 'listening' to the student voice: The undergraduate researcher's contribution to the enhancement of teaching and learning. *Journal of University Teaching & Learning Practice, 7*(2). Retrieved from http://ro.uow.edu.au/jutlp.vol7/iss2/4.

Reeve, J. (2013). How students create motivationally supportive learning environments for themselves: The concept of agentic engagement. *Journal of Educational Psychology, 105*(3), 579–595.

Robertson, J., & Bond, C. H. (2001). Experiences of the relation between teaching and research: What do academics value? *Higher Education Research and Development, 20*(1), 5–19.

Tight, M. (2012). *Researching higher education* (2nd ed.). Maidenhead, UK: McGraw-Hill.

Tight, M. (2016). Examining the research/teaching nexus. *European Journal of Higher Education, 6*(4), 293–311.

Varambhia, A. (2013). Perception of research-teaching links in Natural and Mathematical Sciences. *Higher Education Research Network Journal, 6*, 75–82.

Verburgh, A., Elen, J., & Lindblom-Ylänne, S. (2007). Investigating the myth of the relationship between teaching and research in higher education: A review of the empirical research. *Studies in Philosophy and Education, 26*(5), 449–465.

Walker, E. (2013). An international comparison between the research-teaching links at two Schools of Law. *Higher Education Research Network Journal, 6*, 50–60.

Wheelahan, L. (2010). *Why knowledge matters in curriculum: A social realist argument.* Oxford: Routledge.

Wickenden, J. (2013). Investigating research-teaching links in the undergraduate School of Medicine: Ownership as a means of rebalancing student objectives. *Higher Education Research Network Journal, 6,* 61–74.

Willison, J., & O'Regan, K. (2007). Commonly known, commonly not known, totally unknown: A framework for students becoming researchers. *Higher Education Research and Development, 26*(4), 393–409.

Winch, C. (2013). Curriculum design and epistemic ascent. *Journal of Philosophy of Education, 47*(1), 128–146.

Worton, J. M. (2013). How do we learn? Disciplinary ways of thinking and their roles within the undergraduate curriculum at King's College London Dental School. *Higher Education Research Network Journal, 6,* 29–42.

Zamorski, B. (2002). Research-led teaching and learning in higher education: A case. *Teaching in Higher Education, 7*(4), 411–427.

Zimbardi, K., & Myatt, P. (2014). Embedding undergraduate research experiences within the curriculum: A cross-disciplinary study of the key characteristics guiding implementation. *Studies in Higher Education, 39*(2), 233–250.

18

Engaging Students as Co-designers in Educational Innovation

Karen Gravett, Emma Medland and Naomi E. Winstone

When developing new educational tools and resources, students are often positioned as 'end-users' rather than creators or designers. This position can be problematic and may contribute to the perpetuation of traditional academic and student roles, and notably to the conception of the student as consumer (see Chapter 4). Moreover, whilst we may consider students' needs and views as end-users when designing a new tool or resource, this consideration is often likely to be framed singularly. Inherent within the question: 'what might students want, need and expect from this resource?' lies the implicit assumption of the monolingual student voice, and the significant absence of the diversity and plurality of students' voices.

K. Gravett (✉) · E. Medland · N. E. Winstone
Department of Higher Education, University of Surrey, Guildford, UK
e-mail: k.gravett@surrey.ac.uk

E. Medland
e-mail: e.medland@surrey.ac.uk

N. E. Winstone
e-mail: n.winstone@surrey.ac.uk

© The Author(s) 2019
S. Lygo-Baker et al. (eds.), *Engaging Student Voices in Higher Education*,
https://doi.org/10.1007/978-3-030-20824-0_18

In recent years, the idea of students as co-creators of the curriculum has begun to gain momentum within the literature and within practice (e.g. Bovill, Cook-Sather, Felten, Millard, & Moore-Cherry, 2016; Casanova & Mitchell, 2017; Garcia, Noguera, & Cortada-Pujol, 2018; Mäkelä, Helfenstein, Lerkkanen, & Poikkeus, 2018). Researchers and practitioners are beginning to consider the value of developing partnerships with students in designing learning and teaching experiences from the outset, rather than simply paying heed to what students say about what they have experienced (e.g. via the traditional use of student course representatives within Universities). This might involve co-creation (e.g. of curricula or assessment criteria) or participatory design or co-design (e.g. of tools and resources). Whilst the conception of students as partners has been generating increasing attention for some time (e.g. Bovill et al., 2016; Cook-Sather, Bovill, & Felten, 2014; Healey, Flint, & Harrington, 2014; Matthews et al., 2019), in this chapter, we will argue that co-creation can be viewed as a generative direction for partnership working. Related to the emancipatory idea that students and staff might work collaboratively together in partnership is the notion that staff and students might work in partnership to co-create learning and teaching. This chapter will consider this emerging direction through exploring staff and students' experiences of a particular co-design initiative. Furthermore, we aim to examine what role co-design initiatives might play within the wider move to deconstruct the illusion of a monolingual conception of student voice, as well as noting what constraints may still exist when seeking to engage and empower students in partnership.

Co-design Partnerships

In a traditional approach to design, the process is driven by expert designers, who create a product based on their knowledge of the potential user group (see Fig. 18.1A). Whilst they may involve users in the testing of a prototype, for example, the conceptualisation of the product does not involve potential users. A variant of this approach might involve potential users as consultants, or as part of an advisory group, to have input into the emerging design. In both of these examples, the process is driven

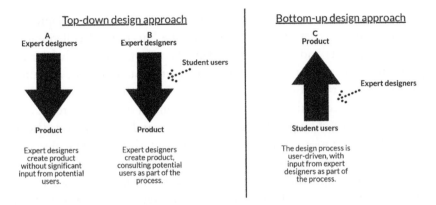

Fig. 18.1 Top-down and bottom-up approaches to design

top-down (see Fig. 18.1B), with expert designers only involving potential users further 'downstream' (Fishman, 2014).

Participatory design, a specific method of co-design, emerged as a counter to these top-down models, positioning potential users as part of the design team. The roots of participatory design can be traced back to 1970s Scandinavia, as a way to enable workers to contribute to the design of new digital systems that would be integrated into their workplace (Spinuzzi, 2005). The workers designed the systems in collaboration with software developers, leading to a sense of control over their work rather than disempowerment. Such 'grass-roots engagement' (Casanova & Mitchell, 2017, p. 10) represents a bottom-up, collaborative approach to design (see Fig. 18.1C), where the design process evolves in partnership with users, not merely on their behalf (Spinuzzi, 2005).

In educational contexts, much interesting work is emerging that devotes attention to the concept of co-design partnerships between staff and students, and to the potential benefits of such collaborations. Mäkelä et al. (2018) argue that co-design confers significant benefits for students in terms of the skills that can be developed through the participatory design process and can offer an authentic learning experience.

In contemporary higher education, the role of students as partners in the co-creation of curricula and learning resources is gaining traction, in part as a mechanism to challenge the common, yet contested, positioning of students as consumers (e.g. Bovill et al., 2016; see Chapter 4). In this context, co-creation is defined as the 'meaningful collaboration between students and staff, with students becoming more active participants in the learning process, constructing understanding and resources with academic staff' (Bovill et al., 2016, p. 197). When participating in the co-creation process, students can occupy a number of different roles: consultant; co-researcher; pedagogical co-designer; and representative (Bovill et al., 2016). Opportunities to act as representatives for their peers are often provided for students, whereas the other three roles often require staff to create opportunities through which students can engage (Bovill et al., 2016). The role of co-researcher necessitates student involvement in research endeavours, whereas the role of co-designer can be more creative and practical. Engaging students as consultants may be more passive, where students are given the opportunity to contribute their perspectives on aspects of pedagogy (Bovill et al., 2016).

There is clear potential for co-design partnerships to give greater prominence to student voices. Garcia et al. (2018) argue that co-design can enable teachers and students to recognise each other's viewpoints, where co-design is:

> not just about listening to students and collecting data for academics to make decisions, it is about promoting students' active participation in shared decision-making and acting according to these decisions. (Garcia et al., 2018, p. 2)

Here, co-design is articulated as being about positioning students' voices to become a fundamental part of the design process. Rather than simply 'listening' to students, students are invited to become active participants in shared decision-making. But do these approaches allow for the surfacing of multiple, rather than singular, student voices? We now turn to examination of a specific co-design endeavour, the 'Feedback Footprints' project, as a lens through which to examine this question.

The Feedback Footprints Project

The aim of the Feedback Footprints project was to engage students in the co-design of a feedback e-portfolio. It was important for students to lead the design of the tool given calls for partnership and responsibility-sharing in enhancing the impact of feedback processes (Nash & Winstone, 2017). In line with a participatory design approach (Spinuzzi, 2005), the project involved ethnography, focus groups, and artefact analysis to inform the design. It is rarely feasible to involve all potential end-users in a participatory design process (Spinuzzi, 2005), so a group of students representing all areas of the university were engaged as co-designers. In the first phase of the project, focus groups surfaced students' tacit knowledge and experience of engaging with feedback; gaining access to users' tacit knowledge is an important part of the participatory design process (Spinuzzi, 2005). This was followed by participatory design events, where students worked with creative media to represent their experiences of feedback and their own design for a feedback e-portfolio. Participatory design is an iterative process involving cycles of prototyping and redesign, which functions as a form of continuous member checking (Spinuzzi, 2005):

> Participatory design studies are not a "listening tour" in which researchers hear the concerns of users, then go away and design a solution; they are participatory top to bottom and must include verifiable, regular avenues for group interaction and definite routines for ensuring that users' concerns are methodically addressed in the resulting design. (Spinuzzi, 2005, p. 170)

Students' designs were used to create a prototype which was then presented to students for evaluation using think-aloud protocols. Over two such cycles, the design was refined to create the Feedback Engagement and Tracking System (FEATS; http://tinyurl.com/FEATSPortfolio).

Student Perspectives

At the end of the project, 28 student co-designers were interviewed by a research assistant about their experiences during the process. Institutional ethical approval was granted, and the semi-structured interview schedule focused on students' perceptions of their role in the process, their contributions, and the finished product. We focus here on thematic analysis of students' responses to the first of these areas of focus. When discussing their experience of the co-design process, participants positioned themselves as occupying different roles, which are discussed under three themes: engaging voices as representatives; engaging voices as consultants; and engaging voices as colleagues. These themes resonate with the representative, consultant, and pedagogical co-designer roles as identified by Bovill et al. (2016). Students are represented by their participant number (e.g. ppt.1).

Engaging Voices as Representatives

Whilst it would be ideal to include all students within the community of the co-design process, practicality demands that a core group of students act as *representatives* for their peers. In other words, those participating in the co-design process need to recognise that whilst their own views and opinions are important, they have a responsibility to step back from their own perspective and try as best as they can to represent the diverse views of their peers. This is particularly important because the students who volunteer to be involved in partner initiatives may not be those whose voices most need to be surfaced. When participants discussed their experiences, there was evidence that students recognised their responsibility to '*represent the voice of students*' (ppt.24) and ensure that the tool would have a positive impact on other students, describing their role as to '*shape… learning of future students.*' (ppt.18), by '*being a representation of what we'd like to see on the portfolio*' (ppt.2).

Many students spoke about representing the views of the wider body of students and looking beyond their own perspectives, where they felt they were '*just helping a lot of the students*' (ppt.16) by '*representing other students and giving a general idea of what would be helpful for other students*' (ppt.12). Many students described this element of their role as a positive experience: '*I liked putting my input and giving a good account from a student…I liked standing as … a representative*' (ppt.8).

Beyond representing the general student body, some students positioned themselves as representatives for the voices of particular groups according to discipline or learning needs and recognised that varied representation within the co-design team enabled these voices to be heard. One student from a School which is quite separate physically and culturally from other areas of the University explained that '*I represent a different part of the university it was important to show what our perspectives on things are*' (ppt.5). Some students also saw their role as representing the particular needs of their discipline; one student from engineering felt very strongly that their voices are rarely heard in educational design due to the focus on essay-based subjects. He reflected on his role in the design sessions: '*I made it very clear that there weren't enough resources for people doing maths-based subjects*' (ppt.9). Similarly, a student with dyslexia expressed the importance of representing the voices of those with particular learning needs: '*so in the designing session I brought up that as there's quite a few people that are dyslexic at university maybe have the option of a colour change background or even just a font change*' (ppt.10).

Engaging Voices as Consultants

There was also evidence that students positioned themselves as *consultants*, where they perceived their contribution to involve sharing their expertise as students who go through the process of receiving and using feedback, voicing their '*opinions on how [the portfolio] should be designed*' (ppt.3). They expressed a sense of responsibility to '*make the portfolio good for students of our age*' (ppt.8), because '*students are going to use it first of all, so definitely consult…the users, rather than just make it and put it there*' (ppt.28).

Many students expressed a belief that if the aim was to design a tool for use by students, then they are best placed to comment on what is likely to be useful for fellow students: '*I just feel like in order to just give a student voice as opposed to just going on what, say that the lecturers have got an impression of, or more professional bodies so to speak, so just to give that student voice, just to give that student opinion as well*' (ppt.16). This was echoed by a student who argued that '*We're going to be the people using it, and it's good to get a varied opinion from everyone'* (ppt.17). Students also showed their investment in the project by wanting to ensure that the outcome was something students would be likely to engage with: *'I think my role was for me as a student that uses feedback and uses [the VLE] to get my opinion on how to make it in a way that students will get involved with it and actually like it, instead of it being not helpful'* (ppt.7).

In some of their discussions, students seemed to position their role as consultants in terms of their representation of the 'target audience' for the feedback portfolio. Whilst they were not necessarily positioning themselves as consumers in the sense of potentially investing money in the product, they did see themselves as representing those who would be investing their time in using it:

> It's really absolutely essential that people who are going to use it have a big hand in how it's designed because they're going to use it and you want it to be most effective for them…and that's why when I was contributing to the discussions exactly the things that I felt should be in there because I thought I'm going to benefit from this so this is what I think needs to happen. (ppt.23)

Many design processes beyond academia incorporate the perspectives of experts, and students recognised that in the Feedback Footprints project the benefit of their expertise was *'to steer the direction of it'* (ppt.18). Students appeared to value the fact that they were being treated as experts and recognised the authenticity of that element of the partnership.

Engaging Voices as Colleagues

Students recognised that they were positioned as colleagues alongside staff involved in the design project, even though they indicated that they had not anticipated playing this role: *'I didn't think I could do this, like, I didn't think the Uni would take us and ask us to actually build things for future students and for ourselves as well'* (ppt.4). Students' roles as partners in the e-portfolio design were validated by seeing that their voices had been taken seriously and that *'the points that were raised and what we wanted from it did come up in the actual [e-portfolio] at the end'* (ppt.11). This visible impact of their contributions was a source of satisfaction for some students: *'I knew that from looking at the prototype, I saw that the ideas that in my group that we came up with, a few of them were in there, and I think I did like the sense of involvement, because I think when you're part of something that's being developed, and having your ideas used, that does feel good'* (ppt.14).

Students also recognised that their *bona fide* role as colleagues in the process was important, and that the outcomes would have been less positive if students were not part of the design team:

> I think from a student's perspective what happens is sometimes the teachers or people designing things may have an idea of what we want but actually it doesn't correlate with what we would actually utilise best…in [the design session] it worked amazingly and there were some brilliant ideas coming up and it was because we were all students sat there. (ppt.13)

> the way we all came up with our own ideas and gave feedback on each other's ideas, and then we all came to a conclusion of the best thing to do to make this work for students, and the way the students definitely have a big hand in it shows it's going to be really effective for other students. (ppt.23)

Staff Perspectives: A Map-Mediated Reflection on the Co-design Project

This concept map-mediated interview enabled us to explore how student–staff partnership, and particularly co-design, was conceptualised by Naomi as a lead member of staff working on the FEATS project. The interview surfaced a number of themes, values, and beliefs regarding student partnership and co-creation that we now consider (see Fig. 18.2).

Concept Map-Mediated Interviews

The aim of the map-mediated interview (Kandiko & Kinchin, 2013) is to surface beliefs, values, and understanding of perspectives with the map functioning as a dialogic learning tool. In this study, the interviewer

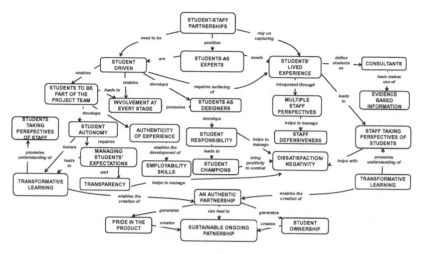

Fig. 18.2 Concept map interview with project lead

(Karen) began by asking the interviewee (Naomi): 'from your perspective what are the factors that contribute to a successful staff–student partnership?' The interviewer then wrote down key concepts onto post-it notes, employing subsequent probing questions as appropriate. The interviewer then asked the interviewee about the relationships between these concepts and invited the interviewee to position them on a piece of paper. After the interviews were finished, the interviewer electronically drew the concept map and sent this to the participant to review.

The Values Underpinning Co-creation

This concept map-mediated interview highlighted a number of the values that underpin Naomi's approach to and conception of co-creation. A pervasive theme within the interview and concept map is her belief that students should be re-positioned within staff–student relations. Students are ascribed new identities: as 'consultants', as 'designers', and as 'experts'. Their lived experience is highly valued, and they are viewed as an integral part of the project team, involved at every stage. Reconceptualising students in new ways—as 'designers' and 'experts'—disrupts normative assumptions about student roles, student knowledge, and student–staff relations. This depiction shows a clear belief in the need to destabilise power hierarchies, and of the potential of co-creation to do this. The map also reminds us of the untapped value of students within higher education: here, they are not just identified as partners but as 'experts' with recent and valuable lived experiences to share.

The map-mediated interview evinces Naomi's belief in the power of co-design to offer transformative learning. 'Student-driven' projects that enable 'student autonomy' are shown as offering a means for students' transformative learning. As we have seen, the transformative benefits of partnership and co-creation approaches are widely cited in the literature. However, notably within the map, transformative learning is identified as a potential outcome of the process for staff as well as for students. Arguably the benefits of collaboration for staff are equally as significant as the benefits for students; however, the discussion of positive outcomes of partnerships for staff in the published literature is not usually accorded the same attention (Ollis & Gravett, in press). Here, the transformative learning for both parties is shown as instigating a truly 'authentic' partnership.

The map highlights the importance of co-creation initiatives being both sustainable and ongoing. This is a crucial but difficult challenge for partnership projects. It can be difficult for institutions to support projects that require time and staff resources to manage on an ongoing basis, yet how the valuable and generative relationships developed can be sustained beyond the initial co-design, as well as how the output from these projects can be managed, are important questions. Bovill et al. remind us that 'in some institutions, staff may feel that institutional structures, practices and norms are in tension with co-creating learning and teaching' (2016, p. 201), and Taylor and Robinson write that the responsibility to 'empower' students is often placed with teachers, without a recognition of the wider constraints impacting upon staff within a larger sphere (2009, p. 167). How to ensure that partnerships remain sustainable, and that they have an ongoing position within institutional structures, is thus a challenging but important consideration. In the case of the Feedback Footprints project, this was achieved by engaging students not only as designers, but subsequently as ambassadors for the final e-portfolio product.

The very useful skills that partnership working can help to develop in students, for example, employability and responsibility, are also significant themes that emerged within the map-mediated interview. Transferable skills and experiences are often cited as important benefits of partnership work for students by learning through doing (Bovill et al., 2010; Maunder, 2015). Maunder (2015) suggests that working in partnership with staff allows students to gain research methods skills, and Jarvis, Dickerson, and Stockwell (2013) argue that engaging in a partnership can increase employability skills for both students and staff (see Chapter 13). However, as well as these skills, the map also makes explicit other significant affective outcomes, for example, pride. Affective outcomes of learning and teaching such as pride and joy have traditionally been given less attention but can be hugely significant to students' engagement within teaching and learning and may be a noticeable aspect of students' experiences of co-creation (e.g. Gravett, Kinchin, & Winstone, in press).

Staff defensiveness, dissatisfaction, and negativity are also prevalent themes that arose within the interview and the concept map. Resistance from colleagues to co-design work and feelings such as defensiveness and negativity are very real challenges for staff seeking to foster partnership approaches and may arise from the genuine concerns of staff regarding additional workload, sharing of responsibilities, or just a general resistance to change. Here, Naomi identifies that these challenges can be managed through sharing understandings and through gaining multiple perspectives and that the positivity of students can work to alleviate such tensions.

Having discussed some of the significant themes and values that underpin a staff member's approach to and conception of co-design, it is evident that the map-mediated interview serves as a useful way to unpack co-design practices. Naomi's map shows recognition of the emancipatory possibilities of co-design but also a realistic awareness of the institutional and emotional challenges that individuals face when looking to foster co-design opportunities and to create an ongoing culture of partnership working.

What Are the Obstacles That Stand in the Way of Student Empowerment?

We have seen how co-design can offer a wealth of meaningful benefits for both students and staff. Nonetheless, it is important for staff to remain mindful of obstacles that may still inhibit truly transformative outcomes. Robinson and Taylor remind us that power 'inhabits all processes of social communication and...has become recognized for its diversity, subtlety and complexity' (2007, p. 12). This exposure of the subtlety and complexity of power relations suggests that no matter how emancipatory the aims of staff, co-design approaches cannot be isolated from existing power structures that lie within all processes of social communication. Robinson and Taylor describe power as 'hidden' and as 'micro-practices' (2013, p. 39; p. 41), for example: 'unequal student–teacher power relations mean that teachers get to decide what counts as knowledge, and that this in turn influences the approach to research and restricts the feedback and opinions students give' (p. 39). Likewise, Mäkelä et al. (2018) caution that co-design experiences can be disempowering for students if they perceive that their views have not been taken into account; however, explaining to students why specific ideas could not be taken on board can be a valuable space for discussion. Staff may need to be mindful of these challenges in order to destabilise rather than perpetuate existing hierarchies. This can be particularly problematic when considering class, gender, and racial inequalities, as well as students' inexperience of co-design processes when participating in initiatives (Garcia et al., 2018). Thus, while communication and dialogue are a fundamental part of co-creation, we cannot assume that such dialogic experiences will inevitably lead to student empowerment, or that any relationship can entirely escape power relations.

Representation is also problematic. Even when we recognise the need to include a diversity of voices, it can be challenging to get a diverse group of students involved in a co-design process. Marquis, Black, and Healey (2017) note that it can often be the most privileged or high-achieving students, rather than the disengaged, that take part. Similarly, Robinson and Taylor (2007) explain that it is often the case that students active in student voice projects are students who have the cultural capital to participate.

It will thus be important for staff to be mindful of these obstacles to 'true' student empowerment and engagement inherent within co-design practices, in order to ensure that the potential for co-design work to include more diverse voices and greater engagement and empowerment for students is not lost. If staff are careful to attend to the challenge of reconceptualising students' roles and are conscious of the need to problematise and recognise micro-power relations, then co-design can offer new and generative opportunities for collaboration.

Conclusion: From Voice to Voices

In this chapter, we have reviewed one example of a co-design partnership through the eyes of students and the project leader. Students identified with a number of different roles in the process, and there was evidence of authenticity in the partnership as described by both the students and the project leader. We conclude by considering key points of learning from the project that demonstrate how co-design offers one way to bring multiple student voices to the fore.

First, co-design processes involve not just the 'views' of students but their creative involvement. In the Feedback Footprints project, valuable information was gained from the first round of focus groups that would have been sufficient to inform the design of the e-portfolio. However, this would have necessitated multiple translations of the unilateral student 'voice', rather than enabling student voices to permeate all elements of the design, prototyping, refinement, and evaluation processes.

Second, this approach did not merely 'listen' to the voice of students as a way to inform the work of expert designers, but involved a genuine sharing of power and responsibility, where staff had to relinquish control. Dismantling traditional power hierarchies in this way has the added benefit of enabling both staff and students to see each other's perspectives and to facilitate learning and empowerment. Third, the co-design process recognises students as experts; rather than seeking student perspectives 'after the fact', this approach positions students as qualified to shape educational experiences for themselves and future cohorts.

However, we have also sought to problematise the process in reflecting upon the question of how representative co-creative opportunities can really be. Power is still contained within these endeavours by the realities of staff–student relations and the power relations inherent in all social communication. Whilst we might be engaging multiple student voices, do they represent the full range of student experiences? The students spoke most prominently of representing their disciplinary communities; returning to Chapter 2, it is unlikely that Alexander would have perceived members of his disciplinary community as those who could best represent his perspectives. However, if we remain mindful of these potential obstacles, co-design can offer the means to disrupt traditional staff–student hierarchies, to recognise the plurality of students' experiences, and demonstrate a willingness to share responsibility in educational endeavours.

Acknowledgements The Feedback Footprints project was supported by a Catalyst Funding grant from the Higher Education Funding Council for England (Ref: PK60). The authors thank the students and staff who participated in the Feedback Footprints project.

References

Bovill, C., Aitken, G., Hutchison, J., Morrison, F., Roseweir, K., Scott, A., ... Rija, F. (2010). Experiences of learning through collaborative evaluation from a masters programme in professional education. *International Journal for Academic Development, 15*(2), 143–154.

Bovill, C., Cook-Sather, A., Felten, P., Millard, L., & Moore-Cherry, N. (2016). Addressing potential challenges in co-creating learning and teaching: Overcoming resistance, navigating institutional norms and ensuring inclusivity in student-staff partnerships. *Higher Education, 71*(2), 195–208.

Casanova, D., & Mitchell, P. (2017). The 'cube' and the 'poppy flower': Participatory approaches for designing technology-enhanced learning spaces. *Journal of Learning Spaces, 6*(3), 1–12.

Cook-Sather, A., Bovill, C., & Felten, P. (2014). *Engaging students as partners in learning and teaching: A guide for faculty.* San Francisco, CA: Josey-Bass.

Fishman, B. J. (2014). Designing usable interventions: Bringing student perspectives to the table. *Instructional Science, 42*(1), 115–121.

Garcia, I., Noguera, I., & Cortada-Pujol, M. (2018). Students' perspective on participation in a co-design process of learning scenarios. *Journal of Educational Innovation, Partnership and Change, 4*(1). Retrieved from https://journals.gre.ac.uk/index.php/studentchangeagents/article/view/760.

Gravett, K., Kinchin, I. M., & Winstone, N. E. (in press). 'More than customers': Conceptions of students as partners held by students, staff, and institutional leaders. *Studies in Higher Education.*

Healey, M., Flint, A., & Harrington, K. (2014). *Engagement through partnership: Students as partners in learning and teaching in higher education.* York, UK: Higher Education Academy. Retrieved from https://www.heacademy.ac.uk/engagement-through-partnership-students-partners-learning-andteaching-higher-education.

Jarvis, J., Dickerson, C., & Stockwell, L. (2013). Staff-student partnership in practice in higher education: The impact on learning and teaching. *Procedia-Social and Behavioral Sciences, 90*, 220–225.

Kandiko, C. B., & Kinchin, I. M. (2013). Developing discourses of knowledge and understanding: Longitudinal studies of PhD supervision. *London Review of Education, 11*(1), 46–58.

Mäkelä, T., Helfenstein, S., Lerkkanen, M. K., & Poikkeus, A. M. (2018). Student participation in learning environment improvement: Analysis of a co-design project in a Finnish upper secondary school. *Learning Environments Research, 21*(1), 19–41.

Marquis, E., Black, C., & Healey, M. (2017). Responding to the challenges of student-staff partnership: The reflections of participants at an international summer institute. *Teaching in Higher Education, 22*(6), 720–735.

Matthews, K. E., Cook-Sather, A., Acai, A., Dvorakova, S. L., Felten, P., Marquis, E., & Mercer-Mapstone, L. (2019). Toward theories of partnership praxis: An analysis of interpretive framing in literature on students as partners in teaching and learning. *Higher Education Research & Development, 38*(2), 280–293.

Maunder, R. (2015). Working with students as partners in pedagogic research: Staff and student experiences of participating in an institutional bursary scheme. *Journal of Educational Innovation, Partnership and Change, 1*(1). Retrieved from https://journals.gre.ac.uk/index.php/studentchangeagents/article/view/162.

Nash, R. A., & Winstone, N. E. (2017). Responsibility sharing in the giving and receiving of assessment feedback. *Frontiers in Psychology, 8*, 1519.

Ollis, L., & Gravett, K. (in press). The emerging landscape of student-staff partnerships in higher education. In K. Gravett, I. M. Kinchin, & N. Yakovchuk (Eds.), *Enhancing student-centred teaching in higher education: The landscape of student-staff research partnerships*. London: Palgrave Macmillan.

Robinson, C., & Taylor, C. (2007). Theorizing student voice: Values and perspectives. *Improving Schools, 10*(1), 5–17.

Robinson, C., & Taylor, C. (2013). Student voice as a contested practice: Power and participation in two student voice projects. *Improving Schools, 16*(1), 32–46.

Spinuzzi, C. (2005). The methodology of participatory design. *Technical Communication, 52*(2), 163–174.

Taylor, C., & Robinson, C. (2009). Student voice: Theorising power and participation. *Pedagogy, Culture & Society, 17*(2), 161–175.

19

When All Is Said and Done: Consensus or Pluralism?

Simon Lygo-Baker, Ian M. Kinchin
and Naomi E. Winstone

Throughout this book, we have seen examples of the power and potential influence of student voices in terms of identity, agency, and responsibility, across a variety of contexts such as the framing of students as educational consumers or as partners in the creation of educational resources. We have also seen that the power and influence are often limited by the selective hearing of institutions so that a particular voice is enabled and privileged under the guise of consensus or as an attempt to balance perceived inequalities. As a consequence, there are potentially a range of lost voices. These may not always be from those perceived as marginalised and may include voices of the assumed majority, such as Alexander (see Chapter 2). In exploring these issues, the authors of the chapters in this book have posed

S. Lygo-Baker (✉) · I. M. Kinchin · N. E. Winstone
Department of Higher Education, University of Surrey, Guildford, UK
e-mail: s.lygo-baker@surrey.ac.uk

I. M. Kinchin
e-mail: i.kinchin@surrey.ac.uk

N. E. Winstone
e-mail: n.winstone@surrey.ac.uk

© The Author(s) 2019
S. Lygo-Baker et al. (eds.), *Engaging Student Voices in Higher Education*,
https://doi.org/10.1007/978-3-030-20824-0_19

315

a series of challenges which, whilst to some extent uncomfortable, should cause us to reflect on the assumptions we make and to question the current trends exposed.

The Mask of Consensus

The issues pertaining to the apparent consensus underpinning the dominant 'voice' are not specific to higher education. As we are writing this final chapter, the UK is facing political deadlock. In 2016, an in-out referendum was held on the UK's membership of the European Union. The British people voted to leave the EU, by a very narrow margin of 52 to 48%. Three years later, the UK has not left on the scheduled date because of deep and chaotic disagreements about the nature of the withdrawal terms. The Prime Minister, Theresa May, has been criticised for staunchly standing by her withdrawal agreement and has continually vowed to deliver on 'Brexit' because it represents 'the will of the people'. The notion of a consensual 'voice' has been employed in political rhetoric, within claims that 'the country has spoken', and that the government needs to listen and honour this mandate. The apparent consensus of those who recorded an identical vote on their ballot papers masks deep division and widely contrasting perspectives; those who voted leave did so for very different reasons, and many have since changed their minds. Even in the face of the largest petition ever recorded which sought a reversal of the Brexit decision, and evidence that the leave campaign misled voters, Mrs. May did not waver, still arguing that Brexit represents 'the will of the people'. Yet a decision made on the basis of a majority vote, representing the 'voice' of the people, does not represent consensus of opinion.

On the basis of the arguments put forward in the preceding chapters, the perception that the student voice represents some form of consensus appears to be a dangerous over-simplification. As Rescher (1993) previously suggested, whilst we may yearn for consensus for reasons of perceived fairness, a more pragmatic response is to acknowledge that making more incremental improvements that may not be approved of fully but that all can accept is more appropriate. This greater pragmatism has the potential for recognising more voices within higher education which is particularly important at a time where the increasingly complex learning environment is becoming even more diverse. This is again mirrored in the Brexit negotiation process, where it has been argued that the government should have sought not a perfect Brexit agreement that satisfied everyone (which was never going to be the case) but rather an acceptable agreement that represented as wide a range of perspectives as possible.

What has been surfaced in this book is a situation in which the myriad of different voices often become labelled under particular banners and that these, through a variety of compromises, come to be seen as representative of a particular consensus. Thus, the different voices become conflated as *the* voice that covers not only those represented by a particular identity (i.e. mature students) but also then becomes extolled as representing all, or at least a majority, of the students. As the number of people entering higher education has increased, more voices enter and the temptation and pressure to respond to these may have further encouraged such behaviour by institutions. This may also have been further encouraged as universities, aware of increased competition and pressure to meet particular performance indicators, seek to find a consensus in order to be seen as responsive. The transactional 'You said – we did' approach is indicative of such.

For some, this has corresponded with a fragmentation of the authority of the disciplines (Rowland, 2002). As a consequence, policies and responses become more centralised and led top-down by institutions rather than bottom-up by disciplines or departments. Henkel (2005) agrees, arguing that as the university has undergone significant change, this has led to the emergence of a more centralised, powerful, and corporate organisation. Alongside diminishing influence at the departmental level, academic autonomy has also reduced (Martin, 2016). Whilst the discipline retains a central focus for the learners, communication has become more of a central responsibility, reducing the potential opportunity for student voices to be heard.

Ultimately, this leads to the different voices being funnelled into a 'representative' student voice. This is complicated by the fact that the representative voice does not remain static: it shifts. Why is this the case? Because at different times institutions have found it politic to respond to a particular voice, encouraged perhaps by government policy or funding opportunities, such as those from the widening participation agenda. Whilst there is clear merit in much of this work, it also helps to highlight the challenges created by a pretence that the student body is represented by a particular singular and monolithic voice.

Although the notion of a consensual approach remains seductive when we consider the complicated and shifting network of different voices that this work has highlighted, it remains highly problematic. As suggested above, it can appear to privilege particular groups. Rose et al. (1995), for example, warn that although consensus suggests homogeneity, such a state does not exist. Instead, they suggest a reinterpretation:

> Against notions of monolithic and homogenous representations, we propose the idea of a representational field, susceptible to contradiction, fragmentation, negotiation and debate. In such a representational field, there is incoherence, tension and ambivalence. Yet, permeating all these disparate elements there is a consensual reality, which forms the common ground of historically shared meanings within which people discuss and negotiate. (p. 153)

However, this adds significant complexity by recognising what Wittgenstein (1958) expressed through his later work regarding language. He argued for the importance of expressed language, coming to the view that the subtleties of how things are voiced are key. Individual meaning and expression are not fixed, but rather subject to change. Rather than viewing the voice as expressing a seemingly fixed and singular structure, it is more fluid. As such we can see an individual as giving rise to a fluctuating set of voices that become part of social practice, reminiscent of Harre's (1998) notion of the self in reality being expressed through different selves. Although an individual may consistently express particular opinions, these are subject to change through subtle shifts depending upon the context within which they are aired. We therefore need to recognise how individuals forming different groups within our student body portray their voices—or indeed withhold them—remaining silent. If we do not, we may risk a further shift, whereby what the university hears and responds to is an increasingly selective minority voice at the expense of a silenced majority—many of whom appear on the surface to be representative of a satisfied mainstream and yet, like Alexander, are increasingly disaffected. This is not to say that the voices from those within other groups should not be heard. They should, but not to the exclusion of others, whether representing a majority or a minority perspective. What has become apparent from the chapters within this book is that once we ascertain the importance of talking to different people and groups, we need to ensure that we are actually talking together, listening, and responding so that the dialogue remains open and can respond to the subtle shifts and changes as these are surfaced.

Is Pluralism the Cure?

This far, our discussion appears to question the utility of seeking consensus as an approach and suggests that an alternative—pluralism—may be a more effective framework to adopt. As Spickard (2017, p. 169) argues, with an increase in diversity now a 'fact', working towards pluralism is a worthwhile and important endeavour. Further, reflecting on this increased diversity at the outset of this book, we suggested that an aim was to examine the potential for engaging with different voices, so that a greater pluralism was achieved. This was put forward under the assumption that pluralism appears to offer a balance within which each group has a voice in shaping social decisions and also works to constrain the authority of others (Connolly, 2017). Ultimately, this works towards a sharing of a broad system of beliefs. Pluralism aims to engage with the diversity, which we have seen is broadening within our universities. It seeks not merely to tolerate difference but to actively seek to understand and work with it, holding on to our own identity whilst finding ways to acknowledge others and their commitments. Ultimately, and perhaps why this has surfaced in a book looking significantly at voices, pluralism is grounded in dialogue.

It would appear then that pluralism has elements that may appeal. It allows for the challenging of consensus and enables opportunities to offer alternatives often rejected by a broader or more powerful group. This is particularly viewed as the case when the consensus is seen as representing an established or traditional perspective—something that universities may be perceived as often representing. It also offers an opportunity to oppose, so that when change is proposed, those who feel uncomfortable in embracing a 'new way' can offer an alternative or at least suggest a period of reflection before the new and shiny idea is fully embraced without due care and attention.

So it would seem that pluralism may at least recognise the existence of different voices in a way that consensus may not. Consequently, adopting a pluralist approach may encourage engagement with different opinions that exist and that may shift as context alters and perspectives respond to change. In a globalised world where change is now a constant, this appears to be a more rational approach. However, the challenges that have been identified within this book are not insignificant. Whilst the pluralist ideal may appear to offer hope through the establishment of dialogue with some who are lost or unheard at present, this remains a significant challenge.

Four Key Stages to Enable Pluralism

The first step, as outlined in the first chapter of this book, is to acknowledge the diversity of student voices underpinning apparently simplistic group-ings and categories. Too often voices are conflated into first belonging to a particular group, and then on the basis of consensus, these different voices are drawn together, or one is promoted as if it were representative of a homogenous student voice. This fallacy has been exposed. The con-sequence is that diverse student voices from within particular minority perspectives are not always heard. Furthermore, there is potential for the majority to also become disenfranchised, as Alexander's case demonstrates (see Chapter 2). Whilst this may raise a fundamental question of whose voice is actually being put forward, rather than search the wind for an answer, we have concentrated on exploring the landscape and from this four key themes emerged. By recognising and giving genuine authority to student voices, a more engaged, responsive, and thoughtful learning environment can be established. To achieve this aim, the authors in this book suggest a need to: rebalance the opportunity to establish a dialogue; challenge the context within which this dialogue occurs; recognise the context within which this dialogue shifts as the learner progresses; and engage in meaningful collaboration as part of this renewed and exciting dialogue.

Rebalancing

Universities are populated by a significant number of people progressing through or returning to study. They represent an increasingly diverse group of people, enabled through greater technological advances and opportunities to travel. Recognising these people for what they represent and who they are so that effective dialogue can be achieved is an important step, a point raised by Hosein and Rao (see Chapter 5). A rebalancing of the relationship is required, and authors within this work have suggested how this may occur. In Chapter 3, for example, Sutherland and colleagues suggest how an institution has valued their work with students and on the basis of a more collegial approach begun to enable a broader set of voices to be heard at different levels of the university. This does not equate, as they present, to representing all the voices within the student body, but is an important step in acknowledging that these other voices exist. However, if reflecting on the notion of 'students-as-consumers' as discussed by Bunce in Chapter 4, engaging students as partners does encourage students to take responsibility for their learning, something academic staff are often heard to question. Bunce argues that if students' voices are recognised in an authentic way, this may reduce the typical, and perhaps understandable, fall-back position: that of being only a consumer. Bunce calls for a rebalancing that acknowledges the commitment of the learner both to their financial outlay and their study engagement. However, creating the space for voices to be heard will only work if, as Heron and Palfreyman (see Chapter 6) explain, students have the necessary communication skills to engage in an appropriate dialogue. Therefore, in order to engage with the diverse student voices that exist, it is necessary to rebalance the university landscape; to recognise where the students have arrived from and what this means they bring with them. If we are to offer them access to spaces for dialogue, opportunities to work as partners, and space to grow as effective learners, we need to ensure that the voices they develop are supported.

Challenging the Context

For students' perspectives to make a real impact on the university land-scape, many authors in this book have suggested that reducing the student to a mere data point is problematic. Beyond rebalancing the dialogue so it is more meaningful, authors of the chapters in this book have argued that the context within which this rebalancing takes place must also be reframed. If we are to encourage the learner to enter into a dialogue with their staff and their peers and to take responsibility for their part within this conversation, we need to ensure that the context within which this takes place does not merely reflect the consumer persona of the student (Gravett, Kinchin, & Winstone, in press). Whilst metrics such as the NSS may offer universities an opportunity to take the temperature of students' perceptions and experiences, they cannot diagnose the root cause of the problems. Furthermore, they reduce students to individual data points that are then collated to calculate a mean response from a particular group. Rather, as Winstone and Boud (see Chapter 7) argue, the learner needs to be actively engaged in a dialogue about their work and their experiences. The university therefore needs to encourage and establish an environment which encourages such a dialogue, rather than seeing assessment as merely an important indicator of outcomes. This draws us further towards mea-surement of attainment and the argument put forward by Herrmann (see Chapter 8) that a narrow focus limits the true value of a higher educa-tion. He argues that we should welcome and encourage a broader set of dialogues that embrace different student trajectories and not narrow these by seeking merely to rank the apparent success on one scale, such as the DHLE. These sentiments are echoed by Dowle, Hopkins, and Spencely in Chapter 9 who highlight the value of doctoral researcher voices. Here are particular examples of those undertaking different journeys and for whom there is often a limited recognition within the broader university of a series of potentially diverse and informed voices who have a significant amount to contribute. So, not only do we need to ensure that all the voices have a space within which to be heard and the capacity to project within this space, we need to respond as institutions beyond merely reporting the conversation as a statistic. This is not to suggest that the responsibility lies entirely with the institution and staff, far from it. The learner, as part of the endeavour, has a responsibility to respond and take responsibility for the voice they project and the actions they suggest.

Adapting Over the Journey

The complexity of the learner experience within higher education and the society within which universities are situated requires us to recognise that individual student voices are not static: they are likely to shift to take on new and more nuanced perspectives over time as they develop as members of a university community. This can offer significant opportunity for each student to develop a range of different responses but can also be disconcerting. As Winstone and Hulme (see Chapter 10) remind us, many students are adept at responding to transition and rather than always seeing particular periods as potential hurdles, we need a greater sophistication to recognise how each individual may experience their journey and then describe and respond to the challenges they encounter. This greater sophistication also resounds within the work of Gravett (see Chapter 11) who recognises that students often struggle with developing appropriate academic and information literacy skills. She suggests that a more integrated approach is necessary, that establishes collaboration and partnership, echoing arguments put forward in earlier chapters. Whilst many students make excellent progress and are, as noted above, very capable of adapting as they arrive and proceed through their time at university, this is not the case for everyone. Querstret (see Chapter 12) argues that whilst there is greater recognition of mental health and well-being as important factors within contemporary higher education, a collaborative approach whereby students and staff explore appropriate responses would benefit the whole community. Finally, there is a further call in Chapters 13 and 14 for greater collaboration to understand how student voices interpret employability (Zajacova, Hepper, and Grandison) and the attributes they may take with them from their time at University (Jones and Pate).

Collaboration with Student Voices

Whilst it is accepted above that much of the collaboration that is needed surrounds the broader living and learning experience on or around the campus, this does not negate the need for these voices to also be heard as we examine the academic work undertaken. Curriculum development is influenced by all dimensions of the university landscape and given the importance that has emerged of the need for collaboration, it is perhaps unsurprising that this theme resonates within the final section of the book. With the added responsibility ascribed to students within partnership working models comes a pressure on academic staff to create the conditions within which this can be authentically experienced. Lygo-Baker (see Chapter 15) argues that this can only occur if we value uncertainty in learning. This theme continues in Chapter 16 where Okupe and Medland argue for greater collaboration in the development of teaching. Simplistic teaching evaluation measures are acknowledged as exactly that, and greater dialogue is promoted whereby students' views can have an immediate and meaningful impact on their learning environments. Students also bring valuable perspectives to work that may, erroneously, be considered to require the expertise of academic staff. In Chapter 17, Kinchin and Kandiko Howson suggest a reconceptualising of the research-teaching nexus, such that students and staff engage in disciplinary learning together. In Chapter 18, Gravett, Medland, and Winstone provide an example of students engaging in co-design of an educational tool.

Conclusion

Each individual student voice changes and can be seen to be in transition during their time within the university, whether negotiating an initial position on arrival at campus or looking to the future upon graduation. As we have seen, there is a danger that these shifting individual voices become synthesised to a series of soundbites, often decontextualised but presented as indicative of a singular and clear student voice. The limitations of this approach have been exposed in this book. Rather than seeking consensus, to simplify the complex processes that exist, we should celebrate the plurality offered and use this as the basis to collaborate and create new and exciting situations through which different voices can express ideas and ask future questions. The chapters within this book have put forward a range of strategies through which those working in higher education can engage with and learn from diverse student voices. Without embracing these different voices from all areas of the campus, universities are in danger of ending up in conversation with a disembodied voice that represents nobody.

References

Connolly, W. E. (2017). *Pluralism in political analysis*. New York: Routledge.

Gravett, K., Kinchin, I. M., & Winstone, N. E. (in press). 'More than customers': Conceptions of students as partners held by students, staff, and institutional leaders. *Studies in Higher Education*.

Harre, R. (1998). *The singular self: An introduction to the psychology of personhood*. London: Sage.

Henkel, M. (2005). Academic identity and autonomy in a changing policy environment. *Higher Education, 49*, 155–176.

Martin, B. (2016). What's happening to our universities? *Prometheus, 34*(1), 7–24.

Rescher, N. (1993). *Pluralism: Against the demand for consensus*. Oxford, UK: Oxford University Press.

Rose, D., Efraim, D., Gervais, M.-C., Joffe, H., Jovchelovitch, S., & Morant, N. (1995). Questioning consensus in social representations theory. *Papers on Social Representations, 4*(2), 150–176.

Rowland, S. (2002). Overcoming fragmentation in professional life: The challenge for academic development. *Higher Education Quarterly, 56*(1), 52–64.

Spickard, J. (2017). Diversity vs Pluralism. *Religions, 8*(9), 169–179.

Wittgenstein, L. (1958). *Philosophical investigations*. Oxford, UK: Blackwell.

Index

A

Academic misconduct 183. *See also* Plagiarism
Activism 46, 47
Agency 1, 10, 13, 32, 41, 91, 115, 121, 131, 137, 153, 180, 185, 267, 315
A Levels 23, 166
Approaches to learning 60, 64
  deep 64–66
  surface 21, 64
Assessment 10, 21, 57, 60, 90, 97, 98, 109–116, 118–120, 182, 183, 198, 214, 217, 240, 263, 266, 285, 298, 322
Australasian Survey of Student Engagement (AUSSE) 44
Autonomy 31, 191, 246, 247, 252
  academic 317
  student 307

B

Big-Fish-Little-Pond (BFLP) effect 164
Boud, David 111, 112, 116, 117, 119, 273, 280, 322
Bovill, Catherine 6, 10, 39, 42, 43, 72, 82, 89, 90, 185, 245, 284, 298, 300, 302, 307, 308
Brew, Angela 279, 280, 285–287
Buckley, Alex 41, 42
Bunce, Louise 61, 62, 64, 65, 252, 321

C

Carless, David 116, 117, 184, 273
Change agents, students as 10, 72, 284

© The Editor(s) (if applicable) and The Author(s) 2019
S. Lygo-Baker et al. (eds.), *Engaging Student Voices in Higher Education*,
https://doi.org/10.1007/978-3-030-20824-0

Co-creation 129, 245, 298–300,
305–309. *See also* Co-design,
Participatory design
Co-design 43, 50, 298. *See also*
Co-creation, Participatory
design
Communicative competence 94, 96,
97
Concept map 22–25, 27, 29, 306,
308
Consultants, students as 273, 274,
284, 300, 302–304, 306. *See
also* Experts, students as
Consumer orientation 61–65
Consumers, students as 3, 5, 12, 41,
55, 56, 58–61, 63–66, 132,
274, 297, 300, 321, 322. *See
also* Customers, students as
Cook-Sather, Alison 1, 6, 7, 9–11,
13, 39, 42, 43, 71, 83, 85, 89,
284, 287, 298
Course Experience Questionnaire
(CEQ) 5, 7, 109, 261
Course representatives 254, 298. *See
also* Student representatives
Cultural capital 92, 162, 163, 183,
309
Curriculum design 38, 42, 49, 63,
72, 82, 89–91, 93, 101, 127,
134, 136, 198, 213
Customers, students as 3, 50, 56–58,
60, 65, 66. *See also* Consumers,
students as

D

Destinations of Leavers from Higher
Education (DLHE) Survey 12,
125, 126, 128–132, 136, 137

Dialogue 2, 4, 8, 9, 22, 41, 90–95,
98–101, 117, 119, 120, 149,
177, 185, 213, 216, 219, 240,
254, 255, 264, 270, 273, 274,
309, 319–322, 324
Diversity 2, 5, 12, 20, 71–74, 76,
100, 137, 144, 160, 169, 170,
175, 177, 198, 210–212, 215,
219–221, 256, 262, 267, 273,
274, 283, 297, 309, 319, 320
Dunne, Elisabeth 6, 10, 42, 72, 284

E

Employability 12, 26, 31–33, 57, 92,
94, 125–137, 209–221, 226,
229, 232, 234, 237–239, 251,
308, 323
Employers 3, 59, 125–130, 133–137,
209–221, 225–228, 231–233,
236, 238, 239, 263
Employment 26, 59, 85, 94,
125–136, 181, 209, 210, 212,
213, 216–220, 226, 228, 229,
232–234, 236, 237, 239, 246,
282
Engagement 2, 3, 7, 8, 10–13, 26, 31,
38, 39, 41–44, 46, 49, 55, 59,
62, 81, 84, 89–92, 94, 96, 99,
112, 129, 135, 162, 211–213,
217–219, 221, 245, 267, 270,
273, 274, 280, 290, 299, 308,
310, 320, 321
Experts, students as 288, 304, 306,
310. *See also* Consultants,
students as

F

Feedback 3, 6, 10, 21, 24, 40, 42, 57, 58, 63, 72, 82, 90, 98, 109–120, 147, 149–151, 153, 183, 184, 230, 240, 262, 264, 266–269, 271, 282, 301, 303–305, 309
Feedback Engagement and Tracking System (FEATS) 301, 305
Felten, Peter 6, 10, 39, 42, 72, 89, 284, 298
Funding 38, 44, 47, 55–57, 75, 128, 144, 263, 317. *See also* Tuition fees

G

Graduate attributes 12, 26, 92, 129, 133, 135, 225–228, 230–240

H

Healey, Mick 42, 43, 170, 185, 280, 298, 309

I

Identity 1, 5, 13, 20, 23, 26, 28–31, 60–64, 84, 131, 132, 137, 160, 164, 168, 170, 176, 181–183, 192, 199, 214, 235, 238, 239, 246, 315, 317, 319
Inclusion 2, 5, 22, 40, 182, 212, 218
International students 12, 72–85, 93, 99, 210, 212–214, 217, 220, 262
Internships 210. *See also* Placements, Work experience

K

Kahu, Ella 41, 42
Kinchin, Ian M. 21, 22, 27, 28, 33, 74, 175, 176, 179, 180, 280, 282, 283, 287, 291, 305, 308, 322, 324

L

Land, Ray 161, 184, 287
League tables 126, 262
Learning advisors 177
Learning analytics 248
Librarians 177, 180
Liminality 161, 285, 287
Literacy
    academic 175–180, 184, 185
    assessment 177
    digital 177
    feedback 116, 120, 273
    information 12, 175–179, 323
    mental health 12, 193
Longitudinal Earnings Outcome (LEO) 130

M

Marketisation 13, 56, 59, 62, 71, 181, 261
Matthews, Kelly 43, 185, 298
Mature students 8, 111, 212, 317
McLeod, Julie 5–7, 9, 11, 19, 28
Mental health
    anxiety 179, 197
    Cognitive Behaviour Therapy (CBT) 197
    depression 197, 201
    help-seeking 192–194
    mindfulness 196, 198, 199

psychoeducational interventions
195, 196
resilience 199, 200
skills training interventions 195,
196
stigma 193, 194, 200, 201
suicide 198
Mercer, Neil 91, 92, 95–98
Metrics 5, 7, 12, 57–60, 66, 109–115,
132, 136, 246, 322. *See also*
Surveys
Meyer, Jan 161, 287
Module evaluation questionnaires
(MEQs) 24, 264–272. *See also*
Student evaluations of teaching

N

National Student Survey (NSS) 5,
7, 9, 12, 19, 20, 44, 57, 58,
109–111, 114, 115, 136, 150,
214, 240, 261, 322
National Survey of Student Engagement (NSSE) 44, 261
National Union of Students (NUS)
39, 42, 43, 81, 200, 201
Nicol, David 114, 115, 117

O

Office for Students (OfS) 57, 126
Oracy 12, 90, 96–98, 102

P

Parents 59, 125, 191, 249
Participatory design 202, 298, 299,
301. *See also* Co-creation,
Co-design

Partnership 2, 9, 13, 38–40, 43–46,
48–51, 65, 66, 72, 101, 110,
120, 129, 146, 170, 185, 273,
274, 286, 298–301, 304–308,
310, 323, 324. *See also* Students
as partners
Placements 26, 135, 210, 213, 216,
219. *See also* Internships, Work
experience
Plagiarism 164, 183. *See also*
Academic misconduct
Postgraduate Research Experience
Survey (PRES) 12, 148, 150,
151
Postgraduate Taught Experience
Survey (PTES) 12
Power 1, 11, 13, 43, 45, 72, 94, 101,
128, 133, 152, 178, 179, 221,
246, 261–263, 287, 288, 291,
307, 309–311, 315

Q

Quality assurance 5, 40, 41, 44, 45,
50, 56, 57, 110, 249, 263, 265.
See also Quality enhancement
Quality Assurance Agency (QAA) 5,
147
Quality enhancement 5, 45, 267. *See
also* Quality assurance

R

Reflection 21, 118, 170, 227, 263,
268, 270, 272, 273, 289, 319
Researchers, students as 282, 284,
288, 290
Research Excellence Framework
(REF) 27, 57

Research-teaching nexus 27, 281, 283, 290, 324

S

Seale, Jane 3–5, 7, 8, 10, 91, 99, 100, 268, 269
Signalling theory 225, 227, 228, 236, 240
Skills 12, 21, 25, 26, 38, 60, 64, 89–102, 116, 127, 129–135, 137, 146, 164, 165, 167, 175–180, 183, 191, 193–198, 200, 209, 210, 212–218, 221, 227, 229–239, 280–282, 289, 299, 308, 321, 323
Spoon-feeding 181
Staff-student liaison committees 5, 82
Stress 152, 191, 192, 196, 197, 199, 281
Student association 47, 49. *See also* Student union
Student evaluations of teaching 13. *See also* Module evaluation questionnaires (MEQs)
Student expectations 246, 261, 266
Student experience 2, 3, 8, 9, 12, 33, 38, 43, 44, 48, 49, 57, 58, 65, 91, 109–111, 127, 130, 181, 198, 213, 251, 261–264, 267, 274, 279, 311
Student representatives 37, 45, 47–49, 72. *See also* Course representatives
Students
    doctoral 144
    international 71–79, 81–85, 93, 212, 213, 215, 220, 262
    LGBTQ+ 20, 212

    mature 8, 111, 212, 317
    non-traditional 92, 168, 181
    postgraduate 77, 214, 215
    undergraduate 38, 77, 144, 163, 228, 268
Students as partners 6, 12, 37–39, 42, 43, 46, 50, 72, 274, 298, 299, 321
Student satisfaction 57–59, 110, 112, 113, 265
Student union 5, 28, 45, 47, 72, 81, 83, 201, 254. *See also* Student association
Surveys 12, 13, 20, 21, 31, 40, 44, 49, 57, 61, 65, 109–114. *See also* Metrics

T

Teaching Excellence Framework (TEF) 40, 57, 126, 136, 150, 246
Technology-enhanced learning 10
Theory of Met Expectations 163
Threshold concepts 161
Transition 12, 128, 133, 159–162, 164–170, 179, 182, 323, 324
Tuition fees 23, 55, 58, 61, 62, 73, 75, 76, 125, 126, 245, 261. *See also* Funding

V

Value for money 56–58, 65

W

Wellbeing 12, 39, 180, 191, 192, 195–202, 323

Widening participation 20, 31–33, 181, 182, 211, 218, 317

Winstone, Naomi E. 21, 24, 28, 33, 112, 114, 115, 119, 120, 163, 167, 182–184, 301, 308, 322–324

Work-based learning (WBL) 12, 210–221

Work experience 135, 210, 228. *See also* Internships, Placements

Z

Zandstra, Roos 6, 10, 72, 284

Zepke, Nick 41, 42

CPI Antony Rowe
Eastbourne, UK
January 08, 2020